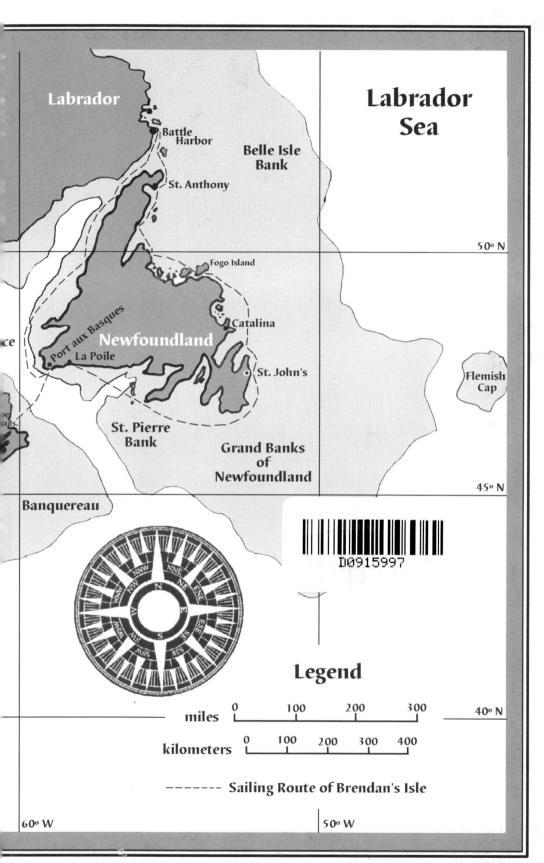

Labrador

Labrador
Sea

Battle
Harbor

Belle Isle
Bank

St. Anthony

50° N

Fogo Island

Port aux Basques

Catalina

Newfoundland

La Poile

St. John's

Flemish
Cap

ce

St. Pierre
Bank

Grand Banks
of
Newfoundland

45° N

Banquereau

D0915997

N
NNW NNE
NW   NE
WNW   ENE
W   E
WSW   ESE
SW   SE
SSW SSE
S

Legend

miles

| 0 | 100 | 200 | 300 |

40° N

kilometers

| 0 | 100 | 200 | 300 | 400 |

- - - - - - - Sailing Route of Brendan's Isle

60° W

50° W

Advance Praise for Servants of the Fish

"Myron Arms' *Servants of the Fish* is a lucid and impassioned account of a journey to the outports of Newfoundland and of the collapse of a fishery—the northern cod—that was once one of the largest and most productive on Earth. Set in the context of a small-boat voyage to the heart of the fishing ground, the book weaves together a history of Newfoundland, a requiem for a depleted natural system, and an encounter with a people struggling to survive in the aftermath of disaster. The characters in Arms' tale are convincing, the prose is powerful, the science is accurate and timely, and the message is one that no concerned citizen of our planet can afford to ignore."

—Christopher Flaven, co-author of *State of the World 2004* and president of Worldwatch Institute

"*Servants of the Fish* accomplishes what non-fiction writing seldom does: it conveys an important story with all the intensity and immediacy of a good novel."

—Carl Safina, author of *Eye of the Albatross* and *Song for a Blue Ocean*

"As one who has lived and worked in the outports that Arms writes about, I am particularly sensitive to the accuracy of his landscapes and to the honesty of his portraits of the fishermen and their families. The places and people I know in Newfoundland come alive in this heart-rending tale of loss and survival."

—Craig Palmer, Anthropologist, University of Colorado, co-author of *When the Fish Are Gone*

"In this compelling portrait of the fishermen of Newfoundland, sailor and environmentalist Myron Arms documents the human side of an ecological catastrophe. On one level it is the tale of a gritty and resilient people, the hauntingly beautiful place they live, and the fishery they helped to destroy. On a more universal level, it becomes a kind of environmental morality play—a voyage to Everyland, an encounter with Everyman, and an urgent call for what the author terms 'a different kind of caring' for the Earth."

—Lester Brown, president of Earth Policy Institute, author of *Eco-Economy* and *Plan B*

"*Servants of the Fish* is a triple treat: a fine sailing yarn, a series of insightful encounters with the people of outport Newfoundland, and a passionate environmentalist's plea for recognition of the damage we are doing to the Earth's oceans . . . . There are, by Arms' own admission and integrity, few answers here—but a great deal to think about."

—Alan Wilson, Professor Emeritus,
History and Canadian Studies, Trent University

"In *Servants of the Fish* author/sailor Myron Arms voyages with his readers on a tour of Newfoundland's outports under sail, taking the pulse of a wounded province after the collapse of the cod fishery which had sustained it for hundreds of years . . . . As the voyage progresses, he tries to understand what this catastrophe may foretell about the future of humanity itself, utterly reliant on a planet whose intricate web of life we do not properly cherish or even comprehend. Like *Riddle of the Ice,* Arms' new book is lucid, stimulating and deeply moving—an important achievement."

—Silver Donald Cameron, author of *The Living Beach*

"*Servants of the Fish* is a delightful read. The combination of sailing, landscapes, people, fishing, history, and science is riveting . . . . In this book Arms presents a well-rounded picture from one geographic center of fishing effort. The story is applicable to other places and useful for both the general reader and the fisheries scientist."

—John Teal, Scientist Emeritus,
Woods Hole Oceanographic Institution

"Written with sensitivity, insight, and an eye for telling detail, Arms' narrative is not just about Newfoundland fishermen but about all of us. It is a parable, a wonderfully readable journey around an island that has become symbolic of the severe stressing of marine ecosystems everywhere. It is a wake-up call about what we are collectively doing to our planet."

—Mark Pendergrast, author of *Mirror Mirror*
and *Victims of Memory*

Servants of the Fish

Also by Myron Arms

Cathedral of the World: Sailing Notes for a Blue Planet

Riddle of the Ice: A Scientific Adventure into the Arctic

Touching the World: Adolescents, Adults, and Action Learning (with David Denman)

Servants
of the
Fish

A Portrait of Newfoundland
after the Great Cod Collapse

by

Myron Arms

Upper Access, Inc., Book Publishers
http://www.upperaccess.com

Publication Date: September 15, 2004

Upper Access, Inc., Book Publishers
87 Upper Access Road, PO Box 457, Hinesburg, Vermont 05461
(802)482-2988 • http://www.upperaccess.com

ISBN: 0-942679-29-6

Library of Congress Cataloging-in-Publication Data

Arms, Myron.

Servants of the fish : a portrait of Newfoundland after the great
cod collapse / by Myron Arms.-- 1st ed.
  p. cm.

Includes bibliographical references.

ISBN 0-942679-29-6 (alk. paper)

1. Groundfish fisheries--Newfoundland and Labrador. 2. Fishery
closures--Economic aspects--Newfoundland and Labrador. I. Title.

SH224.N7A76 2004

333.95'6'09718--dc22

2004007036

Printed in the United States of America on acid-free paper

Cover design by Kitty Werner
Maps by Skip Crane. Copyright © 2004, all rights reserved.

For my Mother and Father,

with love and gratitude

Servants (fishing servants): men or women indentured or engaged on wages or shares for a period
in the [cod] fishery. . . sharesmen . . . usually paid
very low wages.

—*Dictionary of Newfoundland English*

"Salmon is salmon, trout is trout. The same with
herring, caplin, and the rest. But to a Newfoundlander cod only is fish."

—Anonymous

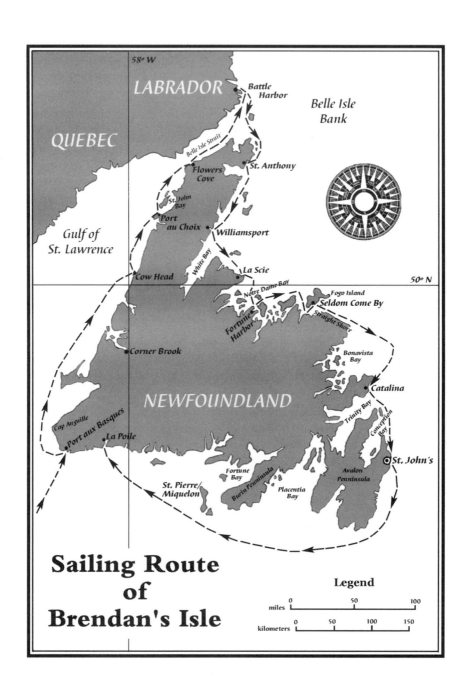

58° W

LABRADOR

QUEBEC

Belle Isle
Bank

Battle
Harbor

Belle Isle Strait

St. Anthony

Flowers
Cove

St. John
Bay

Port
au Choix

Williamsport

Gulf of
St. Lawrence

White Bay

Cow Head

La Scie

50° N

Notre Dame Bay

Fogo Island

Seldom Come By

Fortune
Harbor

Straight Shore

Bonavista
Bay

Corner Brook

Catalina

NEWFOUNDLAND

Trinity Bay

Conception Bay

Cap Anguille

Port aux Basques

La Poile

St. Pierre/
Miquelon

Fortune
Bay

Burin Peninsula

Placentia
Bay

Avalon
Penninsula

St. John's

Sailing Route
of
Brendan's Isle

Legend

| miles | 0 | 50 | 100 |
| kilometers | 0 | 50 | 100 | 150 |

Contents

Author's Note

All the people in this book are real, although I have changed the names and identifying details of certain individuals in order to protect their privacy. All the events in this book are also real, although for the sake of narrative economy, I have occasionally exercised the storyteller's prerogative to alter the order and timing of particular episodes and encounters. Whenever the narrative strays in this way from strict nonfiction, I have made every effort to remain faithful to the individuals involved and to the essential spirit of events as they actually happened.

Prologue

La Poile, Newfoundland
July 2, 1992

THE OLD MAN STOOD at his kitchen window, staring down at the rooftops of his village. His shoulders were stooped. His hands and forearms glistened with a maze of scars, like the back of an old whale. His cobalt eyes, framed in a full beard and a shock of steel gray hair, focused vaguely on the empty streets below. Behind him, a TV set droned in measured cadences from its place on the kitchen table.

The man waited, as I did, for an event that everyone in Newfoundland had been talking about: a news conference due to be televised at seven o'clock that evening by the Canadian Federal Minister of Fisheries and Oceans. Rumor had it that the minister was about to make an announcement about the future of a fishery that had once been the largest in Newfoundland—possibly the largest in the world—the northern cod.

The fish had been growing scarce in recent years; fishermen all over the island were worried. The old man had been saying for days that the news would not be good. "Get it in your minds," he'd said to several neighbors gathered on the government wharf earlier that morning, "there's going to be another round of cuts." One of the men rolled his eyes and cursed under his breath. Another coughed up a great dollop of phlegm and spat it against the side of the government storehouse.

Later, after the others had left, the old man admitted to me that he didn't have the slightest idea what new austerities the fisheries minister might be planning to announce. "We needs to prepare for the worst," he'd said. "For 'tis like heading out onto the banks in your dory fishing. Count on fine weather and you're sure to wander into a gale. Prepare for the worst and maybe you'll find your way back home."

The old man's name was Henry Coyne. I'd met him five years earlier in this same village of La Poile, an isolated community of about two hundred people nestled into a narrow rockbound finger of the sea on the mountainous southwest coast of Newfoundland. The village was little changed from the way it had been for four centuries: a small cluster of buildings perched tenaciously on the rock, connected by a network of footpaths. Nobody owned an automobile in La Poile, for the only access was by boat. The nearest paved road lay fifty miles inland across caribou trails and abandoned logging tracks.

Henry Coyne, like many of his countrymen, was a natural born talker, gregarious, generous almost to a fault. Perhaps he'd become this way because of the intimacy of the village setting and the close family ties that bound virtually everyone in his community. Or perhaps he'd just grown tired of the long months of isolation and the scarcity of visitors "from away." But whatever the reason, he had adopted me and my crew of young American sailors from the first moment he'd spotted us five years earlier in the summer of 1987.

"You like fish?" he'd hollered that first summer, pulling his dory alongside our sailboat as she entered La Poile Bay. When the answer came back in the affirmative, he'd grabbed a fat, thirty-inch cod from the heap that lay at his feet, held it up by the tail, and tossed it onto the sailboat's deck. The fish was so fresh its gills were still quivering.

We met again two years later. I was traveling that year with a different group of sailors—but the boat was the same: my 50-foot fiberglass cutter, *Brendan's Isle*. Once again the old fisherman spotted our dark green hull sailing up the bay, and once again he graced our arrival with a fresh fish. That evening I found myself sitting at a table in the kitchen of his little house, talking until late into the night about the growing problems in the fishery. I met his wife Ruth—since passed away—and his two daughters. One was living at home taking care of her ailing mother. The other was recently married, working as a clerk in a small dry goods store in the village.

Thus it was that on my third visit to La Poile I felt I was coming back to visit old friends. My crew and I had set out that summer on yet another lengthy sailing voyage around Newfoundland, traveling along the coasts of an island that had become, for me, a kind of obsessive destination. I just couldn't seem to get enough of this place, partly because of the grand scale and stark beauty of its landscapes and partly because of people like Henry Coyne—honest, good-hearted people who would befriend you in a heartbeat and for whom generosity was a way of life.

The first sign that something was wrong came moments after our sailboat had passed the lighthouse at Ireland's Island and cleared the ledges at the Naked Man. No sooner had we turned up into La Poile Bay proper than the familiar shape of Henry's open dory appeared out of the mist. The fisherman hollered out a hello. I eased the boat into the wind to slow her progress. Henry pulled his dory alongside and grabbed onto the sailboat's gunwale.

We stood face to face exchanging greetings for nearly a minute before I glanced down into the belly of the dory. Under the foredeck lay half a dozen ocean perch—"redfish" as Newfoundlanders call them—their bulging eyes glazed over with a thin gray film. Beneath the center thwart lay a trio of scrawny cod, each one no more than a few pounds in weight. The rest of the boat's floorboards were clean—and utterly empty of fish.

The old man looked sheepish, almost embarrassed, as he followed my gaze. Then, as if he'd just remembered something, he reached down and grabbed one of the cod by its tail. Before I could stop him, he'd flipped the fish over the gunwale and onto the sailboat's deck. "She's small," he said. "But she'll make a meal." I didn't have the heart to tell him to take it back.

That afternoon in the village the talk was all about the news conference that the fisheries minister was scheduled to deliver in a few more hours. Henry asked me if I had a TV aboard my sailboat. When I indicated that I did not, he invited me to come to his cottage after supper for a coffee. If I had the stomach for it, he said, I could witness an announcement that might change the lives of every man, woman, and child in Newfoundland.

At seven o'clock sharp, the TV in Henry's kitchen went silent. Several seconds later, the screen switched to the figure of the Canadian Federal Minister of Fisheries and Oceans, John Crosbie, appearing live from a conference room in the Radisson Hotel in St. John's, Newfoundland.

"My fellow Newfoundlanders and Labradoreans," the jowly, white-haired minister began, "it is about the northern cod that I wish to speak to you this evening . . . ."

Henry turned from the window where he had been standing and stared at the screen. The minister continued speaking in a flat brogue, explaining the historic importance of the cod fishery to the people of Newfoundland, describing its central place in the island's economy. Finally, he arrived at the subject everyone had been waiting for.

The cod, he intoned, was in trouble. Population numbers for all major breeding stocks around the island had been shrinking. The "total allowable catch," as defined by his own department, had been falling for a number of years. Suddenly, however, population numbers for the largest and most important of the breeding stocks, the northern cod, had collapsed catastrophically across huge areas of the Grand Banks and Labrador Sea.

In response to this crisis and after long and careful deliberation, the minister said, the Canadian Department of Fisheries and Oceans had decided to impose a two-year moratorium on all fishing for this species in the waters of eastern Labrador and Newfoundland—effective immediately. This moratorium period, he said, would give the fish a chance to replenish their numbers. Fishermen, meanwhile, would have one week to remove all traps, nets, and other fixed gear from the water, after which they would be compensated on an emergency basis for income they would lose after the closure.

During a brief pause in the minister's words, I looked across the kitchen at the old fisherman. He was standing next to a chair, gripping it with white-knuckled fingers. "God help us," he whispered, staring at the TV screen. "God help us all."

Crosbie's voice droned on, enumerating the details of the government's plan, even as the image on the screen switched to a hallway outside the conference room. The doors to this room had been barred, forcing the general public to assemble outside and listen to the minister's remarks over closed-circuit TV. Several hundred people—many of them fishermen—were milling around this area when a small group began calling Crosbie's name, insisting on admission to the conference room, demanding that the minister hear their grievances.

When the square-faced Crosbie continued to speak, seemingly unmoved by the events taking place outside, the men charged the conference room doors, ramming into them repeatedly with their arms and shoulders.

"Poor bastards," said Henry, gazing glassy-eyed at the melee on the screen. "Poor simple bastards, for what are they going to do now?"

He walked slowly up to the TV set, stared at it for several seconds longer, and switched it off. Then he turned and looked at me. "Prepare for the worst, is what I said. But how does a man prepare for the end of everything he's ever known, everything he's ever depended on? How does a man prepare for the end of the world?"

For Henry Coyne, the impacts of the cod-fishing moratorium were not as immediate as they were for many of his countrymen, for the areas affected by the original ban did not include the southwest coast of Newfoundland and the fishing banks surrounding La Poile. But, here as elsewhere, the fish had disappeared, and ten months later, in response to mounting evidence of dangerously low cod stocks, the terms of the moratorium were extended to include all fishing areas around the island and to carry forward into the indefinite future.

I did not return to La Poile for six years after the summer of 1992—did not return to coastal Newfoundland at all except for a few brief stops two years later during a voyage to Labrador and western Greenland. Yet the impressions of that evening with the old fisherman have remained burned into my memory. I've not been able to forget his face or his words, have not been able to forget the helplessness and devastation he felt at the collapse of what was, for him, the foundation of his way of life.

The original cod-fishing moratorium was set for two years. Despite official assurances to the contrary, however, the fish did not rebound. Instead, estimates of the "total biomass" of northern cod actually decreased to the point of commercial extinction during that period, while other major breeding populations were added to the list of those that were in trouble. The no-fishing ban was expanded to include several additional species of ground fish (turbot, white hake, American plaice, witch flounder, redfish) whose numbers had also fallen dramatically. By the summer of 1994, the closures had idled some seven thousand fishing boats and thirty-eight thousand fishermen and plant workers. It was the largest layoff in a single industry in Canadian history.

As I traveled along the coast of western Newfoundland during that summer of 1994, I was preoccupied with another matter—headed north to investigate some of the relationships scientists have discovered between Arctic ice production and changing global climate. Yet everywhere I looked I saw signs of the failed fishery. Fishermen whose families had settled this land and who had lived here for generations were pulling up stakes and leaving; communities that had once been active fishing centers were turning into ghost towns. The fabric of an entire society was coming apart.

I began talking with a few people that summer—people like Henry Coyne, whose fathers and grandfathers and great grandfathers had fished here and who couldn't conceive of any other way of life. When I returned home to the United States in the fall, I began talking with others—ecologists, fisheries biologists, fishing company executives, university professors, politicians, and sociologists. I began reading everything I could about the crisis in the world fishery, about ocean ecosystems, about the Grand Banks, about the life-cycle of the northern cod.

Perhaps, I thought, if the situation in Newfoundland were a unique and isolated event—affecting only a handful of people in a remote and seldom visited corner of North America—perhaps then the rest of the world could afford to ignore it. But I knew this was not an isolated event. As scientists had been observing for more than a decade, traditional fisheries were in trouble everywhere. Some had already collapsed; others were poised to do so. The same devastation that was now taking place on the Grand Banks and in the fishing communities of Newfoundland had been occurring in similar settings all over the planet.

And indeed, the ocean fisheries were not the only natural systems being threatened by the impacts of human exploitation. Observers had been expressing increasing concern in recent years about retreating rain forests in Brazil, dying coral reefs in Hawaii, shrinking glaciers in Antarctica, drying rivers in China, falling water tables in California. In this context, at least, Newfoundland was Everyland and we were all Newfoundlanders—for what was happening on this island was but a single instance of what was happening on the island we call Earth.

When I returned to the United States and began thinking about the events that had been taking place in Newfoundland, I found myself grappling with a number of questions. First came a series of environmental and scientific questions centered around the collapse itself: Why had a species of fish once as abundant as the ripples on the waves suddenly disappeared? Why had the crash happened so abruptly? And why, after nearly six years of moratorium, were the fish still not coming back?

The second set of questions was even more complex, for these had to do with the Newfoundlanders themselves and their inevitable involvement with the cod collapse. No matter who or what was finally blamed for the catastrophe—foreign factory ships, destructive fishing technologies, poor government management, bad "in house" science—there was a sense in which almost everyone had played a part. "There are no clean hands in this," one fisherman exhorted to me during my last voyage north. "Everybody was catching fish."

Everybody was catching fish—yet clearly, nobody had intended to destroy a natural resource that formed the social, economic, and, some would say, spiritual backbone of an entire society. Everybody was catching fish because, from the time the first Europeans had sailed to this place more than five hundred years earlier, everybody had always been catching fish. Catching fish in Newfoundland was as natural as breathing.

Were the people of Newfoundland the *victims* of a huge natural disaster, or the *architects*? If the victims, how did such an event occur? If the architects, how did their design get so far out of control? How did an entire society, intelligent and wise in so many ways, fail to perceive what was happening? Fail to respond to the warning signs? Fail to modify its behavior in time to avert catastrophe? These are large questions—many of them still unanswered.

The scientific literature that has emerged since the cod fishing moratorium suggests a few answers. The small but thoughtful body of social analysis suggests a few others. But the more I thought about these questions, the more I realized that the most important answers still lay hidden out there in the remote fishing villages of Newfoundland. If I ever hoped to learn them, I would need to sail once more to these places, pay attention to the changes that had taken place, and listen to people talk.

The book that follows is the story of this quest. The journey itself began in early June 1998, as a crew of young sailors and I set out from the northeast coast of the United States aboard *Brendan's Isle*, bound once again for the island of Newfoundland. During the next three months we traveled almost four thousand miles, exploring bays and sounds, visiting towns and villages all around the twelve-hundred mile perimeter of this island, talking with the people who lived there.

Some of those we met were old friends—people like Henry Coyne whom former crews and I had encountered during the seven previous voyages that *Brendan's Isle* had made to these coasts. Others were new. But every person we met—dory fishermen, government employees, trawler captains, scientists, fish brokers, schoolteachers, politicians, artisans, university students, shop-keepers, pensioners— all shared a common bond with the sea that surrounds this place and with the incomprehensible numbers of fish that once had flourished here.

I understood from the beginning that the story I would learn from these people would not be simple. I knew there would be no villains or heroes in this story, no criminals or saints. There would only be human beings—kind, generous people, for the most part, trying to get along in a difficult situation, doing the best they could. I also knew that the story was going to change me—although in the beginning I wasn't certain how. I knew only that what had happened in Newfoundland was an event that had to do with all of us— a result, some would say, of the way we think about ourselves and the way we understand our relationship with nature.

Newfoundland is a victim, both of her own and of the world's excesses. Newfoundland is a warning signal, a microcosm of the planet itself. For three months my crew and I sailed there, trying to learn what had happened, trying to understand why. Our task, however, was not easy—for like fishermen lowering their nets to scour unseen depths, we soon found ourselves searching across a vast expanse of human hopes and ambitions, aspirations and fears, exploring a complex terrain that would surrender its secrets only to those who were patient and willing to listen.

Servants of the Fish

Chapter 1

Port Aux Basques

THE WIND GROANED in the rigging. Gray-green seas grew steep and oblong. The tops of Table Mountain and the Blue Hills of Garia emerged in a dark line along the northern horizon. Even at forty miles away the land felt dense and solid, announcing its presence like a giant rising out of the sea.

The sailboat shuddered and plunged, scooped green water over the foredeck, lifted, shuddered, plunged again. Amanda looked at me, recognizing the signs. Time to tie in a reef, her eyes announced.

We moved forward along opposite sides of the deck, each clutching a wire lifeline with one hand, the tether of a safety harness with the other. We met at the mast and worked without talking.

Once the boat was properly canvassed and under control, Amanda settled behind the helm again. Nat, her watch mate, moved to the windward rail. I climbed below, stripped off wet foul weather gear, glanced at the radar. No traffic.

What was it, I wondered, that felt so strange this morning? I poured myself a cup of coffee and glanced at an odd-looking map lying open on the navigation table. It was a government fishing map of the banks surrounding Newfoundland, published by the Canadian Department of Fisheries and Oceans and showing the treaty boundaries that Newfoundlanders use to define the five major fishing areas around their island. According to this map, our sailboat had just crossed into fishing area 3Pn, a trapezoidal section of sea that jutted southwestward from the Newfoundland coast into the Cabot Strait. In previous years, the transit across 3Pn had been a busy one, with auto-ferries plying the route between Nova Scotia and western Newfoundland, ocean freighters following the shipping lanes into the Gulf of St. Lawrence, fishing boats steaming north or west or south, on their way to their summer grounds to drag for haddock or redfish or cod. On this particular morning, however, as *Brendan's Isle* made her way toward the harbor at Port aux Basques and her first Newfoundland landfall of the summer, the horizon was empty and the radar screen showed no targets anywhere. Fishing area 3Pn felt like a dead zone.

Moving at a speed of seven knots, the sailboat required five hours to close with the coast. With each passing hour, the scale of the land grew larger, until it became an overwhelming presence that obliterated half the sky. In spite of the weather forecast, the wind continued to build. The seas stacked up in unruly shapes, tumbling pell mell against invisible currents, echoing against the land. I asked Amanda and Nat to tie in the second reef and called for Liz and Richard to join them on deck.

Two miles from the harbor jetties, the VHF radio erupted with a voice that identified itself as Port aux Basques Traffic Control. Because of the large ferry terminal here and the dangerous harbor approach, all passing vessels were required to participate in a radar-controlled system of ingress and egress. The voice requested the sailboat's position. Moments later it indicated that she was on a converging course with the 580-foot auto-ferry *Joseph and Clara Smallwood*, also approaching Port aux Basques from the south.

Dammit, I thought: an empty sea for a hundred miles, and now, just as we'd committed to running down this narrow channel . . . a traffic jam.

In the dropping visibility, the rumble of the ship's engine was the first indicator that she was somewhere close behind. The noise, like kettledrums, traveled through the water and beat out a sympathetic rhythm in the sailboat's hull. Moments later the white curl of a bow wave materialized out of the gloom, followed by a loom of blue steel, a smokestack, a row of human figures crowded along a railing at the bow.

I glanced over my shoulder, trying to gauge the distance between the ship and the little sailboat. The interval was closing fast. Would there be enough time, I wondered, for *Brendan's Isle* to negotiate the entrance channel and pass between a pair of stone breakwaters and into the harbor?

I glanced astern once more and realized that I no longer had any choice. The channel had narrowed and was bound on either side by rock ledges. The ship had now entered the channel as well, blocking any possibility of retreat. I asked Amanda to check the jibs, and I stared intently at the luff of the mainsail, praying that the wind would not fail us. For the next several minutes the sailboat and the ship both catapulted toward the harbor mouth, the distance between them closing ominously. Finally, with only a few hundred yards to go, a long following sea sent the sailboat plunging headlong past a pair of buoys and into the relative safety of the inner basin.

Port aux Basques: a thousand miles east of New York City, three hundred miles east of Halifax, a hundred miles east of Sydney, Nova Scotia, this tiny natural harbor lies tucked behind a series of ledges and rocky islands on the southwest corner of Newfoundland. A century ago Port aux Basques was an isolated outport—little different than La Poile or Rose Blanche or Burgeo or a dozen other remote settlements that lay scattered along the coast to the east and south. But in the 1930s several accidents of geography conspired to transform this place into the western terminus of a new railroad, the infamous "Newfie Bullet." The railroad was the only overland transportation link between western Newfoundland and the more populous eastern sections of the island, and Port aux Basques, as the harbor closest to the Canadian mainland, became an active ferry terminal and freight depot.

Twenty-five years later a road was built along the railroad right-of-way and the ferry service was expanded. Almost overnight, Port aux Basques became an important commercial seaport. Today, ninety Canadian dollars will purchase a one-way ferry ticket across the Cabot Strait for one standard-sized automobile and one human passenger. Every day in summer, four large passenger ferries arrive and leave from the terminal here, making this harbor the place that most people who travel to this island first see and the busiest port of entry in Newfoundland.

Long before Port aux Basques became a highway terminus and ferry terminal, however, it was a fishing village. The lighthouse that crowns the ledges at Channel Head has guided thousands of vessels large and small past the dangers at Fail Rock, Black Shoal, Pot Rock,

Southeast Sunker, Yankee Shoal. The red beacons on Valdy's Island and the range lights on Flagstaff Hill have marked the narrow thoroughfare between Shoal Point and the village of Channel. A pair of wooden church spires and clusters of square, unadorned fishermen's houses have lined the hills above the harbor mouth. Over the decades, these familiar landmarks have loomed up out of the mist and gloom to deliver their message to generations of fishermen—a welcome message of safe harbor and home.

The hour was late with the light almost gone from the sky as *Brendan's Isle* traversed the last few hundred yards of this approach and passed beyond the double tier of entrance markers and rock jetties. On the right loomed the shadowy silhouette of Valdy's Island. On the left arose a series of buildings: the fish processing plant, a chandlery and engine repair shop, a line of small boat floats and fishing storehouses, and finally a squat, two-story brick building, the Fishermen's Cooperative, fronted by a trio of government piers.

With the *Smallwood* bearing down only a few hundred yards astern, I wheeled the sailboat out of the ship channel and into the turning basin in front of the piers. The sails rattled and snapped in the wind. Moments later, the dark blue hull of the ferry obliterated the lights on Valdy's Island and the ferry terminal beyond. In the brief lull in the wind created by the ship's passing, I started the sailboat's diesel engine. Then, while Amanda and the others dropped the sails, I turned to scan the area behind us for a berth where we could moor for the night.

Shadows dressed the waterfront. A solitary automobile rolled slowly onto one of the piers, extinguishing its headlights. Nothing else moved. Along the three government piers, in a basin that could easily berth thirty or forty coastal draggers, there was not a single fishing vessel. One small sailboat lay dark and unattended, tucked in a far corner near the Fishermen's Cooperative building. A few open dories were tethered to the floats next door. Beyond these, at the far end of the fish plant pier, lay the abandoned hull of a single fishing boat, its paint peeling, its hatches covered with canvas tarps, its superstructure stripped of nets and booms.

I guided the sailboat in a circle in the turning basin, waiting for my crew to finish stowing sails, listening to the clatter of the ferry as it began to disgorge its cargo half a mile down the harbor. I watched as a line of camper trucks and automobiles and RVs rumbled down the ferry's gangway under a bank of floodlights, and I found myself thinking about the hundreds of people back there who might be visiting this island for the first time. As they pulled out of the parking area and headed off toward the motels and campgrounds of Newfoundland's nascent tourist industry, many would never notice what had been taking place at this darkened end of the harbor. The empty piers, the uninhabited buildings, the skeletons of fishing boats would pass in a blur and dissolve into the night. The worry and dislocation of the people living here would go unrecognized; their loss would remain a secret.

Not so, however, for the five who were just arriving in the sailboat. For the next seven weeks as we circumnavigated this island, we would be confronted every day, in every harbor and village we visited, with the harsh realities of this place. As travelers who came from the sea, we would share a world with the people we met—and with this sharing would come an easy camaraderie that seamen everywhere confer upon one another. These five sailors, at least, would not be able to ignore the terrible events that had transpired here, for we would be living in their midst.

Once Amanda and the others had stowed and bagged the sails and set up the mooring gear, I guided the sailboat toward the longest of the government piers. The boat bucked and pitched in the choppy sea, so that Nat had to time his leap to the deck of the pier with care. Richard followed, carrying a second line, and in a few more seconds they had the sailboat safely secured.

The lone automobile parked on the pier a few dozen yards away snapped on its headlights again. With its engine rumbling softly, the vehicle backed, turned, and retreated into the night. I glanced around at the empty berths and deserted roadways of one of the largest government fishing cooperatives in Newfoundland, and I realized that *Brendan* and her crew were now utterly alone.

Sunrise. The wind had dropped. The halyards and rigging had ceased their clatter. In the quiet that followed came the sounds of a village waking up: a factory whistle, the rattle of a machine, the muffled cadences of human voices.

I was seated at the navigation table, taking a few minutes before my crew awakened to assess our situation here and to think about the rest of the day. Several practical matters needed attention—a sail repair, an hour of maintenance work on the diesel engine, a visit to the local shops to purchase fresh stores. Beyond these, I had only one important task: to somehow try to comprehend the changes that had happened in this place and the forces that had caused them.

This was not the first time *Brendan's Isle* and I had called at Port aux Basques and moored at the Fishermen's Cooperative piers. We had come here first in the summer of 1987—the same year that I had sailed into La Poile Bay, fifty miles to the west, and had encountered the old fisherman, Henry Coyne. The harbor here looked about the same as it had that year, with rows of boxy, flat-roofed houses surrounded by the silhouettes of granite hills. The air still carried the sharp, heady aroma of salt brine and seaweed. The waterfront still echoed with the cries of gulls, the grinding of surf against rock-bound cliffs, the shrill horns of the ferryboats as they entered and left.

Yet here the similarities ended. For in 1987 this village, along with hundreds of others like it all around the twelve hundred mile perimeter of this island, was still a working fishing community. The fish processing plant swarmed with activity from before sunrise until after sunset, with local dories lining the piers, rafted in tiers two or three deep, off-loading baskets of beautiful fat fish. A hundred yards away at the Cooperative piers, the larger boats congregated, the ones Newfoundlanders always referred to as "draggers," with their booms hoisted skyward and their nets spread out along the roadways for drying and mending. During summer these draggers did not work the local banks, for the large concentrations of fish that came here to spawn in winter and spring had now retreated to their summer grounds, several hundred miles north or south. Yet the talk among the skippers and crews was all the same: of fish for the catching and money to be made.

Brendan next visited Port aux Basques in the summer of 1991—a year in which I was headed north toward the Labrador coast. I was preoccupied that year by reports of heavy pack ice in the northern Gulf of St. Lawrence and the Strait of Belle Isle, so that I wasn't paying adequate attention to the events taking place in the fishery.

Yet the changes in Port aux Basques were impossible to ignore. Reports of dangerously low fish stocks the previous winter had forced a closure of fishing zones 3Pn and 3Ps, idling the dragger fleet and putting hundreds of fishermen at least temporarily out of work. The fish plant had closed. The Cooperative piers had been almost as empty as they were now.

Many of the local fishermen were expressing shock and surprise over the disappearance of the fish. One who was not surprised, however, was a man who'd been born and raised about a mile from here in the village of Channel: a writer, lawyer, political organizer, and grassroots philosopher named Cabot Martin. Born in 1944 and raised as the son of the local Anglican minister, Martin may have been this area's most famous native son. During the decades of the 1980s and early 1990s, Cabot Martin had become an influential voice in the controversies surrounding the disappearance of the cod. Once described as "the poet laureate of the inshore fisherman," he had earned a reputation all over Newfoundland as the champion of the little guy, a populist crusader who had never forgotten his roots in rural Newfoundland or the fishermen with whom he'd grown up.

I first came to know about Cabot Martin by means of a little book of his entitled *No Fish and Our Lives*, a collection of opinions and editorials that had originally appeared in the St. John's *Sunday Express* during the crucial years leading up to the cod fishing moratorium. At that time Martin was serving as president of the Newfoundland Inshore Fisheries Association, a grassroots coalition of fishermen and concerned citizens working in the forefront of the fight to save the northern cod. His voice in these editorials was strident and impatient. His message rang clear: for fish and fisher-man alike, time was running out. If fisheries managers couldn't find ways to implement severe conservation measures—and find them soon—the entire fishery was going to collapse. Along with it, he feared, might go the traditional way of life for thousands of rural Newfoundlanders.

Cabot Martin's analysis of the forces that led to the fishery's collapse emerged from two sources: first, the unique style of fishing he grew up with, and second, the geographical setting in which it was done. When Martin was a boy, in the years just after the Second World War, the village of Channel was still a small and relatively isolated outport, without roads or automobiles, looking to the sea for its survival. The traditional fishery here, as elsewhere along this southwest coast, had always been the type that Newfoundlanders describe as "inshore." Pursued in small open dories, this was a family enterprise practiced by fathers and sons (and, very rarely, daughters) using either single hand lines ("jigs") or long coils of baited hooks ("trawls"), both methods having been handed down virtually unchanged for hundreds of years. Slow, selective, and labor-intensive, this kind of fishing proved to be almost infinitely sustainable. It provided the basis for a subsistence economy upon which communities in this area had depended for nearly 400 years.

One reason for the long success of the inshore fishery along this coast, as Martin repeatedly pointed out, was the structure of the sea floor here. "The fishing banks all the way from Port aux Basques to Burgeo are narrow and close to shore," he explained, "making them easily accessible by small dories and bateaus. There was never a need for the big offshore vessels along the sou'west coast—never any reason."

Reason or not, however, the big boats came, and the inshore dory men had to begin competing with the newcomers for their fish. As Martin grew up, he watched the transition take place, from jigs and baited trawls to large, bottom-sweeping nets (called otter trawls), from small open dories to large offshore draggers.

For years Channel/Port aux Basques served as a kind of battleground between the traditional inshore dory men and the dragger fleets. The topography of its coastal banks made this place especially suitable to methods of inshore fishing. At the same time, its location at Newfoundland's new highway terminus and its easy accessibility to the ice-free fishing grounds of the Laurentian Fan and the southwestern Grand Banks made it an obvious choice as a major service center for the draggers.

Perhaps because of his boyhood memories of Port aux Basques and his long association with the people who lived here, Martin became especially sensitive to this conflict and to its implications for the future. As the fish grew smaller and harder to catch, as the numbers of fishermen increased, as the new fishing technologies became ever more powerful, he came to what was, for him, the only logical conclusion. The intruder here was the offshore dragger. The villain was the otter trawl, an apparatus that he eventually came to describe as a "destroyer of ecosystems," a threat to the health and sustainability of fisheries worldwide.

"The tiger retreats and declines within the shrinking jungle,"

Martin wrote in May, 1991. "We know that. The number of ducks goes down as we destroy their nesting areas; we know that. But out of sight below the waters, our own trawlers destroy the habitat of our cod and, in monumental ignorance, we wonder why our outports are being turned into [welfare] ghettos."

A little over a year after Martin penned these words, Federal Fisheries Minister John Crosbie announced the collapse of the northern cod stocks and the beginning of a moratorium on fishing for this species in Canadian waters. Shortly thereafter, Martin resigned as president of the Newfoundland Inshore Fisheries Association. He put away his pen and withdrew, at least for a time, from the public forum. For the next six years he couldn't think about the fish, couldn't face the fishermen, couldn't contemplate what was happening to the small villages and towns of Newfoundland. "I was depressed," he admitted, "fed up with the people and the politics, sick of the whole mess. I even got out of the cod farming venture I'd been involved in—was forced out, actually, after the hatchery in Placentia Bay burned down. Talk about bad timing . . . it seemed like everything was just falling apart all at once."

Like many Newfoundlanders, Martin was overwhelmed by the magnitude of the fisheries' collapse. For a time he felt helpless, unable to cope. In early 1998, however, like a Phoenix rising from the ashes, his voice re-emerged, this time on the op-ed page of the St. John's Sunday *Evening Telegram*. Not all of his new columns focused on the fishery, but whenever they did, they rang out with the same sense of urgency and moral outrage, the same stubborn opposition to the dragger technology.

"Next time you are down on the waterfront," he wrote in one recent column, "just size up the 'doors' that are hung on each side of a dragger's stern ramp. On the bigger draggers, they are the size of D-9 bulldozer blades.

"These doors, together with 150 feet or so of heavy chain and rollers and even more heavy, wire rope are what do the 'dragging.' From the fishes' viewpoint, the operation would look like an underwater mud and sand tornado bearing down on them."

I spoke with Martin soon after he had penned these words, asking him, if the cod ever did recover, whether he thought the dragger fleets would be allowed to return to the banks to continue their reign of what he called "ecological terror."

A few were already out there, dragging offshore, Martin said.

He'd even seen signs that as limited phases of the inshore fishery were reopened along the southwest coast, the draggers might be "re-injected."

"Talk about short-sightedness!" he railed. "Here we have an area with a geography perfectly suited to the inshore fisherman—an area that has supported a sustainable hook-and-line fishery for hundreds of years, and already we're talking about sending the draggers back in. Common sense says we almost destroyed it once; let's not do it again. But the big fish companies won't give up. Their advocates are unrelenting."

Martin's voice dropped to a whisper, and suddenly he sounded tired. "Will this experience ever teach us anything? Or will we just keep on chasing the almighty dollar, following the cycles of destruction and stupidity and greed, until we're forced to repeat the whole terrible story all over again?"

"Brendan's Isle," a voice intoned, "Brendan's Isle," repeating the syllables with a sing-song rhythm that made them sound like some kind of prayer. "Brendan's Isle . . . . Now where do you s'pose this Brendan's Isle might be? Some way down in the States, I'll venture. Some far way from here."

Glancing up from the navigation table, my mind still filled with the passionate crusadings of Cabot Martin, I slowly came to realize that I was also listening to another voice, quiet, insistent, that seemed to be coming from somewhere outside the sailboat's hull.

I moved to the companionway, climbed the six steps to the cockpit, turned toward the pier where the man I had heard was standing. My head was at about the same level as his black rubber boots. "Good morning," I said, glancing up at the grease-stained knees of his mechanic's coveralls.

"Goodday, skipper," said the man, tilting his visored cap onto the back of his head and running a dirty shirtsleeve across his brow. He was short, broad of girth, with large, stubby-fingered hands. "Budgen's the name. John Budgen. Harbormaster, Port aux Basques."

I moved along the sailboat's deck to a metal ladder bolted to the pier and climbed hand over hand to the paved surface where the man stood. He looked vaguely familiar. Had I encountered him, I wondered, during, one of *Brendan's* previous visits to this place? I moved around until the sun was behind me, the better to gaze into his face. His features were large and deep-set. His hair and stubble beard were flecked with gray. Except for a pale stripe across his forehead where the brim of his cap usually sat, his skin was the color and texture of old shoe leather.

John Budgen ran through the standard set of questions that he had posed, probably for decades, to mariners arriving at these piers. Vessel size? Commercial or pleasure? Last port of call? Where bound? He made a few pencil marks on a printed form that he had taken from a thin canvas satchel slung over his arm and handed me a copy.

"I remember you," I said. "I was here aboard this sailboat the summer of 1987, rafted alongside a big steel sixty-footer."

"Not much room on these piers for a sailboat in them days," said the harbormaster. "Like a carnival it was. Crazy it was. Docks full of draggers. Shops, bars, streets full of fishermen."

"The boat we were tied alongside was from Stephenville," I said. "The owner and his brother were rebuilding the wheelhouse. There was fiberglass and lumber all over the place. They had a table saw set up in the drying room in the main Cooperative building."

"Fellas had money then. Some of the boats was making a lot of money. You know how that goes. Money in the pocket, fella's got to spend it. Skippers with quotas was already gone, fishing down the Gulf. Others was staying, getting ready for the autumn fishery, spending money."

"I was back again with this sailboat in the summer of 1991," I said. "The year the Cooperative building was vandalized."

"Then you seen things change some," said the harbormaster.

"There wasn't much fishing going on along this coast in '91."

"Wasn't much fishing going on anywhere in Newfoundland in '91. But I s'pose you know that." Suddenly the playfulness was gone from his voice and his words had a ring of finality to them, as if he'd had enough of reminiscing.

"Dockage, two dollars," he said, "payable in advance." He reached for the pair of dollar coins that I held out to him and slipped them into his satchel. "Showers, laundry, both in the main building. Any problems, I'm here, eight to five. Welcome to Port aux Basques, skipper."

A white disk of sun emerged from behind the eastern hills and ascended into a cerulean sky. The ship's clock measured the morning with its odd chiming, adding one stroke for each half hour, until it reached eight and began the cycle again. Liz and Nat and Amanda and Richard lugged shower kits and bags of ship's laundry up to the Fishermen's Cooperative building to indulge in the unexpected luxury of fresh hot water. I finished the maintenance work on the engine before setting out for an hour's walk along the waterfront.

Even at midday the piers and roads and promenades around the harbor were still mostly empty. In front of the Cooperative building John Budgen slept—sitting bolt upright—in an aging blue Oldsmobile sedan. At the small boat landing a pair of carpenters worked with nail guns, installing the siding on a new set of fishing storehouses—a government work project, they told me, funded by what they called "TAGS money." At one of the floating piers a man bailed an old wooden dory with a plastic milk bottle. Behind him a whistle blew in the vicinity of the fish processing plant. I watched with surprise as a dozen plant workers emerged from a door at the end of the building, arranging themselves in twos and threes around the fish plant pier to smoke and talk.

What could be going on at this plant, I wondered, with so little fishing taking place along this coast? Almost as if he'd heard my question, one of the plant workers left the others and started down the pier toward me. He stopped at the last piling, standing almost directly in my path.

The man was tall, wiry, with thick brown hair and sideburns that nearly reached his chin. He wore a greasy baseball cap, blue coverall, white wraparound apron, black rubber boots. His sleeves were rolled up, revealing a solid mass of tattoos from his wrists to his elbows.

We exchanged hellos and a few platitudes about the weather. The man obviously wanted to talk. He asked if I was skipper of the green sailboat and queried me about our outbound passage from the States. I could tell from the way he framed his remarks that he had spent a large portion of his life at sea.

"Fisherman?" I asked, more as a formality than an actual question.

"Thirty-seven years."

"Dories or draggers?"

He laughed. "Would you believe both? Fished dories when I was a little fella, I did. Fished with a jigger with my Pap and brothers from the time I could walk. Fished gill nets with my uncles, too, for ten, fifteen years. Then my brother bought a dragger, forty-four footer name of *Gulf Harvester*, working out of Ramea. Fished with him fourteen seasons."

"You've been around some."

"No different than most. Just trying to make a living."

"Where's your brother's boat now?"

The man paused. "St. John's. For sale."

He pulled a wrinkled pack of cigarettes from his coverall pocket and offered me one. When I declined, he withdrew a paper cylinder from the package, tapped it on the back of his hand, lit it, took several long draws.

"When the government first cut the quotas, I was afraid my brother Ray was going to kill somebody."

"What year was that?"

"'Ninety . . . no, 'ninety-one it was. January. They closed the S'pear Bank that winter, closed the whole ground. Said the draggers in 3Pn was taking too much redfish as by-catch, so they closed the whole fishery. Laid up twenty-five boats. Closed down the fish plant. Sent home forty plant workers."

I was here the following summer, I told him. I knew about the trouble that had happened in Port aux Basques that year. I'd seen the wreckage that had been left behind in the Fishermen's Cooperative building—broken windows, ransacked offices, smashed furniture.

"The fellas was angry. Some was ready to burn the place down. We didn't understand, see. Didn't understand that if the fish was really that scarce, then why just close this fishery, with all the others still open? Why should we suffer with the rest of Newfoundland still fishing, with the French still dragging the S'pear Bank, the foreign factory ships still working the Nose and Tail? What was we supposed to do—just stay in port and let our families starve? Stay off the ground so the others could take the fish that should have been ours?

"Eighteen months later everything was closed."

"Eighteen months later didn't make no difference, closed or not closed, moratorium or no moratorium. Because by then everybody knew. The fish was gone. No rioting, no burning, no prayers to Almighty God was going to bring them back."

Silence. The man pulled another cigarette from his pocket, tapped it on his hand, lit it.

"What have you been doing since the moratorium," I asked.

He laughed self-consciously. "Living on the package—the welfare package is what I mean—same as the rest of Newfoundland. Living like Ottawa's whore. But things is better now. Fish plant is open again. Two shifts a day. My shift runs seven 'til three."

I admitted that I was surprised—surprised first that a man with his long experience in the fishery was working in a role that had traditionally been reserved for the women of the community. Even more surprised that the plant was open at all.

"Work is work," he said with a shrug. "Good news is there's plenty of fish—enough, they say, to keep this community working 'til Christmas. Bad news is the fish ain't from here, and won't be neither."

"From where then?"

He shrugged again. "Nobody supposed to know that. It comes across on the ferry—trucked in. Comes frozen in blocks, size of a house."

"From Norway?"

"Could be."

"Russia?"

"That's my guess—though it probably don't matter, long as the fish is good."

The man turned and stared vaguely out at the harbor. The fish plant whistle sounded again. He took one last draw on his cigarette, flipped the button to the pavement, ground out the burning ash with the toe of his boot.

"Strange how the world goes," he said, shaking his head. "Used to be we waited for the fish to follow the caplin up the bays. Now we waits for them to arrive on the Sydney ferry."

Chapter 2

Cabot Strait

DAWN BROKE UNDER RIBBONS of tunnel-shaped cloud that streamed like jet contrails along the axis of the Cabot Strait. The radio forecast promised strong southerlies. The sky, however, spoke of more—an acceleration of wind as it squeezed into the approaches, with gales on the headlands by afternoon.

It was time to go—and soon. In a sailboat such as *Brendan's Isle* there are windows of opportunity, and I knew that if we could punch out of this harbor and put the wind on our quarter before it became too strong, we would enjoy a good, fast ride around the western capes of Newfoundland and into the Gulf of St. Lawrence.

I glanced from face to face at my shipmates as they sat hunched over bowls of cereal at the dinette table, wondering if each was ready for the challenges of this day. The eldest and most experienced of this group, Amanda Lake, was no stranger to this vessel or to this part of the world. She had sailed the coast of western Newfoundland with *Brendan* and me twice before—once on the way to Labrador in 1988, the next time while en route to Greenland in 1994. Both times she had sailed as a deck hand, learning the routines of the vessel, practicing the rigors of an expeditionary lifestyle, proving in a hundred ways that she could handle the daily stresses of such a journey. On this present voyage she was sailing as mate and captain of the second watch—a role she had earned over many months and thousands of miles at sea, and a job she had performed with grace and competence during the weeks we had already been underway this summer.

The other three on board were all university students, all novices to this kind of sailing and strangers to this coast. Nat Pearre, a native of Halifax, sat behind a cereal box staring, absently, at a stack of toasted bread, listening to the wind. Having just completed an undergraduate engineering degree at Swarthmore College in the United States, he was taking a few months to travel before going back to look for work or further education. As the son of Dalhousie University oceanographer Sifford Pearre, Nat had a particular interest in the science that surrounds the disappearance of the northern cod. As a Canadian, he was also on a pilgrimage of sorts, journeying to a remote part of his own country to meet a people and learn about a way of life that neither he nor most of his countrymen had ever witnessed.

Nat's cabin mate, Richard Griffiths, was a person I had known since he was a child. Richard had grown up in a remote island community in northern Scotland similar to many that we would be visiting this summer—a village called Mossbank, Shetland Islands. Fifteen years ago I'd been befriended by Richard's father and mother when *Brendan* had called at the Shetlands during a passage across the North Sea. Richard had only been five years old at the time, yet both he and I remembered the encounter clearly. He remembered the big green sailboat in Lerwick Harbor and the American sailor who visited his home; I remembered the bright little Shetland boy with the brown wool sweater and rubber boots and the mop of tousled blond hair. Our mutual decision to sail together a decade and a half later represented a leap of faith—on both our parts—as we sought to discover how each had changed over the years and to learn whether each would live up to the other's expectations.

The fourth member of the crew, Liz Bogel, was another person I had known, at least by reputation, since she'd been very young. Liz's mother and I were first cousins, and although I'd never met Liz in person until she was in her teens, I had known her mother since we were both children.

In at least one respect, Liz was the most unlikely member of this crew—for until *Brendan* actually left the States in the middle of June, she had never set foot on a sailboat. But she had done many other things that counted for almost as much—and a few that counted for more. She was a gifted student, a talented jazz musician, an all-American fly-half on the Princeton women's rugby team. Just a month before she'd come sailing, in fact, she had broken her arm in a scrum, and the first thing she had worried about—even before acknowledging the pain—was whether the break might keep her from going to Newfoundland.

As for learning how to sail, Liz's progress during the first weeks of this voyage had been nothing less than astonishing. With the help of her shipmates and her own powers of concentration, she had mastered the basics of the sailor's craft as quickly as anyone I'd ever sailed with. The lessons keep coming, of course, and there is a sense in which no one ever stops learning what the sea has to teach. So far, however, Liz had proven herself equal to the challenge.

I was about to engage my shipmates in a little pep talk about the wild conditions we were likely to encounter out in the strait when a sudden gust of wind heeled the boat, causing bowls and cups and cereal boxes to slide across the dinette table. Nat lurched forward, corralling a cereal bowl and several coffee cups with his arms. Others grabbed for whatever they could reach, and together they managed to keep everything but a box of Corn Flakes from spilling onto the floor.

I suddenly realized that there was no time for sermonizing. "Give me five minutes to settle up with the dock master," I said, "and we'll be out of this place, heading for old John Cabot's Strait."

According to the Canadian *Sailing Directions*, the Cabot Strait is a body of water fifty-six miles wide, bounded on its western side by Cape North and the coastal palisades of Cape Breton Island, Nova Scotia, and on its eastern side by Cape Ray, Newfoundland. A glance at any sailing chart will verify that Cape Ray is indeed the headland closest to the Nova Scotia coast and thus the official terminator of the strait. For any mariner transiting the area, however, Cape Ray appears low and hummocky, one of several unsubstantial nubs of land that make out from this coast for forty miles under the great rectangular loom of Table Mountain. Cape Ray does boast a lighthouse, which makes it recognizable from sea in a way that adjacent features are not. But as to the actual shape of the land, it presents a rather unremarkable contour, as if there were no real boundary here, as if the land just fell away from the mountainous interior to strike a feeble truce with the sea.

Twenty miles due north of Cape Ray rises another terminator—a massive granite headland called Cap Anguille. Here the land soars nine hundred feet from the water's surface to become a kind of geological anchoring point, the great western elbow of Newfoundland. When seen from the deck of a little sailboat, this dark and ominous promontory does not simply begin: it intrudes, it overwhelms, it dominates the sea, announcing with its hulking form that whatever erosive forces may have conspired to carve the ancient river bed and sever this island from the rest of North America, such forces are hereby contradicted and rendered powerless. Here, at the blunt western end of the Cap Anguille Mountains, an ancient orogeny reasserts itself to proclaim this single truth: that Newfoundland is a rock, monolithic and immovable.

The wind rattled in *Brendan's* rigging and a white curl of foam tumbled at her cutwater as she doubled Cape Ray and bore off, running almost dead downwind, toward the loom of Cap Anguille. Once again she carried a deep reef and tiny patch of headsail, but here the seas were regular and the boat remained well under control. My shipmates passed the wheel from hand to hand in half-hour shifts in order to get the feel of the boat's motion as she skidded downhill. Meanwhile, I sat somewhat apart, gazing at the hunchback cape as it slowly grew on the horizon, thinking about this forbidding land and about the waves of Europeans that had once sailed here and had dared to call it home.

It is easy, when confronted by a coastal geography such as this, to understand why so many of the early visitors did not become permanent residents. This is a coast unlike any other in eastern North America. Bold and windswept, denuded of topsoil by the scouring of glaciers, empty of all but the most tenacious vegetation, the land presents a bleak and unforgiving aspect to the passing mariner. Protected bays and coves abound, providing thousands of safe harboring places for visiting ships—yet the interior of the land is nearly as inhospitable as the outer coast, being mostly comprised of high, rubbly plateau, crisscrossed with a maze of ponds and bogs, ribboned with stunted forests of spruce and tamarack.

In more temperate latitudes farther south, even when the coast is harsh, the interior beckons to the prospective settler with the promise of protected valleys, fertile river basins, great continental plains. But Newfoundland's interior plateau is so little suited for human habitation that to this day, except for the crudest lumbering operations, most of it has seldom been entered—and some not ever explored. With the exception of a few mining and lumbering communities, virtually every human settlement in Newfoundland has been established along the narrow strip of coast, its back braced against the harsh interior, its face directed toward the sea.

Another reason (besides the inhospitality of the land) that early visitors chose not to settle here was that the purpose of their journeys often pointed them elsewhere. Beginning with John Cabot, who made the first historically recorded voyage to Newfoundland in 1497, most had no intention even of stopping in this place. Some, like Cabot, were searching for someplace else: looking for a northwest passage to the Orient, dreaming of the riches of Cathay. Others had come on a simpler mission: to fill their little ships with dried cod, then to return with their bounty to the markets of Europe.

The huge numbers of cod to be found on the banks surrounding this island and the ease with which they could be captured was common knowledge among European fishermen long before Cabot uttered his famous remark about casting baskets into the sea and raising them up "filled with fishes." By 1436 an island had appeared on European maps of the western Atlantic whose name was "The Land of Stockfish" (dried cod). Fifteenth century Portuguese ship logs referred to "La Terra de los Bachalaos" (Land of the Cod Fish). Bretons and Normans described a place they called Terre Neuve. Bristol fishermen talked about Newland or the New Founde Land. But whatever its name, knowledge of this western isle seemed always to be accompanied by news of the prodigious quantity of cod fish—in shoals so thick, it was said, that the sea would sometimes turn black with their bodies and a dory could barely pass through them.

Despite the large and growing presence of European ships plying these waters, however, it was the particular character of this fishery that it did not require that the fishermen actually live here. All that was required, for those willing to take the risk, was a voyage out to the western fishing grounds each spring and a voyage home to Europe again each autumn. During the summer, temporary drying stations were established in the harbors and coves that dotted the island's coasts. Here small crews would be put ashore to clean and split and dry the fish. Then in September when their work was done, the summer crews would stow the fish aboard, leave the shore, and rejoin the mother ship for the voyage home.

According to most historians, this system of seasonal "ship fishing" predominated from the earliest period (probably the mid-fifteenth century) right through the sixteenth and well into the seventeenth century. For most of these fishermen, the land was too barren and inhospitable to invite year-round residence, and, in any case, the fish had to be transported back to Europe to be sold.

Slowly, however, patterns of permanent settlement evolved. The first European residents were probably small parties of men detached from the fishing ships, known in the local vernacular as "winter crews," who remained on the coast to cut wood and build drying racks ("flakes"), small boat landings ("stages"), and cooking rooms for use in the summer fishery—and possibly also to maintain possession of strategically located harbors and coves for their own ship captain's use the following season. In the beginning, these winter crews may have been semi-permanent, with individual fishermen only remaining for a year or two. But eventually the captains began to understand the usefulness of transporting women to the new land, and soon afterwards the winter crews found themselves building more permanent structures, raising families, and becoming what they called "livyers" (people who "live here").

Few written records remain from this earliest period of European settlement in Newfoundland, yet it is clear from the surviving place-names that many nationalities were involved. Port aux Basques speaks of the presence of the early Basque whalers on this coast. Table Mountain, looming behind it, indicates an English presence; Cap Anguille tells of the French. The Spanish were also here—especially in the years before the defeat of the Great Armada—as were the Dutch and the Portuguese.

By the beginning of the seventeenth century, however, the patterns of coastal settlement had become centered primarily on the presence of two national groups: the French and the English. By 1600, each nation had on the order of two hundred small ships plying the fishing grounds around Newfoundland; by 1630 England had perhaps three hundred ships. Following the voyages of Jacques Cartier (1534–1541), the French began actively exploring and colonizing the St. Lawrence Gulf and River areas and the vast continental lands to the west. Along with this activity, the French fishing ships quickly became the dominant presence along the north and west coasts of Newfoundland, establishing their claim to a portion of coastline that eventually came to be known as the "French Shore."

Meanwhile, the English concentrated their fishing—and colonizing—mainly along the south and east coasts of the island. With thousands of square miles of fishing banks and dozens of deep bays at their disposal and with the ever expanding European markets for fish, the English ship fishery continued to flourish. Not so, however, for several abortive attempts at colonization. Beginning with Sir Humphrey Gilbert's triumphant arrival at St. John's Harbor in 1583, several attempts were made to establish a bona fide English colony here. Like Cecil Lord Baltimore's "first colonial capital" at Ferryland (1623), however, most were abandoned and all were eventually deemed failures.

The reason was simple: with an active and profitable ship fishery already in place, the powerful merchants and ship owners back in Bristol and Devon had no interest in competing for their fish with year-round residents. The west country ship fishermen had influential friends in Parliament and the attention of the Crown; the scattered residents of Newfoundland had neither. Thus, whenever policy was established having to do with permanent settlement in the ports and harbors of English-speaking Newfoundland, such policy was always strongly influenced by what amounted to a "lobby" of ship fishing interests.

Seasonal ship fishing, they argued, with its long sea voyages from England to the fishing banks and home again, served as an excellent Naval training ground, providing a steady supply of experienced English seamen to the Admiralty and the Crown. This advantage, combined with the continuing profitability of the ship fishery and the "vexing problems" of administering a colony that might not otherwise be needed, led the English Parliament to pursue a policy of "limited settlement without government" in Newfoundland for most of the seventeenth century, finally culminating in the so-called Newfoundland Act of 1699. Under this Act, official authority in each permanently settled village or outport was given to the first fishing captain to arrive in port each spring (the so-called "fishing admiral"). Such person became the sole ruler of the village and the supreme arbiter of disputes for the year. Residents were thus left at the whim of fate as to which admiral they might get for the coming season and how they might be treated by him and his crew.

One of the great mysteries of Newfoundland's early history, given the many injustices of such treatment, is that the residents of these tiny communities chose to remain in Newfoundland at all. Yet remain they did, and somehow, over the decades, many found ways not only to overcome the hardships visited upon them from almost every quarter but actually to make their communities thrive and grow.

The reason that stands out for this success—beyond the strength and resiliency of the people themselves—is the fish. Nearly everything else was set against them. The climate was harsh. The interior of the island was barren and unproductive. The English government's treatment of the settlers was, in the words of one of Newfoundland's most famous historians, "stupid, cruel, and barbarous." The fishing admirals were vacillatory and self-serving.

The fish, however, persisted through every uncertainty and every hardship. In a barter economy, the fish became the common currency. In a land ravaged by storms and haunted by famine, the fish became the single dependable food source. In a society that promised nothing but the product of one's own efforts, the fish became the people's wealth and their salvation—the substance that held their communities together and, very often, the reason they were able to survive at all.

One of the most obvious measures of the importance of the fish to the lives of the island's early residents can be seen in the geographical locations of their towns and villages. In the rest of colonial America, early settlers nearly always tried to establish their communities in places with the best harbors or the most convenient access to transportation routes or to arable land. In Newfoundland, however, people seemed rather to settle in the places most accessible to the fishing grounds. Often this meant that they would find themselves living on wild, windswept promontories or in small coves or "tickles" (passages between islands) where boats could be quickly launched and either rowed or sailed out to the fish. As long as there was a beach or flat area on which to dry the fish and an adequate supply of fresh water, here is where the community would be established and where the people would live out their lives.

Dependent upon the cod and wedded to the vast expanse of ocean, the little clusters of families that populated these settlements began to form a unique identity as a kind of maritime proto-culture.

Theirs was not a society tied to any particular European nation state, for they lived in a place without a name, without political boundaries, without an army or a flag or even a government. Many ceased giving allegiance to any political entity but merely paid lip service to whatever European power held sway over them at the time, changing allegiances as the currents of war and peace in Europe also changed.

Seemingly out of place and time, many of these communities carried on in this manner for centuries. Habits of speech that had been brought over from the wharves of Bristol or the cottages of Cork or the tenements of London became fixed in particular settings. Boat building technologies and fishing methods that had been used in Europe since the Renaissance became frozen in time. The extreme isolation of many of the locations forced inhabitants to organize themselves into tightly knit kinship groups. Family fishing ventures, shared root gardens, communal building projects became the norm, resulting in a network of tiny coastal communities with strong traditions of altruism and interdependency.

Over the years, the outside world proceeded in its tumultuous pace. Disputed boundaries between English and French fishing territories shifted. Fishing admirals failed to return. International treaties were signed and broken. Wars were lost and won. Yet throughout every circumstance, the people of the outports persisted. Bound together by the natural cycles of their maritime environment and by their knowledge and skill as fishermen, they had forged a common identity. As long as they could follow the cod up the bays each spring, as long as they could fill their dories and spread their flakes with fish, they would continue to bind their lives to the sea and to depend on its bounty for their sustenance and survival.

Afternoon shadows painted the land in deep relief as *Brendan's Isle* drew abeam of the lighthouse on Cap Anguille. The wind-driven seas stacked up like moguls. Nat stood behind the helm, both hands on the wheel, concentrating on keeping the boat tracking straight. The others joined me at the rail to witness the drama that unfolded along the shore.

Dead astern, the silhouette of Cape Ray had already started to drop beneath the horizon. Ribbons of chinook cloud streamed along the face of Table Mountain, dividing the high terrain into kaleido-scopic layers of dark and light. To the left of the mountain, just on the sailboat's quarter, the land dropped away to form the valleys of the Little Codroy and Grand Codroy rivers. Here the coast became almost level for a time before beginning its climb again toward the headland at Cap Anguille.

With the exception of the lighthouse, this entire coast presented only one visible sign of human habitation, this being the tiny fishing village and harbor-of-refuge at Codroy Island. Tucked behind a low, kidney-shaped bar, this settlement boasted the only all-weather harbor between St. Georges, fifty miles to the northeast, and Port aux Basques, thirty-five miles to the south. As such, it had been a favorite stopping place and base of operations for the west coast dragger fleet for many decades. The government piers here were once almost as crowded as those in Port aux Basques. The shallow banks to the west and south were a popular ground for draggers.

On this particular afternoon, however, the village roadways appeared deserted and the near shore waters remained empty of traffic. The one sign of activity in the harbor, a cluster of masts near the government pier, turned out to be a row of electric transmission poles.

Due north of Codroy, the headland at Cap Anguille rose like a battlement from the valley floor. Its southern and western faces, stripped of vegetation, framed the backdrop for the lighthouse as the sailboat tumbled past. For a moment it appeared as if this tower of rock might form an abrupt terminus to the entire island of New-foundland, for there was nothing but open water visible ahead. Seconds later, however, the north face of the cape exploded into view, revealing a densely forested palisade that angled steeply back to the east for twenty miles and disappeared into the horizon: the Cap Anguille Mountains.

The wind accelerated into a clear air gale as the sailboat drew away from this coast. Somewhere ahead was the Port au Port peninsula and the rest of western Newfoundland. From deck level, however, nothing was visible but empty sea. The sailboat plunged down the backs of waves, streaming through ribbons of spindrift, and I suddenly felt the deep and inexpressible solitude of this place, as if we might have been sailing off the edge of the world.

Chapter 3

Cow Head

BRENDAN'S ISLE STOOD in the center of a shallow basin, sails furled, engine turning over slowly. A stone breakwater and wooden piers surrounded the basin on three sides, facing a small fish plant and shingle beach. At the seaward end of the basin a trio of lobster boats and a decommissioned dragger lay bow to stern, moored against one of the piers.

"Can I tie alongside?" I called to a small group of men standing on the pier next to the dragger.

"Yes, boy, no problem," one of the men hollered back. He leapt to the fishing boat's deck and climbed a set of steps to the bow. "Come ahead now," he called, waving his arms.

Amanda waited until the sailboat had pulled close to the flared steel hull, then tossed a coil of mooring line neatly across the dragger's bow. The man retrieved the line and, just as neatly, led it through a hawsepipe and made it fast on a steel cleat. Amanda repeated the same maneuver at the stern with another of the men while Liz and Richard dropped several orange fishing floats between the hulls.

Once the lines and bumpers were made fast, the first man climbed to the roof of the dragger's wheelhouse. His movements were rabbit-like, and he seemed to bounce from one place to the next. He sat facing the sailboat, dangling his legs. When he spoke he addressed Amanda, as having obviously been the leader of the deck during the docking maneuver. He introduced himself as Tobias Foley, owner of one of the lobster boats down the pier. "How far you fellas sailed in this boat?" he wanted to know. "How much wind can she handle? How far will she tip before she goes over?"

Amanda stood at the mast answering the man's questions while slowly stripping off her foul-weather gear. "Damn few fellas here be out on a day like this," Foley said, "even if there was any fish." Amanda pushed her orange rubber parka hood onto her neck, peeled back her gloves, unbuttoned her parka. "Too much sea for most of these boats," said Foley. Then he looked up as Amanda pulled off her wool watch cap and shook out her shaggy blond curls.

The fisherman stopped talking, practically in mid- sentence. In the embarrassed silence that followed, he gazed around as if he were trying to find a place to hide. He would not meet Amanda's eyes again but only looked from face to face at the men who stood on the deck below. "Holy Jesus boys," he stammered at last. "He's a girl."

An unrelenting surge rumbled among the boulders at the base of the breakwater, the residue of last evening's gales, and the wind keened in the rigging. Here, in the tiny fishing harbor of Cow Head, there was little protection from the elements. The harbor was built on a headland that jutted out half a mile from the coast and was attached to the mainland by a low, rocky causeway. The headland itself stood several hundred feet high, providing at least a modicum of shelter for the cluster of wooden buildings and storehouses nestled along its shore. The man-made harbor, however, faced directly into an open bay where its stone ramparts seemed ineffectual against the fury of the northern Gulf.

Once Tobias Foley and company had left the dragger's decks and had returned to their own vessel, I asked Amanda and Liz to accompany me on a walk into the village. Amanda had traveled on this coast before, and I knew by her reaction to the fisherman's remark that she had not been offended. I was not as certain, however, about how Liz might have been feeling in response to the man's knee-jerk chauvinism.

"Seems you're a bit of an oddity in these parts," I said to my two shipmates as we climbed across the dragger's decks and up onto the pier.

"I'm not sure I got that last remark," said Liz. "Was it an insult or some kind of backhanded compliment?"

"Simple gender confusion," said Amanda. "Nothing to get excited about. What you heard was just ten generations of tradition talking."

"Then I think you were being mean."

"Mean?"

"He was embarrassed. You should have left your cap on."

"Or maybe taken my shirt off," said Amanda, and both erupted with peals of laughter.

I parted ways with my shipmates at the foot of the pier, as they had both elected to hike up into the hills above the village, while I decided to follow a gravel roadway that wound among tattered buildings toward the fish plant. The village—if that was indeed how it should still have been termed—was mostly deserted. On the left, a few yards beyond the breakwater pier, was an abandoned two-story frame building with picket fence, a pair of barricaded garden plots, several crumbling outbuildings. The doors and windows were shuttered and boarded over. The picket fence and much of the main structure were weathered gray. The yard and gardens were overgrown with weeds.

Beyond this building were several small fishing storehouses (or "stores" as Newfoundlanders called them), most of them closed and barred shut. Alongside each store was a cache of lobster pots, cleaned and mended and stacked like firewood. One store was open, its doors ajar. Inside were buoys, pot warp, gillnets, tubs of trawl lines, oars, an outboard engine, jerry cans of fuel. A man worked in the adjacent yard, cleaning a gillnet that he had spread on a slab of rock. He picked over the fine plastic filament one section at a time, pulling off tufts of seaweed and small bits of fish. He did not look up as I passed but only raised his hand in a half-salute.

Around the next bend the road widened to reveal a long red building with a shipping bay and sliding steel door: the fish processing plant. I had learned that the inshore fishery had been opened along this coast on a limited basis for several days that month and was hopeful that this might translate into an opportunity to buy a bit of fresh cod or turbot or halibut. The plant appeared to be operating. A pickup truck was parked in front of the building, and the sliding door was unlocked. I did not enter, however, but sat on a step near the loading bay, waiting for someone to happen by, pondering the strange state of affairs in this place.

It was hard to tell from appearances exactly what was going on here, for Cow Head seemed a bundle of contradictions. In certain ways it appeared to be mortally wounded. In others it seemed to be struggling on, like a patient in an intensive care unit hooked up to a series of life support systems.

I knew something of the recent history of this place, for the events that had taken place here were essentially the same as those that had been taking place in small fishing communities all along this western coast. I knew, for instance, that the precipitous moment of crisis for this village had occurred five years before, in the summer of 1993. For reasons that were still being debated, the cod fishing moratorium had not been imposed in the Gulf of St. Lawrence until that summer, a full year after John Crosbie's original announcement. This delay had taken place because managers at the Canadian Department of Fisheries and Oceans had considered the so-called "Gulf cod" to be a separate breeding population, and their 1992 stock assessment had not shown these fish to be in the same trouble as the northern cod. A year later, however, the DFO's mistake became obvious when the Gulf cod, too, collapsed. At this point, the moratorium was extended to include fish stocks in the Gulf area, effectively closing down the cod fisheries around the entire island.

That closure, had it not been accompanied by some sort of government compensation package for out-of-work fishermen, might have transformed this place (and others like it) into a ghost town virtually overnight. John Crosbie understood this fact perhaps as well as anyone in the Canadian government, and his willingness to declare the moratorium when he did was tied directly to assurances from Ottawa that such compensation would be immediately forthcoming.

The first of the compensation packages was a hastily conceived stopgap measure created to provide economic relief to Newfoundlanders who had been hardest hit by the closures. Poorly planned from the beginning and inadequately funded, this program was replaced in May 1994 by a massive bailout plan, The Atlantic Groundfish Strategy (or TAGS, as it became universally known), a $1.9 billion initiative designed to support and retrain some thirty-eight thousand fishermen and plant workers throughout Atlantic Canada. In addition to unemployment compensation and retraining,

TAGS was also charged with the task of reducing capacity in the fishery by fifty percent—a goal that was to be achieved by eliminating redundancy in the processing sector and by buying back fishing licenses from retrained fishermen.

TAGS was the key to survival in places like Cow Head, although rumor had it that the program was going to end, at least in its present form, by the end of summer 1998. Several secondary fisheries were still operating here: shrimp, scallop, turbot, halibut, skate, caplin. The most obvious of these in Cow Head was the lobster fishery, as witnessed by the small fleet of lobster boats in the harbor and by the huge inventory of traps stacked in the village. Lobstering had been an important part of the economy in western Newfoundland ever since canneries had been introduced here in the early part of the twentieth century. This fishery was highly seasonal, however, and was limited by government regulation to a few weeks in the spring and early summer—a fact that would probably insure its sustainability even as it also limited the amount of income that any one fisherman could expect to earn from it.

The most dramatic rescue measure that was being applied here, it seemed, was the reopening of the inshore cod fishery, even if on a limited basis. This one surprised me, for even though I'd been forewarned, I wasn't expecting to see so many signs of activity in this place: dories moored in the harbor, nets being mended, fishing stores filling up with gear, even the fish plant showing signs of life. Nothing I'd read or heard had suggested that the cod were coming back. In fact, most reports seemed to point in the other direction. Maybe scientists in the Department of Fisheries and Oceans had come up with new data. Or maybe this was a political move, designed to provide fishermen a few days on the bays and nearby banks—not enough days to make a living—perhaps not even enough to cover the costs of gear and boats—but enough, at any rate, to remind people of better times and to inspire hopes of returning some day to the way life used to be.

I looked up from where I was sitting just in time to see the now familiar figure of the lobsterman, Tobias Foley, bounding around the corner of the fish plant. He stopped when he saw me, and I waved and called out a greeting. Almost before I'd finished speaking he was by my side, as if he had somehow been catapulted across the intervening terrain. He asked what I was doing here. When I told him I was looking for someone who might be able to sell me a bit of fish, he held up his hands and skittered backwards toward the fish-plant door. "Don't move, Cap. I'll be only a minute."

True to his word, the fellow reappeared moments later with a large slab of fish wrapped in a piece of newspaper. The fish had been gutted, split down the middle, and laid open flat like the leaves of a book. The smooth white flesh was caked with gray crystals.

The expression on my face must have given away the fact that I had never tried to cook a piece of salt cod. "The way we does it," said Foley, "first we soaks it in a bucket of fresh water—to get rid of the salt taste. Then we boils it, adding whatever's handy—onions, potatoes, cabbage, a handful of carrots." A smile played around the corners of his mouth as he spoke, and I thought I could see him beginning to salivate. I was about ready to reach for my wallet, but before I could make a move, he placed a hand on my elbow. "You'll not even think about paying Tobias Foley for a bit of salt fish," he said, then turned and retreated across the roadway.

"Then you'll come by the sailboat tomorrow noon," I called after him, "for a bowl of boiled supper." Without turning around, he waved an arm over his head and disappeared in a single bound around the corner of the next building.

The following day served as a much needed layover for *Brendan* and her crew as we rested and waited for clearing weather. Nat took on the task of soaking the salt fish and preparing the vegetables for the noon meal. The fisherman showed up on the deck of the dragger in the late morning. Once again he came bearing a gift, this time in the form of a two-gallon bucket of white tundra berries, known in the local vernacular as bakeapples.

I invited him to step aboard and sit and talk a while in the cool sunshine. He placed the bucket of berries on the seat next to him and offered me one. I declined as politely as I could, knowing that until they are cooked and sweetened with sugar, bakeapples are hard and acidic—an acquired taste. He shrugged, grabbed a handful, popped one into his mouth, and passed the rest of the bucket down the companionway—a peace offering, perhaps.

We talked for a time about the recent gales, the ice last winter, the spring lobstering. Eventually I got around to asking about the opening of the cod fishery, admitting that I was not prepared for all the activity we'd seen in this community. "Must be nice to have the fish coming back," I said.

"Begging your pardon, Cap, but anyone thinks the fish is coming back just ain't opened their eyes. Oh, yes, there's the scattered cod out there. Fellas is only allowed to use trawl lines for them. The gillnets you seen are for winter flounder, plaice, turbot, even though gillnets ain't ever been too particular about what sort of fish gets caught in them.

"Cod fishery's open on a quota system. But where the government gets their numbers, I don't know. Three thousand tons, seven thousand tons, seems like they just pulls the numbers out of a hat. Quota is regional, set for the whole coast, from Cape Ray all the way down to Belle Isle. Opens the beginning of the month, then when the quota gets filled, don't matter where the fish is caught, the coast is closed again."

I asked if he'd been out fishing in his own boat since the lobster season ended.

"No, boy, I only jigs, only ever did. The fisheries agent, fella from Rocky Harbor name of Kenny Goss, he come down here this spring and tell us the government don't want us jigging. Cuts the fish, he says. Nobody wants to buy a fillet in the store with a big cut across it, he says. You boys ought to know that. So now the government don't want us jigging, not even to catch a fish for our family.

"So many rules, a fella has to carry a briefcase when he goes fishing now. So much damn paperwork. It's like this every time a fella leaves the harbor. [He held his hands apart, one above the other, indicating a stack of papers several inches thick.] So many rules you can't keep 'em all straight. No jigging on this coast. No traps in that bay. Each place a fella goes, the rules is all different."

"Who makes the rules?"

"Government, boy. Government makes the rules. People talks. Somebody complains. Then they makes a new rule. No telling why. No telling why the government does anything they does."

The fisherman paused, popped another bakeapple into his mouth, chewed loudly. "Funny thing is, we seen it coming. Long time before they told us anything, we little fellas seen it. Starting in 'eighty five, maybe 'eighty six, we seen the fish getting smaller, the catch dropping every year. All around Newfoundland we seen it. But the big boys in St. John's, the bureaucrats, the scientists, they wouldn't listen. We tried to tell them, but who are we? Simple fishermen. No education. No fancy titles after our names. We tried to tell them the caplin wasn't coming in on the beaches like they used to and the fish wasn't running up the bays. We tried to tell them and they wouldn't listen."

"What was happening?" I asked. "What was causing the fish to disappear?"

Foley stared at his hands. "You know how it goes, Cap. Inshore blames the nearshore. Nearshore blames the offshore. Everybody blames the fish companies and the foreign factory ships. Well, it could be one of them and it could be all of them together, and maybe there's nobody's ever going to know for sure. But what I says is there's more than just fishing that's to blame."

"What else, then?"

"Think about when the fish started getting scarce. Think about when the fellas here first started noticing. Was it in the 'sixties when the factory ships first showed up on the Banks? Was it in the 'seventies when the local draggers come along? How about the early 'eighties when we got the two hundred miles to ourselves? No, boy, there was plenty of fish until one thing happened and one thing only. Nineteen-and-eighty-four it was when Greenpeace and that man Brian Davies come along and stop the seal hunt. Come out here with their helicopters and cameras and destroyed one fishery, and not eight years later another fishery destroyed as well."

"Seals?"

"Yes boy, seals. Fish-killing machines. Come down on the ice every winter, six million strong, move north again in the spring with half a million new pups. More every year, ranging farther south, farther into the Gulf, looking for fish. Nobody in Cow Head or any other village along this coast is going to fill their dories with fish again until we gets rid of them seals once and for all."

I listened with care as Tobias Foley described his theories about seals and cod, for I understood how deeply his feelings ran on this matter and how long he had thought about such interrelationships in this place he lived and fished. The subject of seals—which in the Gulf of

St. Lawrence always meant harp seals—was one that had become highly sensitive for many who lived along this coast. Traditionally, the annual spring "cull" of harp seals and seal pups was considered a birthright. More recently, however, it had evolved into a moral and political dilemma, as animal rights groups had started to wage highly visible international campaigns protesting wasteful hunting practices and cruel and inhumane treatment of the animals, and as the Canadian government had been forced to establish conservation measures and to enforce certain humanitarian reforms.

Historically, the hunting of seals had been a part of the subsistence lifestyle in Newfoundland ever since the first Europeans had decided to settle here. The earliest outport livyers had learned from their aboriginal predecessors how to hunt seals, how to use their fur and skin for boots and clothing, how to use their meat and oil for food and lamp fuel.

By the mid-seventeenth century French fishermen had established an organized commercial seal hunt along the shores of southern Quebec and the Belle Isle Strait. English-speaking hunters followed suit soon afterwards along the coasts of northeastern Newfoundland and southern Labrador.

Harp seals are creatures of the ice. For most of the year they live and feed in the high Arctic, migrating south in the late autumn only after the first of the southern sea ice has started to form. They arrive off the Newfoundland coast in November or early December in huge numbers (perhaps as many as ten million in their original state) and spend the winter months living on the pack ice either off the coast of northern Newfoundland or in the western Gulf of St. Lawrence. During the late winter they form into large, loosely organized "whelping patches." Here the females bear their young and nurse them for several weeks before the herd begins its long northward migration again.

At first the seals had been pursued almost exclusively from the shore, on foot or in small ice punts. Later, as markets for seal products grew and commercial hunting became increasingly lucrative, more and more of the population became involved. With the discovery of the offshore whelping patches in the late eighteenth century, sealers began to travel to the "front" (as they called the main east coast whelping area) in small, ice-strengthened fishing schooners, then in slab-sided wooden steamships, and finally in huge iron factory ships that could smash through the ice and penetrate into the very center of the whelping grounds.

By the middle decades of the nineteenth century, during the heyday of Newfoundland's sealing industry, merchant ship owners in St. John's were sending more than five hundred vessels and fourteen thousand Newfoundlanders to the front each spring—a number that may have included almost every able-bodied man on the coast. The average landed catch between 1819 and 1829 was just under 300,000 seals, with a real kill of at least twice that number. During the next three decades the average topped 400,000 seals per year, with a real kill that likely approached a million seals annually.

In spite of increased hunting effort, landings grew steadily smaller during the late nineteenth and early twentieth centuries, reflecting the severe stressing of the seal herd, whose total numbers may have fallen to a million or less by the time war broke out in Europe in 1914. For the next several decades, two wars and a worldwide depression kept sealing activity at a low ebb. Even the end of World War II saw only a modest revival of the hunt, for in the intervening years most of Newfoundland's sealing fleet had either been sunk or had rusted away from age and disuse.

The modern era of seal hunting thus began in the early 1950s as two new players entered the scene: a group of Norwegian whale and seal hunters with a fleet of highly mechanized icebreaker factory ships, and a group of high level bureaucrats at the Canadian Department of Fisheries and Oceans who became convinced that cod and harp seals were incompatible enemies, locked in a struggle between predator and prey that would eventually spell disaster for the cod.

DFO managers granted the Norwegian factory ships a virtual monopoly to hunt both harp and hooded seals at extermination rates in the Gulf of St. Lawrence and at the Labrador Sea front. Airborne "gypsy sealers" flying specially equipped light aircraft from ports all over the Canadian Maritimes were allowed to join the seal hunt in the western Gulf. The hunt—or what some were still calling the "cull"—was becoming an international free-for-all, an "orgy of greed and uncontrolled violence," as critics described it, in which the seal herd was once again being threatened with commercial extinction.

The first widespread awareness of what was happening on the ice occurred in the summer of 1964 when a television film showing violent scenes of the seal hunt ignited public outcry and mobilized the energies of animal rights activists. Underfunded and largely ineffectual at first, the animal rights campaign finally began to gather momentum under the leadership of a young Canadian named Brian Davies and an organization, founded by Davies, called the International Fund for Animal Welfare (IFAW). Year after year, from the mid-1970s to the mid-1980s, activists from IFAW, Greenpeace, World Wildlife Fund, and other animal rights organizations journeyed to the ice with their cameras and pens, dedicated to waging a media war against what they viewed as unconscionable acts of violence against a fellow creature.

Such was the success of IFAW's media campaign of the early 1980s that almost no one who was old enough to read a newspaper or look at a TV set in those years needed to be told what a "whitecoat" harp seal pup looked like. Images of this lovable creature, its mass of downy white fur framing a cupie-doll face and dark, soulful eyes, appeared everywhere in the news, as did the companion images of the same creature with a crushed skull, mutilated face, blood gushing from its eyes and mouth and nose, lying half dead on the ice while it was literally being skinned alive.

Eyewitness descriptions of the hunt published during this period were so graphic that people often could not read them all the way through. One such account by Canadian journalist Silver Donald Cameron describes the hunt as being like a battlefield. "As far as you can see, the ice is splashed with blood. Whitecoats, still living, whose mothers have ducked into the water, cry aloud. [Their] tiny carcasses, . . . not much bigger than a good sized roast once the fur and fat are taken, stare at us with bulging eyes protruding from heads smashed by sealers' clubs."

The media campaign succeeded in arousing public indignation, but it was a 1982 ban on the importation of whitecoat seal products by the European Economic Community that finally moved the Canadian government to begin taking Brian Davies and the animal rights campaign seriously. The European ban was renewed in 1983, followed by a boycott of Canadian fisheries products by British supermarket chains, also organized by Davies, in the summer of 1984. Mounting pressures from world opinion, combined with the threat of further boycotts of Canadian fisheries products by American buyers, finally forced Canadian federal Fisheries Minister Pierre de Bane to admit defeat. After appointing a Royal Commission to study the sealing industry and recommend reforms, de Bane resigned his post as Minister. Seal landings dropped from 170,000 in

1982 to an average of about 36,000 per year for the next four years as the airplanes and factory ships were banished from the front. For a time, at least, the commercial harp seal hunt appeared to be a thing of the past.

"That man Davies," said Tobias Foley, articulating each word as if it were a curse. "He tried to make the name of Newfoundlanders into somet'ing mean and dirty. 'Goons,' he called us. 'Murderers.' 'Bloodthirsty swilers.' He come out onto the ice with his bevy of airline stewardesses to watch the hunt, and the sealers, taking him for friend, says 'Sure m'son, come ahead, come and take our picture while we works.'

"Now you might call them sealers dumb Newfies—and maybe in the end you might be right. Because without knowing, they was asking that man to take away their jobs, showing him just exactly how 'twas done. 'See here, Brian boy, see here is my sealing stick. Here the nail bent over just so to kill the whitecoat in one swipe. You want to take my picture, Brian boy? Why sure, you stand right over there. Now see, I raises my arm like this. . . .' "

Foley exhaled a slow breath between his teeth. "Oh there's blood—blood everywhere. It ain't no pretty sight killing seals. But you ever seen the blood and scales and guts on the deck of a dragger after the cod end gets dumped? Ever seen a giant tuna come aboard and bled to death? Ever seen the bloody fish parts washing down the gutters in every fish factory in Newfoundland? We spends our lives in blood, Cap. It's a nasty job sometimes—a dangerous job that nobody wants to do sometimes—but it's all we has.

"One thing you need to understand—it ain't just the cod or the lobster or the seal that makes a Newfoundlander's year. It's everything together. Turr and eider duck in November, moose in December, seals in March and April, lobster and caplin in May and June, and when times is good, fat blackberry cod in June and July and maybe August.

"Pay me a t'ousand dollars, Cap, and I'll never go sealing again. I'm no 'murderer,' see? I'm no 'bloodthirsty swiler.' I don't like killing baby seals anymore than you. But I needs that t'ousand to mend my boat, buy fuel, mend traps. Just like I needs the next t'ousand from the lobster to get my summer fish. Every certain thing works together. That's how we lives on this island. That's how we've lived for five hundred years."

In December 1987, three years after Davies and the International Fund for Animal Welfare closed down the seal hunt, the release of the Report of the Royal Commission on Seals and Sealing led to a number of reforms, all of which were implemented by the DFO the following spring. Vessels over sixty-five feet in length were prohibited from participating in the hunt. Sealers were required to be trained in efficient and humanitarian methods of killing and were not allowed to "stockpile" stunned or wounded animals. No one was permitted to kill whitecoat pups under fourteen days old or adult seals, male or female, while they were in the whelping patches. And trained observers and enforcement staff were to be made available by the DFO to monitor the hunt and enforce the new regulations.

Aided in part by a continuing ban by the European Community on the importation of whitecoat seal products, harp seal landings remained low (on the order of fifty-thousand seals annually) through the first few years of the 1990s. Based on a DFO census, it appeared that the seal herd was also rebounding, from a total population of less than two million in the early 1970s to perhaps double that number by the early 1990s. Yet this relatively peaceful state of affairs was soon ended, for the collapse of the northern cod set the stage for an emotional battle. Old memories were rekindled, old fears resurfaced, and traditional opponents renewed their arguments about the relationship between seals and cod.

In 1993 DFO managers broke almost a decade of silence as they began lobbying once again for increased harp and hooded seal quotas, arguing that seal predation had been a primary factor leading to the cod's disappearance. Meanwhile, Davies' International Fund for Animal Welfare and the animal rights coalition set out on what they called a "public education campaign" to show that the seals were not responsible for the cod's disappearance. Sealers and fishermen entered the fray, attitudes became polarized, and each side amassed an array of statistics with which to prove its claims.

Seals eat cod—nobody was arguing about that. But serious arguments *were* arising about how much cod the seals eat and about how many seals were out there doing the eating. DFO estimates of the harp seal population in 1994 stood at 4.8 million and growing, with seal predation responsible for the consumption of 150,000 metric tons of Atlantic cod annually. In contrast, estimates from animal rights groups suggested that the seal population might be closer to 3 million (only marginally larger than it had been ten years earlier), and that Atlantic cod represented "only about one percent" of the harp seal's annual diet.

Where did the truth lie? Was this argument destined simply to turn into a shouting match, or were there means by which to evaluate the various claims and counterclaims? What was known for certain about the complex relationship between seals and cod? How many of the purported behaviors had actually been observed? How many had been measured?

These were questions I'd found myself asking during a voyage to Nova Scotia and the western Gulf of St. Lawrence in the summer of 1997. Everyone that year seemed to have been talking about harp seals, for the DFO had recently ended its policy of limited quotas and had reestablished the hunt in earnest. Based on the projected growth of the seal herd, the opening of new markets in Asia, and the introduction of a program of government price supports, the DFO had raised the quota for harp seal landings to 250,000 in 1996 and to 275,000 in 1997 and 1998.

One of the people I talked with about seals during the summer of 1997 was fisheries biologist Jeffrey Hutchings, who was then teaching fish ecology and evolution as an assistant professor of biology at Dalhousie University in Halifax. Hutchings, whose family was from Newfoundland and who was descended from nine generations of fishermen, had been studying the collapse of the Atlantic cod since the height of the crisis in 1992, at which time he had been working as a research fellow at DFO's Science Branch in St. John's.

Of the various projects that he had been involved in at DFO, one had to do with seals and cod. He and several colleagues had become concerned about the DFO's official explanation for the collapse of the fish stocks—an explanation that emphasized "natural causes" such as seal predation. Hutchings and the others began to worry that such emphasis might in fact be a smokescreen, a way to divert criticism away from the DFO's own inaccurate cod stock assessments and poor management decisions.

As a result, he and two staff scientists, Alan Sinclair and Ransom Myers, decided to take a hard look at the scientific record to ascertain exactly what was known about the relation of seals to cod and to clarify the arguments being used to support the DFO's management decisions. What they discovered came as a surprise even to the researchers, for after a thorough investigation of the record, they found no scientific evidence of any sort linking seals with the reduction of the cod stocks.

"This doesn't mean there are no links," Hutchings was quick to explain. "Only that we could find no evidence of any. Marine ecosystems are highly complex, and I guess we shouldn't have been surprised that scientists didn't know very much about this one. The fish that the seals eat may or may not be the same ones that finish up in fishermen's nets. The seals may also eat organisms that prey on juvenile cod—or cod larvae—such that removing the seals might actually lead to fewer cod, not more. Inputs at one place in such a system can result in highly unpredictable outcomes somewhere else. The main thing we discovered was that there were huge gaps in our knowledge about the behavior of cod—and seals—and that we had a long way to go before we could claim to understand all the interrelationships."

At the conclusion of this study, Hutchings and his colleagues wrote a paper stating their findings—a paper they hoped to present to an upcoming conference of DFO scientists. Almost immediately, however, the authors drew a reprimand from their superiors. Strong pressure was brought to bear from within the department to keep the paper from being published. In effect, the department issued a gag order. Copies of the paper that did exist were withdrawn from circulation, and the authors were advised by their superiors not to discuss its contents.

In the wake of this episode, Alan Sinclair chose to continue at DFO (where the official reprimand remains a part of his record). Jeff Hutchings and Ram Myers, however, both decided to leave their government posts to pursue teaching and research opportunities at Dalhousie.

Here, during the summer of 1997, both became deeply involved in a public exposé of the "managed science" that had been going on during their tenures in St. John's. Myers was informed that summer that he was being sued for libel by senior DFO officials (a suit that was later dropped), while Hutchings found himself hounded by newspaper and TV reporters from all over Canada who were eager to learn more about the scandal.

"The odd thing," says Hutchings, "is that I'm not even opposed to hunting seals. Like most people, I'd like to see it done humanely, without unnecessary waste or killing. But I come from an old Newfoundland family. My father and grandfather and great grandfather were all fishermen. I know how important sealing has been to the traditional way of life in Newfoundland. I know how important it is for thousands of rural Newfoundlanders right now.

"The thing I am opposed to, though, is when an outfit like DFO tries to justify quadrupling the sealing quota based on 'scientific evidence'—evidence that we know just isn't there.

"I mean, just for example: if you take DFO's own estimate of the harp seal population—some 4.8 million at last count—and you multiply that number by the amount of cod each seal is supposed to eat in a year, you come out with a number that's larger than the DFO's own estimate for the entire biomass of Atlantic cod in Canadian waters.

"Obviously, one of these numbers has to be wrong. It's unlikely that there's a lot of extra cod out there or somebody would almost certainly be catching it. Which means that there must be a lot fewer seals—or the seals must be eating a lot fewer fish. Whatever way you work them, these numbers hardly add up to the kind of 'scientific evidence' it takes to establish good, rational management policy."

The clatter of a serving spoon against the rim of an iron pot announced that places had been set for our noon meal and the salt cod was finished boiling. Nat, who was cook for the day, emerged from the companionway and waved the spoon in front of Tobias Foley and me, indicating that the meal was hot and ready to be served.

Foley was still talking about seals. I had shared some of what I'd learned from Jeff Hutchings about the difficulties observers had experienced in making a count of the harp seal herd's actual size.

Surprisingly, Foley agreed that getting an accurate measure of the herd could be a problem.

"Nobody can count all them millions of seals from an airplane. There's too many animals—too much ice. But we that lives here, we sees the seals as they pass along the shore. More every year, water black with them sometimes, crowding in on the coast in numbers greater than anyone alive can remember."

"Some scientists have speculated that the seals may have changed their pattern of migration," I said, "—that they may be moving along the inshore banks because of disappearing food sources—perhaps because they're undernourished— possibly even starving."

"If that's so, then maybe we're all up against the same problem."

"Same problem . . . ?"

"All of us hungry—seals and people together—all of us looking for fish."

I gazed for several seconds at my guest, amazed at the easy identification he was able to make with this creature he had hunted, this predator he had felt himself in competition with all his life.

Finally Nat cleared his throat and waved the serving spoon again. "Excuse me," he said, "but did I hear you mention something about 'looking for fish'?" His expression remained a perfect deadpan. "I mean if you're looking for a nice piece of salt fish, I have an idea that might work . . . ."

All three laughed. Foley and I followed the cook down the companionway, joined the others at the dinette table, and buried our faces into steaming bowls of boiled fish supper as good as any we'd ever tasted.

Chapter 4

Port au Choix

THE GREAT NORTHERN PENINSULA presents the bleakest and least hospitable coast of any in Newfoundland. At Cow Head, where the peninsula begins, the ancient mountain range that has defined the coastal landscapes for a hundred fifty miles begins to retreat inland. The shapes of the hills grow softer, their color fades to gray, and they wither in size, as if they had been sinking under their own weight into the miles of marsh and barren that now surround them.

Except for a pair of anomalous pinnacle hills, the coastal terrain for the next fifty miles becomes flat and featureless. The beach is black shale, carved into rough steps by winter ice floes and by the incessant grinding of summer surf. A half dozen shallow creeks and ponds punctuate what otherwise remains a straight and unbroken line, and the land, as one watches it from the deck of a small vessel, dissolves into a hazy blur.

I felt disoriented the morning *Brendan's Isle* left Cow Head and pointed her bows northeast along this coast—bewildered by a pair of responses that pulled me in opposite directions. The day was sunny; the wind was light. The sailboat seemed to float suspended, out of all time and place, and the empty seas ahead inspired a careless ennui.

At the same time, however, the featureless coast ignited an ancient fear: a nagging possibility that every sailor must contemplate in which a sudden change in weather transforms a benign and apparently harmless beach into a lee shore, a dangerous maze of ledge and rock that could break a little boat like ours to sticks in a matter of minutes.

For hour after hour as *Brendan* proceeded northward, I felt myself pulled between these two responses. I watched the shoreline shimmer, mirage-like, as the boat crept across glassy seas—and I studied the sky for approaching weather, straining ahead for a glimpse of the headland that was to be our destination. Finally, just as I was feeling we might never reach our goal, I saw a cluster of coastal mountains emerge out of the haze far off on the eastern horizon. Soon afterwards, I spotted a low silhouette of land rising out of the sea fine on the starboard bow: the Point Riche peninsula and the harbor at Port au Choix.

As one travels along this coast, one comes to understand why this headland and this well-protected harbor have played such an important role for mariners throughout the centuries. Port au Choix is exactly what its name suggests: the haven that a prudent skipper would choose above all others. Indeed, except for a pair of small bays immediately to its south, Port au Choix is the only deep, landlocked harbor that is safe in all winds for seventy-five miles in either direction. As such, it is the natural crossroads of the area, the harbor most accessible to the fishing banks and the trade routes of the northern gulf, and the gateway to the Strait of Belle Isle and all points north and east.

Twenty-five years ago, when the Canadian DFO was trying to decide where in Newfoundland to build a series of major fishing service centers, Port au Choix became the obvious selection for the base of operations for the northern dragger fleet. But the planners in Ottawa were hardly the first to recognize the unique geographical advantages of this place. Indeed, for the last eight thousand years, ever since the Wisconsinian ice sheet retreated from these shores, the Point Riche peninsula has been the locus of wave after wave of human habitation.

Maritime Archaic, Dorset Eskimo, Beothuk Indian, modern Inuit, all have left signs of their passing here in the layers of bog and tundra, and the village site at Port au Choix has been a center of population, trade, and fishing since the time of the Pharaohs in Egypt.

In more recent times, Port au Choix has also been an important landmark in the delineation of the so-called "French Shore" and the administration of the ship fishery that once took place along this coast. After centuries of conflict between French and English fishing captains, a set of formal fishing boundaries was finally established, first in the Treaty of Utrecht in 1713, then in the Treaty of Versailles in 1783. Under the terms of both treaties, the French were granted exclusive rights to establish summer drying stations along the shores of western Newfoundland, but no fisherman, neither English nor French, was permitted to establish a permanent settlement.

The resulting situation soon became untenable for all concerned. Inuit groups who were still using sites along this coast for their fishing and sealing camps were eventually driven out by French summer crews. The French, meanwhile, were allowed to fish along this coast but not to settle, while the English, whose numbers were growing and who were increasingly motivated to claim all of Newfoundland as their own, were officially allowed to do neither.

As the years passed, a few small English settlements began to appear in parts of western Newfoundland due to winter poaching and illegal homesteading. As a result, sporadic conflicts continued to break out between French and English fishermen. For the rest of the eighteenth and most of the nineteenth centuries, however, the entire western shore of the island was officially considered forbidden territory, and places like Port au Choix remained sparsely populated.

As the twentieth century began, this situation became the topic of treaty negotiations once more. In response to waning French fishing presence and continued infiltration by English-speaking homesteaders, the British government was pressured once again to investigate "the French Shore problem" and to devise solutions. Finally in 1904, in exchange for certain lands in West Africa, the French agreed to withdraw from the main island of Newfoundland altogether and leave the French Shore to English settlement. Newfoundland was by this time a bona fide English colony whose centers of commerce and population were all located in the south. Port au Choix thus became the gateway to a new territory—a kind of Yukon of the east—such that even today, nearly a hundred years later, it still has the look and feel of a frontier town.

It was mid-afternoon by the time *Brendan* pulled up into the western end of Port au Choix harbor. A trio of wooden draggers lay moored against the long facing pier of the Fishermen's Cooperative. At the far end of this pier a half dozen dories and motorized bateaus were tethered to a set of mooring pontoons. A boy in a sweatshirt and jeans and rubber fishing boots stared at the sailboat as she slowed and circled in front of the pontoons. As the boat drew near, he set down his fishing pole and busied himself moving dories to make room for the newcomer.

By the time the sailboat was safely moored, a group of men had gathered at the head of the pier and a pair of pickup trucks had pulled into the parking area adjacent to the pontoons. The next few minutes were noisy and confused, filled with loud greetings, comments about the weather, questions about the boat and her recent passage down the gulf. "Did you come to see the beached whale?" one man asked. "Stinks like the devil it does." "You've missed the shrimp festival," commented another. "All the big draggers was here last week. Now they've gone—fishing down the Labrador again."

Once the novelty of arrival had worn off, the crowd began to drift away. Liz and Amanda befriended the boy with the fishing pole and led him on a tour of the sailboat. Nat and Richard headed into the town center to see what they could learn about the beached whale. I also planned to take a walk into town later in the afternoon, for I was eager to visit two old friends, Jack and Rita Farwell, each one in his seventies, each a lifelong residents of this community, and each as irrepressible and upbeat about life as anyone I had ever met. I had a hunch that even the collapse of the cod fishery couldn't keep these two old Newfoundlanders down, and I wanted to spend some time with them, to share their enthusiasm and feel their energy.

First, however, I needed to walk over to the Cooperative pier and take a closer look at the draggers moored in front of the Fisher-men's Cooperative building. Something was different about these boats—something my crew and I had not yet seen this summer—for these were shrimp boats, rigged for a fishery that had survived the cod collapse and that continued to be important to the local economy here.

I had managed to learn a little about the northern shrimp fishery over the past several years—partly from talking with fishermen during previous voyages to this coast, and partly from having corresponded over the past few winters with scientists and fisheries managers who had been working with this species.

The size of this fishery in the Gulf of St. Lawrence had grown—from a total catch of just under six hundred tons when it first opened in 1970, to thirteen thousand tons in 1992 (the year of Crosbie's original moratorium), to almost twenty thousand tons in 1997. Fisheries managers were not certain why shrimp populations had experienced such dramatic growth in the Gulf in recent years, except to note that the disappearance of the cod might have something to do with it.

"Cod eat shrimp," commented DFO fisheries manager Louise Savard during a conversation I'd had with her the previous winter. "So it seems logical to hypothesize that the disappearance of the cod and the growth in shrimp populations may be related. Remove the predator from the food chain, and the prey begins to multiply."

Based on the dramatic expansion of the shrimp fleet and the steady increase in quotas over the last several years, I had expected to see the shrimp fishery booming in Port au Choix when *Brendan's Isle* arrived this summer. The large seafood processing plant across the harbor was freshly painted and appeared busy. But where were all the other boats? Why were there only three moored along this pier? Why wasn't Port au Choix filled to overflowing with shrimp draggers?

I stepped onto the pontoon where *Brendan* was moored, climbed the ramp, and walked along the main pier toward the Fishermen's Cooperative Building. "Hey Cap," came a voice from the bridge deck of one of the shrimp draggers. "How'd you like to swap boats?" The question was followed by a deep, booming laugh.

I gazed up at the maze of nets and booms and metal superstructure of a small wooden dragger named *Cape Harrigan*. "It's a deal," I hollered back, and I heard the booming laugh again.

Moments later, a man dressed in a dark blue coverall and baseball cap appeared at the *Harrigan's* wheelhouse door. He had a lean, wiry build, with powerful arms and shoulders and a narrow, grizzled face. He introduced himself as Gerald Gould, skipper of one of the only shrimp boats working out of Port au Choix this summer.

"Where are the other boats?" I asked. "Why are there so few moored here? Has the Department of Fisheries cut your quotas?"

"No Cap, Fisheries is telling us there's plenty of shrimp. Quotas bigger than ever. But the fishing is off this year, way off. Maybe it's the weather, maybe currents, maybe cold water, maybe something eating them. Nobody certain why."

"The fish plant seems busy."

"Oh yes, plenty of shrimp coming in to the plant, coming down from St. Anthony, trucking in."

"Is that where the other boats are? Fishing out of St. Anthony?"

"All the big boats, yes Cap. Fishing down Hawkes Channel, a hundred miles offshore. That's where *Cape Harrigan* would be, too, if she was big and strong enough. It's been tough fishing on the local ground this summer, the Esquiman we calls it. I've been working just three men—myself and two others. That's bare bones. But a fella can't make no money otherwise."

I pressed the man on why he thought there had been such a drop in the number of shrimp he'd been catching in the Gulf this year. Could the DFO have been wrong with their optimistic stock assessments? Could something have been happening with this species the same way it had happened a few years ago with the cod?

"God only knows," said Gould. "You got to hope, Cap, that the fisheries managers have learned something. You got to hope they've learned their lesson. Is there a fishery here? A real fishery that I can pass on to my son? And him to his son? Hard to imagine, with the quotas going up every year. You saw what happened to the cod. Hard to imagine we ain't just doing the same thing, just taking one more creature, fishing it till there's nothing left."

Gould looked down the pier toward the sailboat—eager, it seemed, to change the subject. "Now if you wants to see something different, Cap, you ought to take them friends of yours out to view the stranded whale. Big sperm. Come ashore down past Gargamelle Cove after a storm near two weeks ago."

I assured the man that my crew and I would try to make the journey out to see the whale. Meanwhile, however, there was another journey that I wanted to make—a pilgrimage of sorts—to meet a pair of old Newfoundlanders who had become important to me. I asked him whether Jack and Rita Farwell were still living in Port au Choix, whether they were still healthy, whether Jack was still farming his potatoes and rhubarb and turnip greens.

"Now there's a fella got more energy at nearly eighty than two others half his age," said Gould. "Him and Rita both, tough as old trees. Jack's out at his farm almost every day now it's summertime. But Rita's almost always home." He gestured toward a cluster of buildings across the harbor. "Little green and white house, center of town. Just ask anybody to point the way. Not a person in this community that doesn't know old Jack."

In the ten years since my first visit to Port au Choix, the village had undergone a number of visible changes. The potholes in the main street had been filled and the roadway freshly paved. The government pier had been refurbished. The fish plant had been painted, left to fade and peel, painted again. A new Visitors' Center had been constructed several miles out on the peninsula to interpret the archeological history of this place to summer tourists. A craft shop had been opened. Many of these changes, I suspected, had taken place as a result of the availability of TAGS money, and some had certainly been designed to employ local citizens idled by the fishing moratorium.

In the town itself several new buildings had been constructed, the largest and most outlandish of which was a three-story Tudor mansion built just before the cod collapse by a wealthy dragger skipper named Martin Caines. After the collapse, several such houses here had been abandoned by fishermen who could no longer afford to keep them up. Others had been modified to reflect the new austerity. The owner of one such house had decided to discard his expensive new electric baseboard heating system in favor of a cast-iron wood stove. He'd installed the stove in a central downstairs room, just as his less affluent neighbors had been doing for a hundred years, and he'd cut holes in the imported hardwood floors of each room above to accommodate the chimney pipe on its way to the roof.

One building that was no longer standing since my first visit here was a dwelling up on Main Street built by one Wilbert Farwell, a fishing skipper from Burin who had sailed out to the Great Northern Peninsula in the first years of the twentieth century. This dwelling was one of the earliest permanent structures erected in the village after the treaty of 1904: a small, double story frame bungalow constructed in the style of the late Victorian era, with steeply pitched roof, cathedral windows, eaves bordered with hand-carved stars and half-moons and hex signs. The wood shutters and picket fence had likewise been adorned with all manner of magical bric-a-brac, and the whole affair had been painted in kaleidoscopic profusion with every color in the rainbow.

At present there was only an empty lot where this structure had once stood, for the place had been torn down after Wilbert Farwell died in 1991. But both the house and its ancient inhabitant had still been firmly ensconced on the afternoon that I had first walked into this village and had stopped to stare at what must surely have been one of the most preposterous structures in all of Newfoundland.

As I'd stood gawking at the building, a shortish fellow with mud-spattered boots and dirty coveralls had emerged from a storehouse on the far side of the road and had hitched himself across the pavement. "My father's house," he'd announced in one of the thickest north-country brogues I'd ever heard. "She's a beauty, eh? Maybe the oldest house in Port au Choix."

The man was a fireplug. His face was square, with ruddy cheeks, a hook nose, a bubble-shaped chin that jutted straight out from his neck. His forehead and scalp were covered with a maze of black fly bites. The rest of his body was almost perfectly cylindrical. His bell-shaped shoulders and barrel chest dropped straight to his hips, then divided like a tree trunk split in two. One of his knees was nearly immobilized, causing him to walk with a limp, and one hand was wrapped in a blood-spattered rag.

"Had an accident?" I asked.

"Oh you mean this?" He looked embarrassed as he unwound the rag from his hand. "Ain't nothing, just a few scratches. Now the leg, that's a different story. Crushed it, see, moving a boulder out of the middle of my potato field."

There was no stopping the fellow after this, for once he had started telling about his battle with the boulder, I could do nothing but follow him back across the street to his own house, nodding every few seconds as he completed the rest of the tale.

It was a story full of braggadocio and derring-do, a larger-than-life encounter between human ingenuity and the natural order of the universe. He showed me the lever that he had used to move the rock. He showed me the scars on his leg where the doctors at the Grenfell Hospital had performed the surgery to put him back together. Later that afternoon, he drove me and several of my crew out to his plantation to show us the offending entity—the boulder itself—and to introduce us to the place he liked to describe as "the finest potato farm in all of Newfoundland."

Every time I've returned to Port au Choix since that first visit, I've made the journey up to that little green and white house across from where old Wilbert Farwell's family manse used to stand, knocked on the door, and asked if Jack Farwell, potato farmer extraordinaire, was perchance at home. Over the years I've been treated to dozens of Jack's stories and reminiscences. I've met his wife Rita, tasted her biscuits and bakeapple jam, learned about how both have lived and survived on the Great Northern Peninsula for nearly eighty years.

Jack's life has spanned most of the history of this peninsula since the frontier was open to English settlement. As such, he is a walking encyclopedia about the life and times of this place. "Used to be lobsters here," he told me once. "First time anybody in Port au Choix saw any real money was fishing lobsters. There was a cannery where the fish plant is now. Not large, only twenty-five, thirty jobs. But the lobsters was plentiful then. We fished them all year, winter and summer. Not like now, see, one or two weeks and they're gone."

Jack joined the inshore fishery when he was thirteen years old, working alongside his three brothers. They fished in a seventeen-foot dory powered by a single cylinder Lathrop "make and break" engine. Most of the year they worked a string of lobster traps. Other times they jigged for cod. "Once when there was fish out there, you could put down a hook to the bottom, see, you could haul on her, haul up a big sucker. That's what we used to call him, see, that's what we used to call a big fish."

Big fish or not, life on the peninsula had been hard in the years before roads or electricity or full time school or modern medical services. Jack recalled one snowy January in 1931 when he and his youngest brother Max had been out snaring rabbits. "One night it got stormy and we had to come home. Max took sick that night—died next day with TB meningitis. He was twelve years old."

Six years later Jack's second-oldest brother died at age twenty, also of tuberculosis, and two years after that, his oldest brother also died.

"It was July sixteen," Jack recalled, "nineteen and forty. I was fishing down to Lynn's Cove when I seen the boat coming straight the bay. I told the fellas fishing with me, I said, I got some trouble coming, see? I guess my brother's dead, is it. There's the boat coming straight the bay from St. John Cove, and I knowed it was my brother gone."

Soon afterward, Jack's mother sent him to the Grenfell Hospital in St. Anthony to get a checkup because, as she said, "you prob'ly got TB too." Fortunately, his mother was wrong. Yet as soon as the all-clear came from the doctors, Jack began thinking that fishing might not be the healthiest occupation for the last of the Farwell brothers. Beginning with a war job at the American airbase in Stephenville, he set about trying his hand at almost every other kind of work that came his way. He never left the fishery for good for another twenty years, but in the mean time he became a literal Jack-of-all-trades: walking proof that there were more ways to earn a living in northern Newfoundland than catching fish.

The afternoon light had started dropping from the sky and thin wisps of fog were curling about the chimneys of the town as Amanda and I paused in front of the little green and white house on Main Street and gazed up at the sign above the door: *John Farwell's Store*. The door was unlocked. It opened into a tiny vestibule where we kicked off our boots, then, in stocking feet, stepped into a room that had been arranged as a dry goods and general merchandise store—one of the many business ventures that Jack and Rita had pursued over the years. The shelves and counters were mostly empty. In one of the windows were several skeins of heavy gray yarn and half a dozen pairs of hand-knit socks—Rita's handiwork. On a back shelf was a tray of pudding-cakes and several large pans of biscuits, so fresh the air in the room was still heavy with their aroma.

I stepped to the counter and rang a bell that sat atop an ancient cash register. A voice called out from the back of the house. Moments later, a short, stocky woman appeared framed in a doorway at the far end of the room. "Goodday," she said, looking for a place to wipe her hands. "I was just finishing some baking." She brushed a trail of flour off the front of her green cotton sweater, fluffed the skirt of her house dress, fussed with her hair.

Amanda and I introduced ourselves: "American sailors . . . green boat down at the Cooperative pier . . . here four years ago . . . do you remember . . . ?"

"Why yes, I remembers, yes. Why Jack was asking just the other day, he was. 'I wonder if that American fella with the college students be coming north, stopping in Port au Choix this year?' Just the other day he was asking . . . ."

Within moments Rita had invited us to take off our jackets and step into her kitchen for a cup of tea. "Jack's at the garden," she said, "living at his camp. A moose broke through the fence last week, got into the strawberries. Jack worries if he breaks in again, he might go after the turnips."

She cleared a pair of places at the kitchen table. "Here, m'dear— sit here. Have a bit of biscuit, a piece of bread, some partridgeberry jam, a piece of rhubarb pie. Made three rhubarb pies last Sunday, I did. Rhubarb is coming in beautiful now. Made three rhubarb pies and Jack stop home and ate a whole pie all by himself." She smiled at the memory of her husband's appetite.

Rita scurried about the kitchen as she talked. On the far side of the room was a tap where she drew water for the tea, then set the teapot on an iron cookstove. She opened the oven and pulled out five loaves of bread, stirred a pot on the stovetop, painted the loaves with a butter-brush, slipped another tray of biscuits into the oven. The room was hot. The aromas were sweet and heady.

"Here's your tea. Here, more biscuits. Another piece of pie? I'll open a tin of cream. Jack loves tinned cream on his rhubarb pie."

When Rita and Jack were both home together, Rita was almost always the silent one. But this afternoon she was on center stage, and she seemed to be enjoying the spotlight. She told us about the warm weather last winter, about a cousin who had just died, about her nephew's scheme for making money with the beached whale. This nephew, it seemed, had organized a group of villagers to help strip away the rotting flesh and save the whale's skeleton. Then he was going to reassemble the whole business in a field, present it as a tourist attraction, charge admission.

"The whale ain't much to see—mostly just a terrible smell. But the garden. Well, m'dears, Jack won't let you leave Port au Choix 'till you seen his garden. Fifteen hundred strawberry plants he set this spring. Twenty-five new rows of potatoes." She stepped across the room to a table with an old rotary telephone, picked up the receiver, tucked it under her chin. "I'll call Doris. She'll take you out this evening after supper. Jack's staying the night, just to make certain the moose don't come back. Jack's worried about his turnips, see. Fourteen hundred dollars he made in turnip tops alone last summer."

She dialed a number, pausing between each digit. "Oh m'dears, that garden's something else . . . onions, strawberries, potatoes, rhubarb, cabbage . . . a regular garden of Eden it is . . . . I swear you'll never see another like it in the world."

Six miles east of town on Eddie's Cove Road, Doris Hamlyn's red Ford pickup truck swerved around a pair of potholes and pulled into a narrow track that tunneled into the underbrush. Several hundred yards along this track, the truck slowed and stopped. Doris got out and unlatched a grid of wires rigged between a pair of fence posts, while I and the rest of *Brendan's* crew sat huddled in the truck bed. In the clearing ahead, we could just make out an old blue Chevy truck and a trio of small wooden buildings.

"Uncle Jack," Doris called as she climbed back into the cab. "You got visitors, Uncle Jack."

She guided the pickup across the clearing and parked next to the largest of the buildings. Rows of leafy vegetation corrugated the land to the right and left, ahead and behind. Rectangular fields, separated from one another by hedgerows of birch and spruce, created the impression of a maze of gardens, one behind the next, receding into the tangle of bog and barren that surrounded them.

"He's done it all himself," said Doris as we climbed down from the truck and stood gazing at the checkerboard fields. "He's cut every tree, moved every rock, worked up every square yard of soil. He's been at it fifteen years."

The garden was immaculate—the result of huge amounts of energy and care. But where was the gardener, I wondered? I found myself searching across broad plantations of potatoes and cabbages, strawberries and onions, looking for the steward of all this profusion. Surely he must have been here somewhere.

Suddenly a voice arose from a distant stand of rhubarb. " 'Twas lightning hit my outhouse, see, hit my turnips too." I looked in the direction of the sound and watched a dark, almost unrecognizable figure emerge from the shadows at the end of the field. His shirt and hat were loamy brown, his overalls and face and hands were caked with dirt. He broke off a pair of rhubarb stalks and wiped his hands on the leaves as he walked.

"I'll show you where the lightning hit," he said, striding straight into our midst. "Stripped the bark off two trees, see, burned my outhouse roof, melted my toilet seat." He turned and extended a muddy paw for handshakes all around. "Just plain lucky, I was. Could've burned the whole place down."

Jack walked on, a mud-splattered dervish embarked on a seemingly endless series of heroic adventures. The others followed. After the outhouse, he led his visitors to the well he had just finished digging, to the new potato field, to the section of fence torn up last week by the marauding moose. At each new station he told a story, each one louder and faster and more outlandish than the last.

As the old man moved across the garden, Doris placed a hand on my shoulder to slow my pace. We hesitated, then stopped a dozen yards behind the others to watch and listen.

"He's a wonder, ain't he?"

"One of a kind."

"He's like Newfoundland itself, Uncle Jack is, for he's had the odds stacked against him all his life. He's seen every kind of trouble, seen it all—yet seems like nothing in the world can keep him down."

She gazed at him, tenderly, the way a daughter might gaze at an aging parent. "Whenever I gets to feeling sad, whenever I starts to worrying about families leaving, houses boarding up, people's lives falling apart, I always think about Jack, about his garden here."

"He calls it the finest potato farm in all of Newfoundland."

She laughed. "Some days when he's really full of piss and fire, he calls it the finest potato farm in all the world. Funny thing is, some days you just have to believe he's right."

Chapter 5

St. John Bay

A GUST OF WIND CLATTERED in *Brendan's* rigging next morning, an hour north of Port au Choix. Overhead, the anvil top of a thirty-thousand-foot thunderhead moved across the sun, while to the east, swirls of dark cloud tumbled down the twin peaks of the Highlands of St. John. Moments later an area of breaking seas, a flash of lightning, and the rumble of thunder announced the onset of a squall line.

The sailboat rounded up to take the initial force of the wind head-on. Richard, my watch mate, sat at the top of the companion-way huddled under a canvas spray dodger, while I took up my customary station at the navigation table below.

In front of me was an array of instruments: a compass, an autopilot console, a radar screen. With these I was able to see and steer electronically without having to leave the safety and comfort of the deckhouse.

The weather forecast early that morning had been for intermittent rain and squally east winds—not an ideal prospect for a small vessel proceeding north toward the Strait of Belle Isle, but one that *Brendan* and her crew had dealt with many times. The factors that had not been mentioned in the forecast, however, were the lightning and thunder—perhaps because they are so uncommon here. For although electrical activity often accompanies storms generated over continental land areas where the temperatures of the colliding air masses are dissimilar, such activity occurs only rarely in maritime settings such as Newfoundland.

A flash of lightning lit the surface of the navigation table, followed almost immediately by the sharp crack of thunder. I glanced at Richard, still seated in the companionway. He said nothing but only stared wide-eyed at the place where the lightning had hit the water.

"How close?" I asked.

"Close."

Even before he finished uttering this single word, there came another flash, another crack of thunder. The boat heeled to a fresh gust of wind; the cabins filled with the smell of ozone.

"Closer," said Richard.

This was bizarre weather, far more suitable to a passage along the coasts of Virginia or the Carolinas than to a transit of the northern Gulf of St. Lawrence and the approaches to the Strait of Belle Isle. I had sailed along this present coast on eight previous occasions—sometimes remaining in the vicinity for several weeks—and I had never before seen lightning or heard thunder. This is not to say that such events never happened—but they were rare enough that they usually made headlines in the local newspaper when they did. Yet this summer we had already witnessed the effects of at least two episodes of severe electrical activity here, for it had only been a few days since Jack had suffered his near miss at the potato farm.

Weather patterns all during *Brendan's* voyage to Newfoundland this summer had been anomalous. Easterly winds had been the rule where westerlies normally prevailed. Gales had been more numerous. The storm track had shifted south from its mean summer position over Quebec and Labrador, such that low pressure systems had been marching across Newfoundland and the Gulf of St. Lawrence like soldiers in a parade. The weather fax map that I'd looked at that morning had showed eight lows—no highs—stretching all the way from the Gulf of Maine in the west to the Davis Strait and Greenland in the east. Yet somehow there still seemed to be enough convective energy in the areas between these systems to spawn electrical storms that would make old Dixie proud.

What was going on? Were we simply experiencing the randomness and unpredictability that meteorologists have long associated with weather? Were we in an odd "El Nino year" (an explanation that had become standard for much of the popular media) in which hemispheric weather events were somehow being influenced by an unusual warming of the surface waters of the central Pacific Ocean?

Or was there something more fundamental going on: a shift in basic patterns of circulation of the atmosphere and oceans that might more properly be described as climate change?

Brendan lay head-to-wind, sails stowed, engine ticking over just enough to maintain headway. She was in no immediate danger but was simply assuming a defensive posture, waiting for the weather to pass. While she waited, I found myself staring into a gray wall of rain, thinking about a subject that had become particularly compelling to me: the possibility that the disappearance of the northern cod might be connected in some way with an episode of climate change.

The study of climate—and in particular ocean climate—is a newcomer to the canon of modern scientific endeavor. Until the advent of computers, electronic navigation systems, modern oceanographic survey platforms, and Earth-observing satellites, scientists simply didn't have the tools to measure and observe such a vast and complex system. Even as recently as a few decades ago, marine biologists and others interested in the health and productivity of the oceans had little dependable information about patterns of climate and their effects upon fish populations. Although researchers could (and did) theorize about possible interactions between climate and fish, most of their conclusions remained highly speculative.

By the early 1980s, however, all of this had started to change. The United States, Japan, Germany, and several other nations had launched satellites that were photographing and tracking major ocean currents, monitoring sea surface temperatures, measuring sea ice cover. Sophisticated floating oceanographic instrument packages were collecting large quantities of new data having to do with sea water temperatures, salinities, vertical and horizontal mixing, rates of current flow. Similar advances were taking place in the measurement of the atmosphere. And new computing systems were providing the analytical muscle to process these data and to model the structure and behavior of the entire (global) climate system.

As a result, by the early 1990s a large body of new information about the ocean climate system had become available to fisheries scientists. Observers had discovered, for instance, that the Labrador Sea and northeastern Grand Banks had been displaying anomalous behavior as a climatological "cold spot" for much of the past thirty years. Recent theories about global ocean circulation (the Great Ocean Conveyor Belt) and regional atmospheric circulation (the North Atlantic Oscillation or NAO) both suggested that the Labrador Sea was an important bellwether of climate change. A series of extremely cold winters across this area during the late 1980s had culminated in 1991 in one of the coldest winters of the century, with unusually cold sea water temperatures, near-record sea ice cover, and the longest sea ice season on record along a six hundred mile section of the coast from eastern Newfoundland to northern Labrador.

As chance would have it, I had been in northern Canada aboard *Brendan's Isle* in 1991, traversing this same body of water, and I had thus been able to witness the effects of the cold conditions firsthand. The contrasts between that summer and this one could not have been more dramatic. That year the northern gulf and the Strait of Belle Isle had been clogged with sea ice until late July, several weeks later than our present timetable. The sailboat had been forced to delay—then delay again—as she waited for a lead of open water. When she was finally able to move, there were no navigational aids to guide her, for the Canadian Coast Guard had not yet attempted to set buoys or other floating aids to the east and north.

On August first, the sailboat followed fresh leads of open water through the strait. At the eastern end, however, she was once again forced to stop, this time by hundreds of miles of sea ice that still clogged the coast of eastern Labrador. Reports from the Canadian Ice Center described the pack ice as extending all the way to Cape Chidley, five hundred miles to the north, with ice concentrations of up to eighty percent of the sea surface. Finally, on August fourth and with time running out, I made the decision to scuttle the summer's sailing plan and retreat westward.

The frustration of having to turn around, combined with the sheer drama of the ice and the questions it raised about changing climate, led me on a three-year quest to try to understand the unique role of this climatological "cold spot"—a quest that eventually resulted in a second northern voyage in 1994 and a book about that voyage (*Riddle of the Ice: A Scientific Adventure into the Arctic*).

In addition to the climate riddle, however, another scientific conundrum had also emerged from the ice: this one having to do with the collapse of fish populations and the possibility that such collapse might be connected with the cold conditions. The longest coastal sea ice season in almost a century across the Labrador shelf and eastern Grand Banks had occurred in the same year and the same place in which the northern cod had met its final demise. Could these events have been related? Could the cold water and sea ice have affected reproduction rates, depleted food sources, or in some other way inhibited the fish's ability to survive?

Having witnessed the drama of the ice firsthand, I found the notion of some kind of link between climate and cod to be compelling. But I wasn't a scientist, and I knew if I wanted a well-reasoned answer founded upon the latest data, I would need to turn to the scientific record to learn what the researchers themselves had discovered.

Among the Canadian government scientists investigating the cod/climate connection, one of the most articulate and fair-minded is Ken Drinkwater, an oceanographer who has worked in the Science Section of the Canadian Department of Fisheries and Oceans for almost two decades. As a young researcher in the early 1980s, Drinkwater served on a team that produced the now-classic analysis of the relationship between cod reproduction and ocean salinity on the Labrador shelf. Ten years later he participated in another investigation of the relationships between cod reproduction and salinity in three areas of the Grand Banks. Together, these studies comprised the most authoritative statements then available about cod and climate—and both supported the argument that the cod collapse may have been significantly influenced by climate factors.

The first study, published in 1983, proposed a connection between cod and climate based on nutrients in the water column— the so-called "food chain hypothesis." Dissolved nitrates, Drinkwater and his colleagues argued, provided essential nutrients for the production of zooplankton, a primary food source for young cod. When nitrate levels in the waters of northern Labrador rose, rates of cod survival also rose; when nitrate levels dropped, survival rates also dropped.

According to this hypothesis, the variable that determined the quantity of nitrates in the sea water was an environmental one: the relative freshness or salinity of the ocean surface. After a particularly cold winter, the researchers explained, the Labrador Sea became flooded with large volumes of spring meltwater flowing down through the Hudson Strait. Such outflow formed a fresh water "cap" that remained trapped on the surface, inhibiting the mixing of nutrients from deeper layers, suppressing the production of zooplankton, and increasing the mortality of young cod. In contrast, a warm year with salty, ice-free conditions reversed this sequence, resulting in greater cod survival.

The first serious challenge to this hypothesis came from Drinkwater himself. In another study completed in 1993, he, along with DFO biologists Ransom Myers and others, compared estimates of cod survival with sea surface salinities for three areas of the Grand Banks. Just as in 1983, the researchers found that the two factors appeared linked in a positive relationship, with the survival rates for young cod in any given year increasing or decreasing along with sea water salinity.

So far, so good. But another set of data, unavailable during earlier investigations, suggested that something wasn't right. The original hypothesis had made sense because a food chain mechanism had been proposed linking cod survival and salinity. But newly examined records of actual zooplankton production suggested that even when nitrate levels correlated positively with the survival of young fish, the mass of zooplankton (the actual food source for the fish) often correlated *negatively*, with years of high food production/low cod survival and low food production/high cod survival occurring together.

The failure of the food chain hypothesis to provide a logical link between cod and climate led Drinkwater and his colleagues to search for other possible mechanisms. One that seemed to make sense was based on the observation that at certain stages of their development, cod larvae will die from contact with freezing or near-freezing water. This proposition, the so-called "larval freezing hypothesis," suggested that it was the presence of sea ice rather than the presence of nitrates that governed the relationship between cod and climate.

What began as a promising idea, however, soon proved otherwise. After a careful investigation of the geography and timing of cod reproduction, the researchers discovered that if such a relationship made sense at all, it only applied to the northernmost stocks, and then only in the month of May, for at all other times and in all other areas of the Grand Banks, the near-surface water rarely dropped below freezing when cod larvae were present.

Given the limited application of this hypothesis and the absence of other explanations for the observed correlations, the researchers' conclusion at the end of their 1993 study was appropriately tentative. While noting the positive relationship between cod survival and salinity, they admitted that "the mechanism underlying the relationship . . . remains elusive."

Elusive mechanism or not, managers at the Canadian Department of Fisheries and Oceans incorporated the argument proposed by Drinkwater and his colleagues into their official explanation of the cod collapse. Somehow, the managers argued, the number of cod that survived in a given year was related to salinity. Salinity was climate-driven. A series of cold, icy winters during the period immediately prior to the cod collapse had contributed to several years of low salinities across the Labrador Sea and eastern Grand Banks. *Therefore*: the collapse had been caused—or at least seriously influenced—by climatological events.

Even in the *sanctum sanctorum* of the DFO, however, not all scientists agreed with the department's "official" rationale. Among the government scientists who remained skeptical was fisheries biologist Jeffrey Hutchings—the same Jeff Hutchings who had challenged the DFO's rationale regarding the relationship between seals and cod. Another who remained skeptical was biologist Ransom (Ram) Myers, a respected senior scientist and veteran of thirteen years with the DFO who had served alongside Ken Drinkwater as a co-author of the 1993 study on cod and salinity. As with seal predation, both Hutchings and Myers were concerned that blaming the cod collapse on changing climate might simply be another way for DFO managers to downplay the role of overfishing and sidestep mounting criticism of their own management errors.

For Hutchings and Myers, the first step in evaluating their department's position was to take a hard look at the arguments proposed in the 1993 study. (As co-author of this study, Myers had a particular intimacy with both its methods and its sources.) What they discovered was a major problem with the data that the research team had used. It seems that several months after the study had been completed, new estimates of cod "spawner biomass" for the critical years of 1984 through 1988 had become available—estimates that were substantially lower than the ones used in the original analysis. Using these revised estimates, Hutchings and Myers re-analyzed the population and salinity figures that Drinkwater and his colleagues had assembled. For all three study areas, their conclusions were the same: "relative to the effect of spawner biomass, [we conclude that] neither temperature nor salinity had a significant influence on recruitment of northern cod prior to the moratorium in 1992."

When asked to comment off the record, both Hutchings and Myers stand firmly behind their published conclusions. "It makes no sense to suggest that a few years of cold, fresh conditions on the Labrador shelf could lead to a collapse of this magnitude," says Myers. "Evidence from ground boreholes, tree rings, and other long-term records shows that the climate in eastern Canada was at least as cold as it has been in recent years during most of the nineteenth and early twentieth centuries—all the way up to about 1920. The cod fishery was alive and well during all that time—with huge landings of fish and no signs of any major stock collapse."

On the subject of ancient climates, Myers is even more adamant. "The cod has been around for more than twelve million years," he exclaims. "It has lived through countless reorganizations of ocean climate, survived half a dozen ice ages. Through all that time it has proven to be one of the most successful fish species ever evolved—and one of the most resilient—until now."

The question Myers keeps on asking is why scientists are even arguing about climate and cod. "Given the scarcity and inconclusiveness of the evidence, it seems the only reason to continue searching for a climate trigger to explain the cod collapse would be if you couldn't explain the numbers any other way. Yet the fact is, we have plenty of other ways to explain the numbers—virtually all of them having to do with overfishing."

Hutchings elaborates upon his colleague's conclusions. "There were many changes in the fishery that began to stress fish populations," he explains. "But I think the back breaker, the condition that finally paved the way for the collapse, came with a shift in what biologists describe as the fish's 'age structure.'

"In layman's terms, age structure is simply a count of the number of fish in each age class—a kind of census-by-birthday of the total fish population. When fishermen start to exploit a given area, they naturally go after the biggest fish first. Net meshes are large, targeting the older fish, allowing the younger ones to pass through and escape. Then, over time, as most of the older fish are caught, the age structure of the population begins to shift downward. Younger, smaller fish become proportionately more numerous, and fishermen, if they are to keep up their quotas, begin fishing down the age classes. Once again, pressure is exerted on the oldest of the remaining fish until they, too, are mostly caught and the age structure of the population shifts downward again.

"You can see where all this finally leads," he says. "The fish population becomes progressively younger. Fishermen begin targeting fish that are seven years old, then six, then five. Commercial landings include a greater and greater proportion of 'preproductive' females—fish that haven't even had a chance to add to the reproductive cycle yet. Finally the age structure becomes so young that virtually no segment of the remaining population is reproducing. At this point, every trawl becomes a withdrawal against the future. Every fish that is caught becomes a nail in the coffin of species extinction."

Ken Drinkwater, in spite of his commitment to environmental influences, has come to embrace many of the arguments proposed by his two former DFO colleagues. He agrees that overfishing was "probably the main cause" of the collapse. ("It's certainly a truism to say that if there hadn't been any fishing, there would still be cod out there.") He admits that Hutchings and Myers have raised "serious questions" about the usefulness of his proposition linking cod recruitment and salinity. He even allows, somewhat begrudgingly, that there is little concrete evidence linking climate factors with the disappearance of the cod.

Yet, in the end, he continues to insist on what he terms "an environmental component." He points to the dramatic impact of the regional cold spot upon almost every natural system, and he appeals to common sense. "It's almost inconceivable," he says, "that thirty years of Labrador Sea cooling would not have had some impact on fish populations."

Perhaps because of the influence of Hutchings and Myers, Drinkwater has tempered much of his earlier language. Now when he talks about the collapse of the fishery, he emphasizes *interactions* between environment and fishing. One such interaction, he says, has to do with growth rates. "It's a well established fact that cold water retards the growth of cod. Down on the Georges Bank, for instance, a typical four-year old cod might be twenty inches long and weigh five or six pounds. Up on the Labrador shelf the same fish would require seven or eight years to grow to this size.

"Now think about what happens when the water gets colder still, as it did in the Labrador Sea in the late 1980s and early 1990s. Colder water means growth rates are going to drop even lower. The fish are going to be smaller, skinnier. But the quotas, which are based on biomass, stay the same. And this means that if the fishermen want to fill their quotas, they're going to need to catch a heck of a lot more fish."

Catching a lot more fish also obviously means catching a lot more undersized fish—fish that can't be legally landed and sold. And this, Drinkwater points out, increases the potential for what fishermen call "hi-grading"—the dumping of small and undersized fish back into the sea in order to fill quotas with larger fish. Nobody likes to talk about hi-grading—neither the fishermen nor the fisheries managers—because the fish that get dumped are all dead or dying. But the sad fact is that it does happen—sometimes at rates that are alarmingly high.

Drinkwater tells of one dragger captain who was interviewed off the record back in the early 1990s and admitted to dumping three hundred tons of undersized fish in order to fill a quota of two hundred legal tons. "Multiply those numbers by the entire fishery," the scientist exclaims, "and you'll get some idea of the potential destructiveness of hi-grading. And the smaller the size of the fish in a given area, the more likely the hi-grading will be happening."

A third interaction between fishing and cold water, according to Drinkwater, has to do with the fish's 'resilience'—its long-term ability to survive when placed under stress. "Jeff and Ram talk about the cold conditions back in the nineteenth and early twentieth centuries," he says, "and they're right about that. The Labrador Sea was cold during that time, with plenty of ice. They're also right that the fish populations didn't collapse, in spite of the heavy fishing that was going on. But there's a reason for the difference.

"Back in the nineteenth century, before the factory ships and the deepwater draggers, there was a huge buffer of age classes in the population—lots of older fish—which meant there was also lots of reproductive potential just waiting there in reserve. It didn't matter if a cold spell came along with a few bad years of recruitment. With twenty or thirty age classes represented in the population, the fish could bounce back quickly as soon as conditions got better.

"But by the 1980s, the older fish were gone. The reproductive potential of the population was down to just a couple of age classes. This time, when the cold conditions came again, the fish had no buffer, no reserve. The last few years before the moratorium, fishermen were still taking fish, but now the pressure was on the last of the reproducers. And this time, when the cold persisted, the fish that were left just couldn't make it."

A rumble of thunder echoed off the Highlands of St. John and faded into the distance. Ahead, a dark silhouette of land appeared on the starboard bow: Ferroulle Point. As the rain and mist moved away, I asked Amanda to join Richard in the cockpit, set up the working sails, and start us moving toward the strait again.

With my shipmates busy on deck, I remained at the nav-station, staring through the deckhouse windows at the dark mass of rain cloud as it receded into the south, thinking about the state of the scientific debate between Hutchings/Myers and Ken Drinkwater. In certain ways, there really was no debate any longer. Both sides now affirmed that fishing pressure was the main culprit. Both pointed to the absence of older fish and the lack of resilience in the fish population as key reasons for the suddenness of the collapse. Drinkwater simply held out for a kind of double-whammy fishing/climate effect in which the fish became the victims of two crises simultaneously.

Is he right? It's hard to say. The available data about the inter-relationships between climate and fish are still sparse and answers remain elusive. Yet the climate variability over the Labrador Sea and eastern Grand Banks has been particularly dramatic of late, with a decade of very cold, icy conditions, followed by a sudden shift in 1996 to the warmest conditions on record in over one hundred years. (Arctic ice in 1991—subtropical thunderstorms in 1998!)

Drinkwater and others have written about one of the climate mechanisms that may be responsible for this shift: a pattern of change in atmospheric pressure over the central and northern Atlantic that climatologists refer to as the North Atlantic Oscillation (or NAO). Our knowledge about the existence of the NAO is nothing new. With the aid of meteorological records, the behavior of this feature can be tracked for at least a century. It is similar in many ways to the oscillation that occurs over the central Pacific, the El Nino Southern Oscillation (or ENSO), a feature that can also be tracked by means of the historical record for more than a century.

The similarities don't end here—for both features have displayed a somewhat disturbing behavior of late—a tendency to oscillate more intensely, with deeper pressure gradients, stronger side effects. As mentioned, the latest oscillation of the NAO was accompanied by record cold conditions and record ice cover over the Labrador Sea, followed in 1996 by record warm conditions (conditions that, from the looks of things, still persist). Likewise, the current ENSO has already proven to be the longest and most severe on record, having been accompanied by a record-shattering upward spike in global temperatures and a tenfold intensification of violent weather events across the northern hemisphere.

What happens, I wonder, if this intensification becomes a pattern? What happens if we are now entering a period (as many climate modelers now predict) in which climate oscillations such as NAO and ENSO begin to fluctuate more and more widely, generating ever greater extremes of heat and cold, wet and dry, distorting the envelope of what used to be considered normal, spawning an increasing number of chaotic weather events?

If such a pattern were to persist, I wonder how many other species besides the northern cod might become threatened by the stress? Other fish species? insects and birds? plankton and other simple organisms? forest plants and trees? agricultural crops?

The irony, if Drinkwater is right, is that the northern cod may merely be an indicator of things to come. As other organisms are stressed by human exploitation, destruction of habitat, depletion of food sources, toxins in the environment, the double-whammy of climate change may become the final straw, the ultimate stress that tips the scale and leads to the species' extinction. Indeed, as humanity itself is forced to confront the mounting problems of food and material shortages associated with exponential population growth, the same double-whammy may some day come to bear on our kind. What would we do, I wonder, if we were to wake up one day to the realization that the climate of our world had changed and, like the cod, we too had lost the resiliency that had enabled us to survive?

Chapter 6

Flowers Cove

AT THE NARROWEST PART of the Strait of Belle Isle, a mere nine miles of open water separate the Great Northern Peninsula of Newfoundland from the coast of Labrador. Here the summer westerlies squeeze between the two land masses and accelerate down the strait, creating some of the strongest winds in northern Newfoundland. At Forteau Head on the Labrador side, the current stacks up against bold headlands in a series of eddies and overfalls. Directly across the strait on the Newfoundland side, an area of ledges and low, rocky islets marks the location of one of the area's most active fishing communities: the tiny outport of Flowers Cove.

The rain and thunder had already moved off to the south and the sky had started to clear as *Brendan's Isle* sailed up into this narrow section of the strait and approached the ledges at Flowers Cove. As the squally weather moved away, the wind filled in from the west and north and the air grew noticeably cooler. Richard stood at the helm, guiding the boat across short, choppy seas as we made our way toward a fairway buoy that marked the entrance to the harbor. Once under the lee of Nameless Point, Richard turned the sailboat up into the wind. Amanda and Nat stowed sails while a small scallop dragger steamed past. Our helmsman then wheeled the sailboat around once more and proceeded slowly, following the dragger into a narrow, nearly landlocked basin.

Once inside, the scalloper moored stern-to along with a dozen others of her kind on the far side of an L-shaped government pier. The sailboat found an empty space on the near side of the pier

behind a large wooden shrimper, the *Craig and Diane.* Liz and
Richard busied themselves adjusting lines and bumpers while Nat
and Amanda and I headed below to strip off foul weather gear and
change into drier clothing, in preparation for a walk into town.

Flowers Cove, I should emphasize, was not an unfamiliar
stopping place, for I had visited this village twice before, first during
the icy summer of 1991, then again during the following winter. The
first visit had been unplanned, for Flowers Cove had provided the
only available refuge when the leads of open water had suddenly
closed in the strait, forcing *Brendan* to stop and seek safe shelter.

There were no buoys to mark the harbor entrance that summer,
for the drift ice was still too heavy, even in late July, and the strait
remained officially closed to shipping. A set of range markers on a
hill behind the harbor and a beacon mounted on a rock sufficed to
guide the sailboat across Flowers Ledges, however, and in to the
government pier. Here she found protection from the moving ice
floes, and here she remained for five days, waiting for a navigable
lead of open water to develop in the strait.

Dozens of people from the community had befriended *Brendan's*
crew that summer, commiserating about the ice, bringing gifts of
food, offering the use of cars and showers and telephones. Two who
had been especially kind were the village postmaster, Calvin
Whalen, and his wife Mabel. Together, this pair had opened their
hearts to the little group of American sailors. "Come by any time for
a cup of tea," said Mabel after our first visit to their small white
cottage on the hill overlooking the harbor. "And don't knock on the
door. Only people ever knocks on the door in Newfoundland are
people you don't know and prob'ly don't want to. Front door is
never locked. Just step inside, kick off your shoes, give a call for
Calvin or me. One of us is sure to be here."

The second time I visited Flowers Cove was by automobile in
March 1992. Ever since I had started sailing here, I'd wanted to visit
the Great Northern Peninsula in winter and experience what life was
like during the dark months. I'd wanted to watch the snow-fog blow
across the tundra at dawn, to climb the massive walls of rafted sea
ice in the middle of the strait, to listen to the shriek of wind at
sunset, to sit around a wood stove and swap stories while winter
gales piled snow against the doors and windows.

During the previous summer I had met an American sociologist,
Craig Palmer, who had been living in Flowers Cove while studying

the local fishery on a grant from Newfoundland's Memorial University.

With Craig's help, my wife Kay and I were able to rent several rooms the following winter from the Whalens' daughter, Donna, and to spend a week in Flowers Cove. Our days there were occupied with visiting neighbors and friends. Our evenings were usually spent with Mabel and Calvin, feasting on braised moose, caribou, roasted turr, salt cod, seal flipper, turnips and salt beef, peas pudding, figgie duff, bakeapple cheesecake, and a dozen other traditional delicacies from Mabel's prodigious culinary repertoire.

One night after dinner, as winter gales piled snow against the doors and windows, Calvin began telling stories about his boyhood in Flowers Cove. He'd been born here, he said, nearly seventy years ago, before there was a road on the northern peninsula, when the present village site was occupied only as a summer fishing camp. In those days the small promontory where the village is now located was considered too exposed for year-round habitation. The winds were too strong, he said, the storms too frequent, the trees too stunted to cut for firewood. As a result, people spent the cold months of the year living "inside" (three or four miles inland) at a winter village site, trapping small game, cutting timber, pond-fishing through the ice.

"We had no Skidoos to get us into the country in them days," said Calvin. "Snowshoes only—or a sledge pulled by a team of dogs. But the dogs had to eat, summer and winter, just like the people, and many times there wasn't enough food. Wasn't the great numbers of moose in Newfoundland, for one thing, the way there is today. Caribou there was, and birds, and fish. Oh yes, all manner of fish. Ponds and streams full of salmon big as this. [He held his hands out shoulder-width, adjusted them wider, then wider again.] And cod— oh my Jesus but there was cod. In summer this little village was nothing but drying cod, hundreds of quintals, cleaned and split and laid out on flakes every place you looked. Every rock, covered with cod. Every place there was a flat surface with a square foot to spare, covered with cod.

"In the evening people would gather up the fish, stack them in sheds, because sometimes a dog would get loose in the night. Then, next morning, they would set them out again. But you'd never feed them fish to your dogs. The fish was what you lived on, the one thing you could sell to the merchant—offer in trade, really—when the buy-boats come along in September. The fish was like gold. They was what people used instead of money."

Unlike most young men of his generation, Calvin never worked in the commercial fishery. Instead, soon after he finished attending the local school, he taught himself Morse code, then found a job as an itinerant wireless operator with Canadian National Telegraph Service.

For a dozen years he traveled allover northern Newfoundland, filling in as a replacement wherever he was needed. Finally, he returned to Flowers Cove, working first as a truck driver for the new road-building project, then as the community's permanent CN wireless operator, and finally, for the past thirty-three years, as the village postmaster.

"Calvin just retired," said Mabel. "See there, the plaque they give him, hanging on the wall. And the pictures of the party they throwed for him. Over thirty years of service. He even got an article written about him in the *Northern Pen*."

When I asked Calvin what he'd been doing since leaving the postal service, he squared his shoulders and pointed to the gun rack in the hall. "That bird we ate for supper—turr we calls it—I shot that bird last week out in Nameless Cove. The moose steaks last night— bagged that moose in January. Mabel freezes the meat—we eats it all year. Same for hare, caribou, seal. Some people don't like seal—but Mabel just about dies for it. She was born and raised in L'Ans au Loup, across the strait in Labrador. All her people were fishermen and sealers."

Through all of Calvin's talking, Mabel sat silently in an over- stuffed armchair across the room. "That's so," she said each time his story met with her approval. Other times, when the fish grew too large or the ducks too plentiful or the rack of antlers too wide, she rolled her eyes, looked away, hid her amusement behind a cupped hand. Finally, however, when the subject turned to seals, she interrupted with a tale of her own.

"Out in the strait in winter is a place where the shorefast ice ends and the pack begins—the 'running edge' we calls it. There the ice stacks up like mountains, slab upon slab, driving together, some of it standing straight up on end. If you climb all the way to the top, you can look up and down the strait, see the bulls, the mothers, the whitecoats—see them riding the slab ice as it moves with the wind and current.

"My father was a sealer—like almost every man and boy on both sides of this strait. In the spring when the seals come down from the gulf, him and the others would head out to the running edge, scale the rafted ice, climb onto the pack. That's where the danger was, but that's where the seals was as well. Sometimes while they was working, the ice would break free, move out into the open strait, carry on to Lord knows where . . . ."

Calvin leaned forward in his chair and interrupted. "'Twas only last spring it happened again," he said. "Couple of fellas from Green Island Cove got caught sealing out on the ice. They was skinning whitecoats most likely—not paying attention—when the slab they was standing on begin to move. Wasn't anything they could do, just hold on, hope they wouldn't get flipped over, take a ride as far as the ice wanted to carry them. They was blowed up and down the strait the better part of a day before the ice decided to jam up over near Blanc Sablon, all the way across on the Quebec shore. If you wants to know the truth, them fellas was damn lucky to get back home alive."

At the end of this tale, Mabel excused herself and scurried downstairs to a basement workroom. She returned a few moments later carrying a pair of hand-stitched boots. The feet and leggings were fashioned of the smooth, silver-gray skin of harp seals, trimmed around the top with the downy white fur of the Arctic hare. A set of red rawhide laces held the boots together, fastened in cris-cross patterns down the fronts and tied in bows with tassels on the ends.

"The women of this community makes these boots at the craft center over at Shoal Cove," said Mabel, "same as our mothers and grandmothers done before us. Now some people will try to say that killing seals is a bad thing, an evil thing to do. But let me tell you something. Without the seals this community would never be here today. Seals and fish together, that's what Flowers Cove is about—what it has always been about.

She set the boots down and stepped over to the window. "P'rhaps you've noticed the little white church across the street—a lovely church, built with wood frames and ribs and knees, like the hull of a ship upside-down. Loveliest church on the northern peninsula it is, if you wants my opinion.

"Now something you may not know. The people in Flowers Cove calls that the Skinboot Church—just like these before you.

Sealskin boots is what we mean, and a hundred years ago the women of this community was making skinboots, just as we do, selling them, saving the money they earned to do the Lord's work.

"And what do you think this work was—this work that cost ten thousand seals their lives?" She paused and gazed from face to face about the room. "Why 'twas the work of building the church—for every window, every door, every carpet and bench and lamp was bought and paid for by the women of Flowers Cove, with the money they earned with their sealskin boots."

She concluded with a kind of swagger in her voice. "So don't let me hear you say that killing seals is an evil thing. For then I'll just have to remind you that for the men and women of this community, sealing is the work of the Lord."

A distant rumble of thunder sounded somewhere far to the south as Amanda and Nat and I stepped over *Brendan's* gunwale and onto the government pier. We walked past the row of scallop draggers, crossed a gravel parking lot, turned west on a paved macadam road. We wandered aimlessly for a time, past a dry goods store, an abandoned community hall, a small white house with a root garden and white picket fence. I'd not visited Flowers Cove since the dead of winter six years before, and I had forgotten much of the geography of this place.

I was on a mission of sorts this afternoon, a promised rendezvous with my two old friends, Mabel and Calvin. Mabel knew that *Brendan's Isle* was due to arrive in Flowers Cove today, for I had telephoned her this morning before leaving Port au Choix. But *Brendan* had been delayed in transit because of the squally weather, and I was concerned that, like a mother hen, she might now be worried that the boat and crew were overdue.

As we walked, I found myself searching among the cluster of buildings ahead for the steeple and pitched roof of the Skinboot Church, for I knew that the Whalen's house would be somewhere nearby. Finally, as we neared the church, a door in one of the adjacent buildings swung open and a woman stepped onto the porch.

"Could this be the place you're looking for then?" she called.

"Mabel," I hollered. "Mabel Whalen."

Brendan's Isle
under sail

The author filleting
a nice bit of halibut

Shipmates (left to right: author, Amanda, Nat, Liz, Richard)

Dories, fishboats, and a visiting sailor

A view of Cow Head harbor

Abandoned dwelling and fishing stores

Underway on a foggy morning

Outport hospitality

A visit to Jack Farwell's garden (left to right: Nat, Amanda, Jack, Liz, and Richard)

Beached whale ("Stinks like the devil, it does")

A peaceful morning

Shrimp-peeling contest

A view of Battle Harbor

Slipway and Salt Store: Battle Harbor

La Poile dory
offloading the
morning's catch

Sorting fish

"Come in all of you. Come in and be quick. 'Tis a miserable evening and you must be cold and wet."

Moments later Mabel ushered me and my shipmates into a small vestibule filled with coats and shoes. The house was sticky warm. The air smelled of salt beef and boiling vegetables and fresh baked bread. Mabel stepped into the kitchen as we removed our over-clothes, and she tied an apron over her cotton house dress. Her face was oval-shaped. Her nose and eyes and mouth were large and soft. "Terrible weather," she said, pushing a tuft of straight brown hair carelessly behind one ear. "Had me worrying after you all after-noon." She set a tea kettle on the stove. "Sit down, now sit. Don't wait for me. You must be nearly starved."

I posed all the necessary questions. "How is your health? Did Calvin bag his moose last winter? How's your daughter Donna? Your son Rex? Your grandson Mark? How old is the little one now—fourteen months you say?"

Mabel grinned from ear to ear at each of my queries, for she enjoyed nothing better than talking about her family.

Eventually I asked about the fishing moratorium and its impacts on the community. At first Mabel put on a brave face and tried to sound upbeat. "There's a new shrimp fishery opened on the Labrador. Large quotas—millions of pounds. All the men talking about it. You remember Jock Gardener—big handsome fella, silver hair—you met him when you was here with young Craig Palmer. Well Jock's got a new boat, *Craig and Diane* I b'lieve she's called, all rigged out for shrimp. Jock says there's good money in shrimp."

I pressed her about some of the other skippers I'd met while I was here in the winter of 1992. Hen Hughes, for instance. Or their old friend and neighbor, Steve Carnell.

"Both retired, both out of the fishery. Steve Carnell, he was getting out even before the moratorium. And Hen, he sold his license a year ago under the TAGS program. He's working on a construction project now down at the Craft Center."

Her talk about neighbors leaving the fishery moved her to reflecting upon the whole matter of the government's program to reduce the number of Newfoundland fishermen by purchasing and retiring their fishing licenses. Her face flushed and her voice grew loud as she described what she saw as the futility of such a scheme.

"Let's say a man decides to leave, to sell his license and get out. So he takes the money—hundred and fifty, maybe two hundred t'ousand—takes the money and goes. But what of the other four that's been working with him, fishing on his boat? They ain't out. They've not promised the government anything, and next thing you know, them four is doing whatever they can to find another boat.

"So for two hundred t'ousand the government has only managed to get one man in five to leave the fishery. Meantime, after paying off the loan on his boat and gear, this one tries to figure out a way to live the rest of his life on what's left. Maybe fifty, maybe a hundred t'ousand, if he's lucky. Now that may be all right for an old man soon to get his pension. But for a young man, 'tis like selling his birthright—selling the only thing of value that he's ever owned. For soon enough the money will be gone, and then he must go, too—leave his family, leave his community—for 'tis certain then that he'll never fish again."

Mabel grew silent. When next she spoke, her voice was broken and full of emotion. "There's so many people without work. So many leaving. So many wanting to come back, wanting to be with their families again, but can't. Grocery store closed two years ago. Hardware store closed. Irving service station up on the highway torn down. Gone. Sure there's TAGS money, but it's not enough. And they say next autumn that, too, may run out. And what will people do then?"

She glanced at a framed photograph of her husband and son and grandson on a shelf across the room and shook her head. "I just hates to talk about it—hates to even think about it." She stared at the floor and closed her eyes, and I could see her chin begin to quiver.

The front door clattered open. Calvin stepped into the vestibule, stomping his feet and calling for his wife. Mabel glanced at the dining room table where her three guests were seated and realized that she must set another place. "We have company, Calvin," she called as she scurried into the kitchen. "Come say hello."

The old postmaster seemed momentarily confused at the sight of three unfamiliar faces seated around his dinner table. He removed his cap, scratched a thinning patch of black hair above his temples, muttered a nearly unintelligible greeting under his breath. I stood up and re-introduced myself. It had been six years since my last visit—no reason Calvin should remember. Yet as soon as I reminded him of our previous meetings, his face erupted into a grin and he extended handshakes all around.

"Yes, yes, the sailor-fellow, the writer. Yes I remembers yes. I been hunting this past three days, see—down in Hawkes Bay. Sit down, sit down. I just didn't expect to find a roomful of American sailors in my house is the only thing."

Mabel served a tray of lemonade and shortbread cookies while Calvin settled in to his customary seat at the end of the table. "Still writing your book about Newfoundland?" he asked. "Mabel and me still going to be in it?"

I admitted, somewhat sheepishly, that yes, six years later I was still writing my book about Newfoundland, and that yes, he and Mabel were most certainly going to be in it. "The problem is, a lot of things have changed since I was here in the winter of 1992."

"The fish is gone," said Calvin. "That's what's changed. And far as I can tell, they won't be coming back—not in our lives, anyway."

Unlike Mabel, Calvin had no problem talking about the troubles that he and his neighbors faced. Mabel was worried, he explained—worried that if any more families moved away, the government might decide to close the elementary school. As things stood now, their grandson was one of a dwindling number of children still living here. Jock Gardener's grandson was another. These two families were among the last to have several generations residing together in the community.

"If the school goes, the young families will follow. Soon there will be no more children playing in the yards. Our own son Rex—house next door—he could be one of those who is forced to leave. Then Mabel will be without her grandson, and Flowers Cove will become a place with nobody but old people waiting to die."

I asked Calvin the inevitable question. What happened? Why did the collapse occur so suddenly? How did things get so far out of everyone's control?

"'Twasn't sudden. Don't let anybody tell you that. 'Twas lots of things that caused the cod to disappear, but none of them sudden.

"The start of it all—the beginning of the end, in my opinion—come with the big foreign factory trawlers back in the late 'sixties, early 'seventies. Large ships they were, black hulls, white super-structures, foreign names painted on their sides and transoms, foreign flags on their sterns. Looking up at one of them from a small dory, 'twas like looking up at a wall. From under the bows, a man might imagine them black iron plates was going to swallow him whole, for they seemed larger than the entire sky.

"All day those ships would drag up and down the strait. Supposed to stay off the coast two miles—out in what was then international waters. But nobody was here to enforce the rules and, fact was, they fished anywhere they wanted. At night or when 'twas stormy they would come up under the headlands, into the bays, to hide from the wind. So close sometimes you could hear the men talking, smell the food they was cooking. Then next day they would drop their trawls right by the traps and gillnets set along the shore, steal the inshore fish before the fellas here had ever a chance to catch them."

Nat asked Calvin if he thought the foreign factory trawlers were the ones responsible for fishing out the cod.

"No, not in those years anyways," said Calvin. "Took our own draggers to do that. But cod was only part of what the foreigners was after. Caplin was the other.

"Now caplin, as you may know, is the favorite food of the cod. 'Tis the very reason the cod come down the strait each year, for 'tis the singular feast they cannot resist. In May and June, back when the fish was plentiful, every bay and cove in this strait was so thick with caplin coming in to the beaches to spawn, so thick that if a man tried to row a dory across one of those coves, he would strike the back of a caplin with every pull on his oars. Beaches piled high with grounded caplin after they was finished spawning, so many the women and boys would come down with barrows and shovels to take them up and pile them on the gardens.

"All during the 'seventies the factory trawlers was taking the caplin—taking them a shipload at a time for fish meal and animal feed and fertilizer. Later, when our own draggers come to this coast, late 'seventies early 'eighties, they just continued on where the foreign trawlers left off. Foreign ships not allowed to fish inside the two hundred miles then, so they sent in the buy-boats—the Russians, the Japanese—large factory processors that would anchor in the bays, set up shop like the merchants of old, purchasing the caplin from our own local draggers.

"Now you'd think they'd have known, them fisheries managers, you'd think they'd have realized when the caplin started to disappear from the beaches, that this spelled trouble for the cod. But it didn't seem to matter. All up and down the strait, first on the

Newfoundland side, then on the Labrador shore, the runs become smaller, the caplin become fewer, until cove after cove saw no run at all.

"'Tis little wonder that the cod disappeared, is what I say, for we fished their food for thirty years. Fished it out in every bay and cove until—to this day—not a single run of caplin come in to the beaches from Green Island Cove to Feroulle Point. Now you can call this 'sudden' if you wants—or you can call it a mystery. But from where I stands, nothing sudden about it, nothing mysterious either. 'Tis a thing that's been going on for thirty years, and 'twill likely take another thirty to make it right again."

The smell of salt beef and cabbage and hot biscuits spilled out of Mabel's kitchen and overwhelmed the senses as if it were a solid thing. "Stop this now," she said to Calvin as she placed a steaming serving dish in front of him. "Stop all this talk about fish, for 'tis a sorry subject for the dinner table. Tell this man something pleasant for his book. Tell him about the moose that wandered in to town last month. Tell him about the string of trout you caught through the ice last winter out at Three-Mile Lake."

Any lingering thoughts that Nat and Amanda and I might have entertained about returning to *Brendan's Isle* for supper were quickly put to rest as Calvin passed each of us a heaping plate of beef stew and potatoes and boiled cabbage. The conversation turned to hunting stories and reminiscences. Rex and his wife Wavey and their infant son Mark showed up at the end of the meal for homemade tarts and bakeapple jam. Donna appeared with her boyfriend in time for coffee.

"Make certain you tell about this in your book," said Mabel. "Three generations of Whalens—just the way it used to be. 'Tis enough, for a time, to make a person forget . . . ."

I awakened the following morning to the moan of wind in *Brendan's* rigging and the chatter of rain against deckhouse windows. Our cruise plan included a layover in Flowers Cove for at least a day. But cruise plan or no, I knew there would be no passage down the strait for a little boat like ours until these gales relented.

There were many people in this village that I hoped to talk with again while we were here—fishermen and their families that Craig Palmer had introduced me to back in the winter of 1992. Among them, the person I was most eager to see again was Jock Gardener, for I remembered him as one of the most forthright and thoroughly likeable people I'd encountered in a long time.

"Jock is a different kind of fisherman," said Craig the day we'd first visited him in his little yellow house down on the harbor. "He doesn't like to follow the crowd. Many times when all the others are fishing one place, Jock turns up fishing someplace else. He kind of marches to his own drummer."

"He's stubborn," said Calvin. "Oftentimes he won't be the one catching the most fish. But that don't seem to matter as much to Jock as doing things his own way.

"And another thing—he don't cheat. You'll never catch Jock Gardener selling illegal fish—selling beyond his quota on the black market, is what I mean."

Two memories about Jock stood out for me as I recalled our winter's meeting six years ago. One was the way he stared at you when he talked—a riveting gaze from beneath black, bushy eyebrows, with pale blue eyes that seemed to pierce right through you. The other was the candor with which he talked about his own profession.

"Things are bad," he admitted as we sat around his kitchen table that winter. "Bad and getting worse. Skippers up and down the strait finding it harder and harder to fill their quotas."

"Why?" I asked. "Is it the weather? The ice? The seals?"

Jock shook his head at each of my questions. "Ice is a fact of life in northern Newfoundland. Seals and cod been living together for thousands of years, doing just fine. No, Mike boy, if you wants to know what's happening to the fish, well there's your culprit."

He pointed through the kitchen window at a heap of chain and rope and rusted steel lying in a tangle under the snow. I squinted into the glare, for at first all I could make out was the snow-covered ground . . . and then I saw it.

"Looks like an old otter trawl," I said.

The fisherman turned to me and stared. "With one of them and time a man can scoop up every last fish in Newfoundland."

Jock's new shrimp boat, the *Craig and Diane*, was moored on the government wharf just a few feet inboard of *Brendan's Isle*. After breakfast I stepped onto the pier, headed down to the dragger's wheelhouse, and called for her skipper.

Jock stepped to the wheelhouse door. He appeared just as I remembered him, a tall man, powerfully built, with a full head of thick white hair, heavy black eyebrows, a square jaw, a prominent nose that appeared as if it might have been broken once in an accident. "Come aboard, Mike boy. Mabel telephoned the house this morning, told Haz you might be coming by."

I climbed over the heavy wooden bulwark and stepped through an aluminum door that opened onto the bridge deck. A bundle of yellow pine two-by-fours lay in a jumble on the floor. Electrical wires ran helter-skelter down the walls. A man in a welder's mask hunched over a hatch on the foredeck, silhouetted in an eerie blue light. The entire vessel reverberated with the clank of a hammer and the hiss of an acetylene torch.

Jock explained, somewhat apologetically, that the boat was new to him and that he was still fitting her out between runs to the offshore shrimping grounds. "She's a good boat—p'rhaps just a bit too lively in a heavy sea. We'll have to do something to damp her down when we fiberglass her hull next winter."

I asked what happened to the boat I remembered—a steel dragger that Jock had used to trawl for ground fish before the moratorium. "Had to sell her. Couldn't afford to keep her with no fishing going on. But I kept my license, thank God. Then a year later they opened the Hawkes Channel for shrimp. I wish I hadn't sold that boat. But I still had the money in the bank—so I went down to Nova Scotia—Yarmouth—picked up one of their local-built wooden trawlers."

Jock gazed out at the rain and wind, heaved a long sigh, and resigned himself, it seemed, to another day in port. He invited me to the galley for a biscuit and a cup of tea. We sat in the crew's mess— silently for a time—eating, thinking our own thoughts. Finally, without looking at me, Jock began to speak.

"I fish with my sons. They're the only reason, really, that I still keeps at it—the only reason for all of this. [He gestured in a circle with his arms.] If Michael should leave here, if David should take his wife and boy and go to work in the oil fields of Alberta or Manitoba, well Haz and me, we would probably leave, too. For it's all that a community like Flowers Cove really is—family. It's the reason our grandfathers came here, the reason our fathers stayed—the reason those few of us remain today.

"This new fishery—the northern shrimp—is a stroke of luck. I don't know what the boys and me would be doing without it. It's a risky business, to be sure, for the new ground is a hundred miles offshore. The old gulf fishery down on the Esquiman Channel near Port au Choix is just a few miles out. When the weather begins to breeze up, the boats there can get back to shelter in a couple of hours. But this new ground is ten hours' steaming time from the Labrador coast—too far to get in when the weather changes and the northerly gales come down."

Jock cleared his throat and stared at me with a steely gaze. "Did you hear about the boat capsized out in the Hawkes Channel a few weeks ago—the shrimp dragger? Five men in the water for sixteen hours before they was found."

I shook my head, explaining that I had only arrived on this coast a few days ago.

"All the men saved, thank God, all of them in survival suits. But they was half frozen by the time they got picked up. Now some people say that all these small shrimp draggers face the same danger—that the booms and trawls make them top-heavy, so they'll roll over in a deep sea. But I think there's another reason. I think on the new ground the men don't know the bottom yet—don't know the dangers. Dragging a trawl in a heavy swell, tide running hard underneath, one of the doors catches on a snag. The boat slews around beam to the seas. Pinned to the bottom she rolls, and suddenly, before anybody can cut the gear free, she broaches and she's overwhelmed.

"And think about the gear, Mike boy—the chain, the doors, the trawl, six hundred fathom of wire—that gear costs as much to replace as the whole summer's profit. So what do you do? For you're damned if you cut it away, damned if you try to hang on."

Jock became silent again. He cast his eyes to the right and left, then touched the bulkhead next to him with his open hand. "She'll do. She's a bit shallow in the forefoot, p'rhaps. But she's steady on the trawl. Doesn't slew around too bad when she hits a snag. She'll do—especially after we get her ballasted right next winter. I only hope this fishery will last long enough to pay for the new gear—long enough to give something to my boys when I'm finished, to give them a future here."

"I've heard that the Department of Fisheries doubled your quotas last year—then doubled them again this spring."

"Department of Fisheries does a lot of funny things."

"Are you worried about overfishing?"

"Fisherman's always worried." He laughed. "But no. Tell the truth, Mike, the shrimp looks good. Plenty of shrimp. What worries me—what worries all the skippers here—is that we're still not seeing any cod. We're dragging the bottom—same area the big company trawlers used to drag before the moratorium—and we're not getting a single young cod as by-catch.

"Remember back in 1992 when Crosbie first announced the moratorium? Two years, he said it would take for the cod to come back. Well that was six years ago, and still no cod. Small turbot, yes. A few small redfish. But no cod. Where are the breeder fish that are supposed to be rebuilding the stock? Where is the spawn? Where is the young tom cod? Over two hundred boats dragging on those banks, dragging all summer, and nothing."

Jock gazed at me with his riveting stare, and I could see the moisture beginning to well up in the corners of his eyes. "The fish is gone—every last one. It's like dragging across a desert out there, Mike boy. Like dragging across an empty desert."

Chapter 7

Battle Harbor

THE EVENING AFTER my meeting with Jock, the weather finally began to clear, and by sunrise next morning *Brendan's Isle* was underway, heading toward the eastern strait. With the yankee jib poled out to starboard and the mainsail pinned against the backstays to port, she raced before a fresh southwest wind, rolling down steep seas, throwing sheets of spray from her bows, leaving a trail of spume and spindrift in her wake. The wind, funneling northward out of the Gulf of St. Lawrence, was warm. The water, however, became progressively colder, with long fingers of the frigid Labrador current swirling and eddying in mysterious patterns under the keel.

Near the end of the mid-morning watch, Richard spotted the first iceberg—a tiny diamond of shimmering white, silhouetted against the barren hills of the Labrador shore. Half an hour later Liz spotted another, almost dead ahead. This one was larger, with a jagged tower that looked like an illustrator's fantasy. Then, in quick succession, various members of the crew spotted another, and another, until the horizon was dotted with dozens of white islands of ice, glistening in the pale sunshine.

I had witnessed this scene several times before. The bergs—intruders from the north—are carried down from western Greenland and Baffin Island by the Labrador Current, moving along the east Canadian coast in an area known as Iceberg Alley. When they arrive in the vicinity of Belle Isle and the approaches to the strait, many of them become trapped in the swirling current. A few actually pass westward through the narrows at Flowers Cove and enter the Gulf of St. Lawrence. Most, however, remain in the large embayment to the east, melting slowly, breaking into large, house-sized sections ("bergy bits") or smaller, nearly invisible slabs ("growlers"), wandering in unpredictable patterns across the surface of the sea.

The ice by itself poses a significant danger to mariners in this windy part of the world. It poses an even greater danger, however, when combined with the frequent fogs that also plague this area, fogs that result from warm, moist continental air masses coming into contact with the cold Arctic surface waters of the Labrador Current.

On this particular morning, at nearly the same moment that the ice appeared ahead, a bank of low cloud appeared on the horizon astern, stalking the sailboat as she entered the area of bergy water. Then, with the ice only a few miles away, the visibility began to drop. The disk of sun grew pale, the surface of the sea turned silver-gray, and the rigging and sails began to drip with condensation. The hills of the Labrador coast, bathed in sunlight only a few moments before, began to lose their definition. Several of the icebergs to the right and left became shadowy ghosts. In a few more minutes, the berg that had been visible ahead vanished altogether, leaving *Brendan,* still moving at seven or eight knots, shrouded in dense fog.

I left the deck and moved to the navigator's station, where I could monitor the electronic images of the ice on the ship's radar. On the screen, the largest of the ice towers were easily visible, and I was able to guide the helmsman around them. The growlers and other shards of broken ice that floated near the foundered icebergs were electronically invisible, however, and for this reason I needed to ask several of the crew to take turns watching at the bows.

Once the lookout was set, I fixed my attention on the radar screen, listening for a call from the deck that I hoped would not come. The wind groaned in the rigging, the spray drove across the bows, and *Brendan* charged into the cottony gloom like a runaway freight train.

During the next several hours, the chime of the ships clock was the only measure of time passing. Down at the nav-station, I was hypnotized by the green pulsing circle on the radar screen. A maze of electronic echoes glowed and faded in rhythmic patterns before my eyes, and I struggled to stay alert.

Suddenly, I was shaken out of my ennui by a series of targets that seemed to be acting oddly. At first I assumed they were icebergs and I initiated a standard pattern of avoidance. Then I realized that, whatever these "icebergs" were, they were organized in a straight line—they were moving at almost the same speed as *Brendan*—and they were slowly, inexorably closing the distance between themselves and the sailboat.

"Starboard twenty degrees," I called to Amanda, "—and listen for the sound of an engine!"

When the line of targets on the screen continued to draw closer, I grabbed the microphone from the VHF radio and hollered into the mouthpiece. I must have sounded somewhat panicky, for moments later came a long belly laugh, followed by the familiar voice of Jock Gardener aboard the dragger *Craig and Diane*. "We thought that was you, Mike boy. Just wanted to be sure."

As I talked with the fisherman, the line of targets veered away and slowly moved past the sailboat. It was a convoy, Jock explained—nine draggers bound for the Hawkes Channel, steaming together for safety. "And where are you bound on this fine summer morning?" he asked.

"Battle Harbor—the old cod fishing capital of southern Labrador."

Jock laughed. "'Twas once a real town, I suppose you know. But only fishermen at Battle Harbor now are in photographs, only fish are made out of metal and paint."

"So I've heard."

Jock paused and cleared his throat. "It's a kind of memorial," he said, as the last of the trawlers steamed past. "Like a stone marker in a graveyard—a memorial for the fishermen and the fish that's gone."

It was early afternoon by the time *Brendan* doubled Cape St. Charles at the northeastern extremity of the strait and pulled into a series of protected bays and channels behind Great Caribou Island. Almost immediately on coming under the land, she sailed out of the fog, and suddenly we were surrounded by low, boulder-strewn hills, barren islands, and a maze of shallow runs and tickles.

There was nothing soft or kind about this land. The color of the rock was mottled gray and black, the shapes were harsh, the rock outcrops right up to the shore were devoid of vegetation. Even though I realized that in decades past there had been a number of small settlements and fishing camps scattered about these shores, it was easy to imagine this place as having never been marked by human presence, so stark and empty did it now appear.

Immediately to port, as the sailboat doubled the cape, was St. Charles Harbour and the site of the deserted outport of Cape Charles. Ahead, as she entered Caribou Run, were Anthill Cove, Shoal Tickle, Green Cove—all sites of former fishing camps now abandoned. On the far side of the Run were more abandoned camp sites at Assizes Harbor, Mouse Island Tickle, Copper Island. A large iceberg lay grounded on the shore near the last of these sites, and the sailboat was forced to feel her way around it, then to circle several bergy bits that lay stranded along the north shore of Great Caribou Island. Finally, she pulled into a sheltered cove surrounded by rocky headlands. Here, after the crew had stowed sails, she made her way slowly past a pair of pinnacle rocks and into a long, narrow passageway: the fabled fishermen's haven and gateway to the northern seas known as Battle Harbor, Labrador.

Despite having been told about the historical restoration that had been taking place here, I was shocked at what I saw—for it seemed as if *Brendan* and her crew had just entered some kind of time machine and had been transported back into a different century. The buildings on the hillside ahead looked prosperous and well cared-for. Many had new roofs, new windows and doors, freshly painted shutters, new wooden clapboard and shingles. A church, an inn, a tiny police detachment building, a general store, and several private dwellings lined the hillside. A cluster of large rectangular ware-houses dominated the waterfront, all of them painted white and crowned with red shingle roofs. A sign on one of the warehouses— also freshly painted—read "The Earle Freighting Service Ltd." The pier in front of these buildings was newly planked and faced with heavy, freshly creosoted pilings. Moored in a slipway between the buildings was a small coastal freighter and several traditional dories, all mended and polished and painted like new.

The only signs of an earlier time that seemed to be missing here were the hundreds of fishing schooners that used to frequent this place during the heyday of the Labrador cod fishery. In those years, Battle Harbor had been the economic and administrative capital of southern Labrador, a provisioning and fueling depot, a marketplace for fish and seals, and, during the late nineteenth and early twentieth centuries, the site of one of the largest outport hospitals on the Labrador coast as well as one of the northernmost wireless radio stations on the American continent. The history of Battle Harbor was virtually synonymous with the history of the cod fishery in eastern North America.

I was happy, in a perverse sort of way, that the fishing schooners were no longer present, for without them, *Brendan* had the harbor nearly to herself. She pulled alongside a pier fronted by a pair of large, double story warehouses. Amanda took charge of setting up bumpers and mooring lines, while I prepared to venture ashore and seek out the proprietor of this place.

I was just about to step onto the pier when a young, clean-cut fellow dressed in blue jeans and a white T-shirt emerged from one of the nearby doorways and approached the sailboat. He was of modest height, with an athletic build, a maze of freckles on his face and forearms, a shock of short, sandy blond hair. He introduced himself as Mike Earle, resource curator, tour guide, and general factotum for an organization he called the Battle Harbor Historic Trust.

"Welcome to Battle," he said with undisguised enthusiasm. "You'll find showers at the Inn up on the hill. Washing machines aren't hooked up yet—we're still getting organized for visitors here. I'll give you a tour of the historical site soon as you're ready. Anything else I can do, just give a shout."

In the late afternoon, as the sun dropped behind a hill on Great Caribou Island, the harbor became shrouded in shadow. The fog, which had been lurking out in the strait only a few miles away, crept into the approaches and curled over the hilltops of Battle Island in long, wispy fingers. Seabirds wheeled in circles overhead, crying like human children as they fought over the carcass of a fish. A trio of large black crows stood in silence at the head of the wharf, watching over the warehouses and buildings of the village like spirits of the dead.

This was a place filled with ghosts, and as the light dropped, it became easier to feel oneself surrounded by them, touched by their presence. I sat on the coachroof of the moored sailboat, watching the shadows grow longer, thinking about the history of this tiny harbor and the people who had once lived here.

It is likely that the earliest human activity in this place, at least since the conclusion of the last ice age, came at the hands of a society of fishermen and traders known as the Maritime Archaic more than eight thousand years ago. What these people discovered here was what every visitor from the sea has discovered ever since: a snug shelter, easy of access, surrounded by high hills, perfectly protected from wind and seas, and located on the outer coast, directly on the path that any small vessel would follow as it plied the trade routes or traveled to and from the fishing grounds of eastern Newfoundland, the St. Lawrence Gulf, and northern Labrador.

It came as no surprise, therefore, that when the first English ship fishermen ventured down the Labrador coast in pursuit of the northern cod nearly eight millennia later, they too chose this tiny, landlocked harbor as one of their primary ports. Some of the earliest of these for whom there are dependable records were fishing captains who sailed for John Slade and Company, fish merchants, of Poole, England. Beginning in the mid 1770s, Slade and Company acquired a license from the English Crown granting it exclusive use of the premises known as Battle Harbor during its seasonal ship fishing operations. At first, this license was granted on a limited basis, so that other fishing interests might also have a chance to make use of the same area. Eventually, however, based on its negotiations with other merchants, Slade acquired a permanent, long-term lease, and Battle Harbor became the first of many "company towns" on the Labrador coast, owned and operated as a private business venture by a single merchant.

For the next several years, Slade and Company operated its premises at Battle Harbor as a seasonal ship fishing business, supplied exclusively by its own captains and ships. By the late 1770s, however, the company had also started to develop a substantial winter and spring seal fishery, pursued in part by resident "wintermen" who had settled in the local area. By the mid 1780s the operation was expanded to include the exploitation of salmon as well, so that by the end of the eighteenth century, the Slade premises and the wintermen formed the nucleus of one of Labrador's earliest year-round communities.

During the early decades of the nineteenth century, a new structure began to evolve in the Labrador fishery. Growing numbers of fishermen began sailing north from Newfoundland in small, home-built schooners and selling their product to Newfoundland-based fish merchants. Perhaps as many as two hundred schooners and five thousand fishermen sailed from southern Newfoundland to the Labrador ground in the summer of 1845. By 1851 these numbers had soared to seven hundred schooners and fifteen thousand men, and by 1880, according to one estimate, to twelve hundred schooners and thirty thousand men. As this fishery grew, the number of fishermen who decided to settle and live year-round in Labrador also grew, thus creating an expanding inshore component to the fishery as well.

At least partially in response to the mounting competition on the fishing grounds, Slade and Company decided to terminate its activities in southern Labrador, and in 1871 the company sold its property, buildings, and equipment at Battle Harbor to a Newfoundland-based fish merchant, Baine, Johnston & Company Limited, of St. John's. Following a pattern that had been evolving for more than a century, Baine, Johnston began purchasing its fish from local schooners and inshore dory men, paying for the product with a line of credit that could be "spent" for food and other basic goods and supplies at their company store. This arrangement, known throughout Newfoundland as the "truck system," was inherently unfair, as the fish merchants almost always commanded monopolies in their retail operations. Not only did they determine the prices that the fishermen were required to pay for their goods and supplies, but they also determined the prices the fishermen received for their fish.

Observers of the Newfoundland and Labrador fisheries during the late nineteenth century became increasingly disturbed by the inequities of this arrangement. One such observer, Sir W. R. Kennedy, recorded these impressions of the effects of the merchant system upon the Labrador fishermen in the summer of 1881: "These poor people, ground down as they are by the detestable 'truck system,' live and die hopelessly in debt, living from hand to mouth without a shilling to call their own. Possible education may in time awaken them to a sense of their degradation, but at present there seems no remedy to this evil."

Another who was similarly disturbed over this state of affairs was a doctor and medical missionary, Wilfred Grenfell, a man who dedicated his life to the fishermen of Newfoundland and Labrador and whose work evolved into a lasting legacy here. Grenfell, moved by the hopelessness and poverty that he witnessed in the small fishing communities of this area, founded his Labrador Deep-sea Mission in the early 1890s to provide medical aid and other basic humanitarian services. Beginning with one small hospital ship, the *Albert*, Grenfell and a team of medical volunteers visited coastal communities from the Great Northern Peninsula to eastern Quebec and southern Labrador. In 1893 he acquired a building donated by the merchant-owner of Baine, Johnston & Company and opened his first land-based hospital at Battle Harbor. Soon afterwards he added several more hospital ships, including a state-of-the-art steel vessel, the *Strathcona,* and established several more regional hospitals in Labrador, Quebec, and finally at St. Anthony, Newfoundland.

Even though the focus of Grenfell's work was medical care for fishermen and their families, he was also acutely aware of what he called "the oppressive 'truck system' of trade," which, he wrote, "keeps its poor victims in a sort of apathetic satisfaction with a hopeless state of slavery." In 1896 he helped to start a small coopera- tive store at Red Bay, Labrador, on the Strait of Belle Isle, with the purpose of breaking the monopoly of the local fish merchant and providing an economical alternative for the settlers. After Red Bay, he also helped to establish cooperatives at St. Modeste and at Flowers Cove, "with very beneficial results to the poorest." The sealskin boot trade that helped to build the Skinboot Church was, in fact, a direct outcome of the Grenfell cooperative at Flowers Cove.

Ironically, one of the places in which Grenfell was not able to establish a fishermen's cooperative was Battle Harbor, for as a tenant whose facility was located on Baine, Johnston property, his Mission was under the control of the fish merchant. The hospital grew and prospered—beginning in 1902 extensions were added, and in 1904 a new doctors' house was built—but like the fishermen themselves, Grenfell's Deep-sea Mission was forced to accept whatever terms Baine, Johnston cared to impose upon its presence here—and to be content to live under the merchant's monopolistic sway.

Both the Grenfell Hospital and the fishing operations of Baine, Johnston continued to flourish at Battle Harbor through the first few decades of the twentieth century. Beginning about 1920, however, the Labrador fishery entered a period of long, slow decline. Inshore landings of northern cod dropped steadily through the 1930s and 1940s, then took another severe drop with the coming of the offshore factory trawlers in the 1950s and 1960s. The Grenfell Hospital at

Battle Harbor, meanwhile, suffered a catastrophic fire in 1930 in which all but the doctors' house was burned to the ground. The schooner fleet that had frequented the harbor for nearly two centuries was slowly being replaced by motor-driven trawlers and offshore "bankers"—vessels that didn't need a fueling stop and supply depot in southern Labrador.

Finally in 1955 the premises at Battle Harbor was sold again, this time to an establishment called The Earle Freighting Service Limited of Carbonear, Newfoundland. Coastal Labrador was actually being depopulated by this time, and Battle Harbor was no exception. Many of the dwellings here were becoming summer "camps" for families that had decided to move back to larger inland communities. The last of the hospital staff was disbanded and the facility moved to St. Mary's River (now Mary's Harbour), Labrador. The Marconi wireless station was decommissioned. Then in 1966, in response to Premier Joey Smallwood's controversial relocation program, the police detachment building was closed and the detachment of Royal Canadian Mounted Police was reassigned to a nearby mainland settlement.

Battle Harbor—and the fishermen of southern Labrador—struggled on. But even before the codfish crash and the moratorium of 1992, this place was becoming a ghost town, a silent reminder of a bygone era, with collapsing roofs, peeling paint, weathered shingles lifting and curling at the edges, piers surrendering to winter ice, footpaths overgrown with weeds. The fabled Battle Harbor, like a corpse left unburied on the Arctic tundra, was slowly decomposing, returning to a state of nature, seeking an equilibrium with the wild, empty landscapes that had spawned it.

Sunrise next morning came with the smell of coffee and the sound of bacon sizzling on *Brendan's* galley stove. No sooner had I drawn myself a mug and climbed into the cockpit than I spotted the young resource curator, Mike Earle, working with a hammer and an apron of nails on one of the restored buildings nearby.

"Good morning," I hollered. "When you're finished with your work, come aboard for a coffee." Moments later the fellow dropped his tools, jogged over to the sailboat, jumped down onto her deck. He was obviously pleased to have visitors in the harbor—and as the members of my crew straggled up one by one into the cockpit, he accepted a cup of coffee, introduced himself, and began to talk about the work he had been doing in Battle Harbor.

He was a former fisherman, he told us—thirty-one years old, married, a father of one. He lived in Lodge Bay, a small mainland community a dozen miles up the river from here. For seven years he had fished for cod and salmon as a sharesman with his father-in-law. Then during the late 1980s, as the fish on the Labrador coast had grown more and more scarce, he had slowly come to realize that if the only thing he could do for the rest of his life was fish, he might soon be sitting on a pier somewhere, living on the dole.

"The problem," said Mike, "was that I couldn't go back home—didn't want to, anyhow. I grew up in Corner Brook, down on the west coast of Newfoundland, the youngest of fourteen children. But even as a boy I knew there was nothing in Corner Brook for me. I knew how hard it was for my friends, how hard finding work. A lot of my family had already moved away to Ontario, and that was something I didn't want to do. I just didn't have any aspirations about moving to a concrete jungle and, you know, trying to make a go."

"What made you decide to come all the way out to Labrador?" asked Amanda.

"'Twas something of an accident, really. Summer of my four-teenth year I took sick, had to go to hospital. While I was there I met a nurse—a student volunteer—name of Dorothy Pye. She was taking care of the floor I was on, and we got to be friends. She began telling me about the community where she lived, a little village of five or six families down in southern Labrador, telling me how nice it was.

"When I got better, I come out on the coast boat to visit for a couple of weeks. Then, when I got here and seen what beautiful country it was, simple life, pleasant people—I decided I wanted to stay. Her father offered me a crewman's job on one of his fishing boats, and that was enough for me. I called my mother, said 'send my gear. I'm staying.' "

"At fourteen years old?" said Amanda, shaking her head in disbelief.

"Well some think it was courageous and some think it was just plain foolish—but I didn't really care about that. When I seen the chance to move out here, get in touch with my roots, you know—I just jumped at it."

"What happened when the fishery began to fail?"

"I was married by that time to Dorothy—we already had a baby. I was a full sharesman by then, and my father-in-law and me, we would talk. Every year we was fishing longer, every year setting more gear, every year landing fewer fish. Just like the others on this coast, we could see the handwriting on the wall.

"Finally in 1990, a little money come along from the Provincial government for some restoration work in Battle Harbor. 'Twas the only thing happening for me here besides the fishery, and I knew I had to get into it. Me and my father-in-law, we both worked as carpenters that year, helping to restore the old church. We kept on fishing—trying, anyhow—until the moratorium. But by then there was an organization, the Battle Harbor Historic Trust, with more people, bigger plans, the promise of some federal grant money. I became what they called a 'restoration carpenter.' For the next five years I worked on almost every historic building on the island—full time—for I knew by then my future was here in Battle."

Later that morning, after a breakfast of coffee and bacon and toast in *Brendan's* cockpit, Mike offered to take my crew and me on a walking tour of the restoration and tell us what he knew of this place. We began with a look at several of the buildings on the hillside: the Church of St. James the Apostle, where Mike and his father-in-law had started their apprenticeship training in restoration carpentry, followed by visits to the Grenfell Mission Doctors' Cottage, the police detachment building, the bunkhouse, the general store. Eventually we wound our way back down to the complex of commercial buildings on the waterfront: the Pork Store and Twine Loft, the Salmon Store, the Flour Store, the Salt Store.

All of these commercial warehouses were empty now, although in the heyday of the Labrador fishery they had often been filled with pallets of salted cod, stacks of sealskins, barrels of meat, sacks of flour, huge white mountains of salt. A number of the buildings were constructed with massive, ten-by-ten wooden beams, many of which had been carved with the names and initials and unreadable scrawls of the countless generations of fishermen who had used these spaces as dormitories and common rooms while they were icebound or weathered in by storms.

One of the subjects Mike and I talked about as we explored these buildings was the relationship between the fishermen and the merchants who operated the facilities here. According to Mike, the most recent of the merchants, The Earle Freighting Service, had been fair to the fishermen. He knew this because his father-in-law had sold his fish here for many years. Earle's dealt in cash—not credit—which meant that a man who worked hard and had good luck on the fishing ground might actually realize a little profit for his labor.

"Not so for the fishermen of an earlier generation," said Mike, "for these men had no choice. Not just in Battle Harbor but in outports everywhere, they were forced to accept whatever the merchant offered for their fish, pay whatever he asked for the goods they needed at his store."

He glanced up the hill at the familiar shape of the Doctors' Cottage. "I've heard that old Doctor Grenfell once tried to set up a cooperative store in Battle Harbor—as a way of forcing the merchant here to charge a fair price. But the merchant threatened to repeal Grenfell's lease if he did such a thing. It seems to me when you hear such a story, it's a pretty good sign of how hard things were for the fishermen here—indeed, for fishermen all over Newfoundland."

I explained to Mike that I was familiar with the legacy of Doctor Grenfell and that I knew how much he detested the merchants' monopolistic system. The surprising thing, however, was that when you read Grenfell's own descriptions of the conditions in the fishery, you realized that he didn't necessarily detest the merchants. At one point he actually described them as "enterprising men of varying fortunes" who made a "modest profit" when the fishing was good but who were often "ruined by bad debt" when times were hard. He seemed to sense that the merchants and the fishermen were linked together—in a kind of life-and-death struggle, perhaps—but linked together nonetheless.

Mike fell silent for a time. I followed his eyes and realized that he was staring at one of the structural beams in the room where we were talking. He was looking at the maze of initials and signatures, dates and ship names that stood in silent witness to the thousands of fishermen who had frequented this place for nearly two centuries.

"It's odd," Mike said. "Sometimes when I look at these marks, I can almost see the faces of the men who carved them—can almost feel myself among them. Hard men, they were. Desperate men when times were bad.

"Many were bondsmen, transported over from Europe, forced to labor for their freedom. These were called servants—'fishing servants' in the local way of talking. Others worked for a wage or fished as sharesmen, same as I did with my father-in-law. But all of them still 'servants' to the merchants here.

"Now I know this might sound strange, but sometimes when I think about them days, I begin to think the merchants might have been servants, too, in a funny kind of way. Just like the fishermen, just like everybody else living on this coast, all servants of the selfsame master…"

I gazed quizzically at Mike, still uncertain what he was driving at.

". . . All of them servants of the fish . . . if only they'd understood."

Chapter 8

St. Anthony

TWO DAYS OF RAIN and westerly gales forced *Brendan's Isle* to remain harbor bound, tethered to the Earle's Freighting Services piers at Battle Harbor. Finally, the morning of the third day broke clear and cold and still. A thousand stars glittered in the predawn twilight. The aurora borealis pulsed across the northern sky, slowly dissolving into the first faint glow of dawn.

As soon as there was light enough to see, my watch mate Liz and I cast off the mooring lines and guided the sailboat, under power, through the narrow channel at the northern end of the harbor. We doubled Great Island, maneuvered around an area of shoals and broken ice, and stood off to the south. Twenty miles ahead rose the dark silhouette of Belle Isle, ringed by a circle of icebergs. In front of these, framed on a perfect mirror of sea, a pair of humpback whales breached and blew in the tangerine dawn.

With the calm seas and nearly unlimited visibility, I felt a kind of peace this morning that mimicked the day. I asked Liz to steer the sailboat toward the humpbacks, hoping to get a closer look. No sooner did she start to turn the wheel, however, than we spotted an even larger group of whales to the west, and then another, due south. Soon the horizon before us was filled with clouds of water vapor that hung suspended in the still air, marking the presence of large numbers of whales.

It was not yet seven o'clock in the morning as the sailboat drew abeam of Belle Isle and bore off toward Cape Bauld and the east coast of Newfoundland. I asked Liz if she wanted a mug of coffee or a bit of food. She seemed barely to hear my question. I asked if she would like me to relieve her at the helm. Without taking her eyes off a dark shape on the horizon ahead, she indicated with a shake of her auburn locks that she was content to remain exactly where she was. "I'll go forward then, and watch at the bows," I said, turning and moving past the deckhouse, "just to make sure we don't run up onto the back of one of these fellows."

I crossed the foredeck, stepped around the jib stays, and slid out onto the bow pulpit. Here, several feet ahead of the cutwater, I felt like I was floating on air. The drone of the diesel engine receded into the distance astern, and soon the only sound I heard was the hiss of breaking water at the sailboat's bow. I wedged myself securely into the forward-most section of the pulpit and hunkered down, thinking about the spectacle of this morning, looking out across the water's surface, watching for whales.

Time and again as I watched, the same sequence repeated itself. A few hundred yards to the right or left, ahead or astern, the sea opened to reveal the black forehead and smooth, dark back of a feeding humpback. A blast of breath exploded like a geyser from the animal's blowhole, marked by a cloud of mist and followed seconds later by a sucking noise of inhale. Behind the blowhole the body continued to rise, culminating in a sharp angle between back and tail—the unmistakable "hump" that makes this species the easiest of all the great whales for human observers to identify. Moments later the blowhole disappeared, the hump flexed, and the giant, twin-lobed tail emerged in slow motion from the sea, hovering in a kind of suspended animation for a few seconds before slipping noise-lessly back under the water's surface.

How many humpback whales were feeding in the mouth of the strait this morning, I wondered? It was hard to tell—perhaps a hundred, perhaps more. These animals, I'd learned, were part of a population explosion of several species of whales that had taken place in recent years along the coasts of Newfoundland and Labrador.

This east-coast humpback population, once reduced to just a few hundred individuals, had recently been estimated at upwards of five thousand—with the numbers growing every year. The animals arrived on this coast each spring, as soon as the pack ice retreated, to spend the summer and early autumn feeding in the nutrient-rich Labrador Current. They congregated around headlands and above precipitous bottom formations where the current ran strong and where the cold bottom-water mixed upwards onto the shelf. Here they fed on summer runs of caplin and herring and shrimp and on dense clouds of krill and other microorganisms that upwelled for nearly a thousand miles along the Atlantic coastal rise—the same rich food sources that once supported huge populations of cod.

Fifty years ago, in the aftermath of nearly five centuries of commercial whaling, the humpbacks were considered by scientists to be an endangered species, threatened with commercial extinction in most oceans of the world. Yet despite their depleted numbers, they were still being hunted along the east coast of Newfoundland into the 1960s by whalers operating from shore-based whaling stations. The commercial extermination of the humpbacks was viewed by many Newfoundlanders as unfortunate but necessary, as these animals were perceived as competitors in the fishery and were blamed for becoming entangled in cod traps, gillnets, and other fixed fishing gear. They destroyed several hundred thousand dollars worth of this gear every year. As an old dory man from Notre Dame Bay once commented to me, "A Newfoundland fisherman has to have a lot of patience to talk kindly of a whale."

Several factors finally conspired to put an end to whaling in Newfoundland. Foremost among these, the severely reduced numbers of nearly all species of whales had rendered commercial whaling less and less economically viable. Like the cod fishermen of four decades later, the whale "fishermen" of the mid-twentieth century had literally nothing left to fish for. This situation, combined with a worldwide ban on killing humpbacks imposed by the International Whaling Commission and ratified by Canada in the summer of 1972, effectively ended the hunt and allowed the whale populations to begin a long, slow process of recovery.

One more set of impediments remained, however, to threaten the return of the humpbacks, for every year fishermen were still placing thousands of cod traps and other forms of fixed fishing gear in the bays and inshore waters all around Newfoundland. Often the choicest "berths" for these traps were areas where bait (such as caplin) was abundant and thus where the whales also hunted. Inevitably, a certain percentage of these whales would enter the traps and would either tear them to pieces, carry them away, or become so hopelessly entangled that without help they would eventually be unable to swim to the surface and would suffocate.

Nobody knew for certain how many whales were involved each year in such incidents—nobody knew how many were shot or harpooned by fishermen trying to save their gear or how many might have suffocated in their own struggle to free themselves—for no one bothered to keep count. Suffice it to say that the problem was large, both for the whales and for the human beings. The death of hundreds of whales became a matter of serious concern for environmentalists and animal rights activists. The loss of thousands of dollars worth of fishing gear became a matter of equally serious concern for fishermen. Traditional adversaries began squaring off on opposite sides of an emotional battlefield, attitudes became polarized, and potentially serious confrontation threatened to erupt.

It took one man, a professor of animal behavior at Newfoundland's Memorial University named Jon Lien, to recognize that the eventual solution to this dilemma was going to be the same, both for the whales and for the people. In the short term, Lien realized, the fishermen were going to need some sort of emergency response team trained to help disentangle the whales from their nets. In the long term, the whales needed assistance in detecting and avoiding nets—perhaps an electronic sound-producing device that would attach to the nets and warn of their presence—thus keeping both the whales and the fishing gear safe from one another.

Lien, the leader of Memorial University's Whale Research Group, first organized his "whale rescue program" in 1978 in response to complaints from a group of fishermen in Newfoundland's Trinity Bay. An unusually large influx of humpbacks that year had been tearing up the Trinity Bay cod traps, and in response, the fishermen had petitioned the Canadian government for a reinstatement of commercial whaling off Newfoundland's east coast. Lien knew that confrontation was not going to help. He also knew that the fishermen faced a serious problem—and he thought he had an idea that might help solve it. With the aid of a handful of student volunteers and a few thousand dollars in grant money, he developed methods of approaching an entangled whale using a soft-bottom rubber Zodiac—methods which often involved landing on the animal's back while avoiding the thrashing flippers and flailing flukes. Gradually, with experience, he became expert at untangling and cutting the animals free of the fishing nets.

After that first summer in Trinity Bay, Lien and his whale rescue program evolved into something of an institution in coastal

Newfoundland. By the mid-1980s, the "Whale Man" (as he became popularly known) and his group of student volunteers were responding to up to one hundred fifty calls a summer, saving at least half of these whales from certain death while also saving fishermen hundreds of thousands of dollars a year in gear and catches. By the early 1990s, with more nets in the water and more whales on the coast, these numbers had increased, and by 1991 members of the whale rescue program were announcing proudly that they had helped to free more than a thousand whales.

"We do a whale almost every day during the summer," Lien said in an interview in 1991. "The animals that get caught are usually juveniles, and it's almost always an accident. They're just like any other young animals, such as kittens or puppies, and they'll just be swimming around and blunder into a net. I've seen them playing with nets and flicking the floats around—like they're bored and want something to do."

The second phase of Lien's program, initiated in the late 1980s, was directed at helping these young whales avoid becoming entrapped in the first place. Beginning in 1988, the Whale Man started experimenting with battery powered, low-frequency electronic beepers. He then turned to a series of experiments with high-frequency clickers that produced a wall of sound in non-repetitive patterns. Finally in 1993, he and a university-based think tank called C-CORE (the Center for Cold Ocean Resources Engineering) developed a low frequency noisemaker that sent out a four kilohertz signal, inaudible to cod but highly audible to a whale's sonar. Produced for about $200 each, this spherical, battery-operated device was marketed under the name "Aqualert." When housed in a steel fishing float and attached six to a net, it proved effective in reducing entrapments by seventy-five percent—a clear victory both for the fishermen and for the whales.

The incredible success of Jon Lien's whale rescue program was evident this morning in every direction that Liz and I looked. Although scientists still have much to learn about the recovery of humpback populations, it is nevertheless arguable that Lien's efforts have saved the lives of as many as one in three of the Newfoundland humpbacks that we were seeing here today. The IWC whaling ban laid the groundwork for the whales' recovery. The activities of environmental groups added to the momentum. But Lien's near-fanatical efforts, driven by his commitment to enlist the aid of the very fishermen who had once opposed the whales, was the factor that finally guaranteed success.

"Human beings cannot be treated as if they are merely an irritant to the natural scheme of things," Lien explains. "They are an integral part of nature and as such are just as much a part of the solution as they are of the problem." By helping to organize fishermen and showing them how to become responsible participants in the deadly business of predator and prey, he not only saved the lives of a thousand whales but also helped to preserve the livelihoods—and the dignity—of thousands of Newfoundlanders.

There was still not a breath of wind as the sailboat proceeded south past Cape Bauld and along the east coast of Newfoundland, making her way toward the village of St. Anthony. I remained wedged into the bow pulpit. The rest of my crew eventually emerged from the cabins to join Liz in the cockpit. The whales were still very much in evidence, with a troupe of white-sided dolphin crossing the path of the sailboat ahead, a trio of Orcas hunting along the bold shoreline to the right, and group after group of humpbacks feeding among the cluster of rocky islets to the left.

The whales presented a dramatic sight, but they also represented a promise, for they spoke of what could happen when human beings agreed to stop the slaughter. Thirty years ago the last of the shore-based whaling stations in northern Newfoundland had ceased its operation. Twenty years ago Jon Lien's whale rescue program began teaching fishermen how to save both fishing gear and whales. And today, as my crew and I made our way along the coastal rise, this place was beginning to feel like some kind of cetacean Shangri-La—a virtual paradise of whales.

At least here, at least for now, the whales had come back. Might it be possible, I wondered, for the northern cod to do the same? If the Canadian Department of Fisheries and Oceans continued to enforce the fishing moratorium, if fishermen agreed to halt illegal landings, to limit by-catch, and in every other way to provide the species time to recover, could the cod eventually rebound?

The official position of the Canadian DFO was that it could. Indeed, some fisheries managers had suggested that specific populations of cod were already showing signs of recovery, leading, as we'd seen in Cow Head, to limited reopenings of the fishery. Others, however—especially those not associated with the DFO— continued to advise caution. And some, such as Memorial University marine biologist Richard Haedrich, were voicing concern that no matter what fishermen might do at this point, the die may already have been cast. Irreversible changes in the structure and organization of the larger fish community may have made it impossible for the northern cod ever to recover to its original condition.

Haedrich, with whom I had spoken during a visit to St. John's this past winter, had spent the last dozen years studying the interrelationships that characterize all marine populations—an area of scientific investigation that he termed "community ecology." Rather than limiting his investigations to individual species, he had been trying to look at entire societies of marine organisms, trying to understand them as complex communities in which all the living members coexist in interactive relationships, both with one another and with their physical environments.

"Fish don't exist in a vacuum," explained Haedrich. "No living organisms do. They cooperate with some members of their communities, compete with others. They prey upon certain neighbors and are in turn preyed upon by others.

"What we keep on forgetting—we human beings—is that when we enter one of these communities with our nets and traps and trawls and remove one of the key participants—especially when that participant is a voracious predator like the cod—we force the entire system into disequilibrium—throw it into a kind of chaos. Organisms like shrimp, caplin, snow crabs, that had once been the cod's prey, enter a phase of explosive population growth. Other predators—including human predators—start to take over the cod's role, and the system begins to reorganize itself, shifting toward a new state of equilibrium.

"The irony is that as fishermen begin to take advantage of their newfound bonanza, dramatically increasing their landings of shrimp and snow crab and caplin and the like, they may actually be helping to eliminate the cod's place in the food chain. Along with an entire cast of opportunistic new predators—skate, sharks, whales, other species of demersal fish—the human beings may actually be usurping the cod's role, helping to create a situation in which one of the most successful forage fishes ever evolved may no longer have a place to return to in the ocean ecosystem."

Twenty miles down the coast, as the sailboat approached Cape St. Anthony, three events occurred simultaneously. The last of the humpback whales slipped silently beneath the oily swell. A convoy of seven small shrimp draggers rounded the cape, booms down, and steamed past the sailboat, heading north toward the Hawkes Channel. And a lighthouse, painted in bold bands of red and white, suddenly emerged into view from beyond a rocky promontory, marking the entrance to St. Anthony harbor.

The sailboat passed the lighthouse, drew abreast of the beacon at Moores Point, and circled northwestward into a long, narrow inlet. A series of commercial piers, several of them in ruins, lined the waterfront. Clusters of small buildings dotted the hillsides. To the right, a dozen shrimp draggers lay rafted together along the face of an old fish processing plant. To the left, a large coastal steamer, the *Northern Ranger*, lay berthed at the end of a newly refurbished government wharf, with more shrimp draggers nested about its flanks.

I guided *Brendan* in a circle around the stern of the steamer, searching for an empty berth along the western side of the wharf. When I saw that none was available, I called to a man standing on the deck of one of the draggers, asking if the sailboat might be permitted to raft alongside.

The man beckoned to come ahead, then disappeared into the fo'castle. He emerged moments later with several of his mates, and together this group made quick work of taking *Brendan's* lines and making her fast to their own vessel.

Once the sailboat was safely moored, all but one of the fishermen retreated to the fo'castle. The one who remained stepped to the fishing boat's afterdeck, adjacent to *Brendan's* cockpit, and rested an elbow against the rail. He was young, probably in his late thirties, clean-shaven, with sandy blond hair, wire-rimmed glasses, an easy, gat-toothed smile. He introduced himself as Derrick Day, skipper of the dragger *Island Voyager* out of Portugal Cove, Newfoundland.

"We'll be lying here until Sunday sunrise," said Day in a soft, almost melodic voice. "Then if the weather holds, we'll be steaming down the Labrador to the new shrimping ground."

"Not a problem," I said. "When you're ready to sail, Skipper, just give the word. We'll be out of your way in five minutes."

I busied myself straightening up the sailboat's cockpit as my crew scampered across the fishing boat's deck and climbed onto the pier. They were obviously ready to get ashore, to stretch their legs and explore the town for a few hours. I understood their eagerness, for after some of the remote areas we'd been visiting, I imagined this little village must have seemed like a major metropolis.

"There's a party tomorrow night in the town center," said Day. "My brothers—the fellas just helped you with the mooring lines— they'll be going. There's going to be two bands, a tent, a couple of Molson kegs—it's called a 'Kin Barsok.' " He laughed. "In the old Viking language, that means a 'family beer bash.' "

Nat gave out a loud whoop, grabbed Liz by the waist, danced her in a circle on the pier. "Paar-teee," he hollered, thumping Amanda on the back and slapping Richard's palms.

"See what you've done?" I said to the dragger skipper in mock alarm. "Now if I stick around until tomorrow night, I might lose my crew forever."

A long blast on the horn of the coastal steamer, *Northern Ranger*, indicated that she was ready to cast off her mooring lines and leave the wharf. No sooner had she withdrawn into the harbor than one of the shrimp draggers moved to the empty berth and began to unroll a long jumble of rope and wire and plastic filament from the drum on its afterdeck. The apparatus was a shrimp trawl—or what was left of one after what seemed a rather serious mishap. Derrick Day and I both climbed to the deck of the pier and offered to help stretch the net onto the pavement and untangle the mess.

"The accident happened three days ago," said Day as we worked. "I listened to the whole affair on the radio. Fella come up over a ridge with his drag, when all of a sudden everything went slack. Right away he knew he'd lost the end."

The net was in tatters, almost unrecognizable. I had seen a shrimp trawl laid out on a pier before, and I knew what it was supposed to look like: the wide-meshed jaws, the long, tunnel-like throat, the patent trap (called the Nordmore Grid) for separating and releasing the unwanted by-catch, and finally, a hundred feet later, the close-meshed "cod end" where the shrimp were collected. The net before us had lost part of the mouth, nearly half the throat, all of the cod end. Unless the owner and his crew could somehow find a way to mend it using scavenged materials, they were going to find themselves in serious financial difficulty.

"Trouble is, everybody's right on the edge in this fishery," said Day. "Almost any problem, lost gear, bad weather, engine break-down, poor fishing, and there goes your summer."

I asked how the fishing had been so far for him and his brothers.

"To be honest, we're still trying to get the hang of this one. I got a quota of two hundred forty thousand pounds—that's six weeks at forty thousand a week—same as a lot of the boats here. But I'm new at this game, don't know the ground, don't know the gear. I been fishing two weeks, landed just twenty-three thousand pounds. That's seventeen thousand in the hole, with four weeks to go."

Clearing his throat, he gazed past me at the nest of draggers rafted together on the far side of the pier. "Part of the problem with this fishery, it's so far away. My brothers and me, we're from St. John's—fished there all our lives. There, we used to steam out to the fishing ground fifty, seventy-five, a hundred miles at the most. We'd fish for a few days, come back home. But here, just to get the boat to St. Anthony is better than three hundred miles, forty-five hours steaming time. Then to get down to the Labrador ground, another hundred and thirty miles, twenty hours steaming time. That's a lot of wear and tear on the machinery, a lot of fuel, a lot of dollars with nothing to show.

"And another thing, there's the food for five men, three meals a day, seven days a week. Back down in St. John's when the boat was in port off-loading fish, everybody used to live at home, eat out of their own gardens, their own freezers. But here it's all part of the boat's expense, every day, every meal, all purchased at a St. Anthony supermarket.

"Tell you the truth, I don't much care for all these weeks away from home, not seeing my wife, not seeing my family. Maybe the boys and me will come back with a few dollars in our pockets—if we can figure out how to start landing our quota, if the weather holds, if the engine keeps on running, if the price of shrimp don't suddenly collapse . . ."

"Sounds like a whole lot of if's," I said, gazing at the mangled net at our feet.

"You got that one right, Cap. Sure do sound like a whole lot of if's."

The following morning broke still and warm. "Perfect weather for a family beer bash," said Nat as he slipped into his customary seat at the dinette table. "The Day brothers have invited us to go with them to the party tonight. You are going to let us go . . . aren't you, skipper?"

I stared at my shipmate with my most ferocious Captain Bligh expression and began listing all the provisioning and maintenance chores that had to be completed today. I had an appointment in town, I told him, with the publisher of the local newspaper, *The Northern Pen*, and I probably wouldn't be back to the boat until mid-afternoon. "But not to worry, my young friend. If you and the others can finish all the jobs that need doing today, the rest of the evening will be yours."

An hour later, with my shipmates busy on the sailboat's foredeck, I climbed across the shrimp dragger, strode down the pier, and turned west onto the two-lane macadam road that led into town. I walked for about a mile along this road, past the post office, the Grenfell Hospital, the Irving gas station, the Vinland Motel, the Foodland supermarket. Finally I came to an unadorned, sandy-colored, single-story building, set back from the road and marked with a green sign identifying it as the editorial offices of *The Northern Pen*.

I entered this building through a large, formal doorway and stepped into a wood-paneled waiting room. Stacked against the wall on one side of the room were bundles of newspapers. In the center of the room was a receptionist's booth, empty. I waited a few moments, listening for the sound of voices from the rear of the building. When I heard none, I mounted a flight of steps and began knocking randomly on closed office doors.

"It's Saturday," came a loud, baritone voice from almost directly behind me.

"I'm sorry, I . . . ."

"The newspaper office isn't officially open on Saturday. We go to press on Friday, hit the streets early Monday morning. Saturday's our day of rest."

I turned to find myself standing only inches away from a tall, heavily built man with a square face, thick blond eyebrows, a prominent nose, curly red hair. He was dressed in a tweed jacket, tan chino trousers, an open-collar sport shirt. "Sorry . . . I didn't hear you come in. I'm looking for a Mister Bernard . . . ."

"Bernard Bromley, that's me," he said extending a large, freckled hand. "Everybody calls me Bern."

"I'm Mike Arms, a writer from . . . ."

" . . . I know," said Bromley. "I've seen your letter—got your phone message yesterday. Sorry for the mess out here. Let's go find a seat in my office where we can talk."

Unlike most of the people I had encountered on this journey, Bern Bromley was a public person: a journalist and community leader who was quite comfortable in a formal interview setting. In the beginning, our conversation felt like just such an interview. I asked a series of questions about the cod crash and its impacts on the people of his community. Bromley answered with a kind of statistical matter-of-factness. Six hundred jobs lost when the fish processing plant here closed down in the summer of 1992. Hundreds of local fishermen suddenly out of work. "Read any edition of the *Pen* during those years," he said. "The story's all there. It was an economic disaster that affected every man, woman, and child on the Northern Peninsula."

I asked him about the new fishery—the northern shrimp. Was it as good as some people were saying?

"Depends on who you're talking to," said Bromley. "The companies with the big offshore draggers—Clearwater, FPI—they're making a lot of money. The little guys with the fifty, sixty-footers, most of them are having a hard time of it. Government wants to give everybody a piece of the pie, so they divide it up in little slices. Two hundred fifty slices, something like that, given out to license-holders from all over eastern Newfoundland. Well now somebody ought to know, even with quadrupling the quotas, somebody ought to realize this single fishery can't be enough to fill the gap left by the collapse of the cod. That's just plain foolish."

"Are the quotas too high?"

"Well that's the big question, isn't it—the one thing nobody seems to know. It's an important question, too, especially since this community is right now in the middle of negotiations to build a new shrimp processing plant. Nothing certain yet—we're talking with companies from Nova Scotia, Newfoundland, even Iceland, trying to put together a ten million dollar package, a state of the art facility."

Bromley leaned forward in his chair. "I've gotten myself involved in this—as one of the directors of the community organization that's spearheading the project—because I know the people in St. Anthony needs this plant, needs the jobs that it represents. If everything works out, we're looking at a hundred and fifty, maybe two hundred new jobs. Our part, the community's part, will be to put up a quarter of the capital, two and a half million, and to guarantee the fish companies our offshore quota of shrimp to catch for fifteen years."

"Fifteen years?"

"Yes, fifteen years. That's the deal."

"But what if this sudden increase in the shrimp stocks is only temporary? What if the shrimp are multiplying mainly because there are no more cod to eat them—so that all that's happening now is that *we're* becoming the cod?"

"I've heard that kind of talk," said Bromley. "And I've heard the other kind, too, that whatever the cod used to eat, the shrimp was only a small part. But it's all intertwined, I know that much. And somewhere along here, somebody better figure out really fast what we're doing. Because, you know, if we catch the last of the shrimp . . . well my gut feeling is there isn't going to be much left."

The newspaperman turned to me with a grim, determined expression, and I realized that the tenor of this encounter had changed. "You understand," he said, "that what we're into here is survival. For my part, the only thing I'm trying to do is find a way to stop people from leaving, stop families from packing their belongings, boarding up their houses, heading for St. John's or Toronto or Alberta. The worst thing in a community like this is to look around and see another house boarding up—it's the worst kind of discouragement.

"Let me tell you a story," he said, dropping his voice to a near-whisper, "a true story about my own brother Paul—for he is one of the people I'm talking about, one of the people may be forced out by this thing.

"Paul is a fisherman—or used to be. He's in his late forties, married, with a son and two daughters. He has a wooden long liner, thirty-four feet, used to fish four or five cod traps out near the Grey Islands before the moratorium. Then, when the fishery was closed, he had no other choice but to take what the government give him, live on TAGS payments for a time, wait for the fishery to open again.

He passed up his chance to retrain, refused to move away. So that now, with the TAGS money about to end, he's facing a real tough time.

"Paul's boat is too small to qualify for a quota of shrimp or snow crab. But still he won't sell his license back to the government—for he sees that as a kind of suicide. So instead, he says, he's just going to hang on, grow his garden, catch whatever fish he can, shoot or trap whatever comes his way, put it in his freezer. He's going to go back to basics, he says, hoping against hope the fish will come back. For Paul, the fishery, the whole of northern Newfoundland is like a ship. If she goes down, he says—well then, he'll just go down with her."

Bromley closed his eyes and folded his hands in front of him as if in an attitude of prayer. "All I wants, all I'm trying to do now is look out for the people that's been hurt by this thing, people like my own brother Paul, trying to make sure they don't give up. I don't know if this new fishery will last for fifteen years. I don't know if it will last for five or even one. All I know is we've got an opportunity here, the promise of some jobs, some money coming in, some reason for people staying. Everybody knows that in the long run there needs to be new industry, new jobs outside the fishery. But right now, today, only one thing we have to do . . . we have to find a way to hold this community together. Somehow, we have to find a miracle."

Saturday night. The thump of an electric bass and the incessant pounding of a drum machine echoed through the sailboat's hull like summer thunder. A voice, distorted out of all understanding, throbbed across the harbor in demonic counterpoint to the wail of a slide guitar. The music was so loud that the rigging rattled and the deck vibrated underfoot.

Derrick Day and I sat a few feet across from one another on the edge of the pier sipping on a couple of beers, trying our best to talk. We didn't talk about torn nets or unfilled quotas or northerly gales, however—for even here, a mile away from the party, we could feel the spirit of the Kin Barsok. Instead, as the last of the summer twilight receded into the west, we talked about the good times at sea: the solitudes, the freedoms, the things that made us both want to go back.

By midnight we had said our good-byes and had retreated, each to his own vessel, in preparation for an early departure next morning. Before I retired to my cabin, I watched the men from several nearby boats making their way back down the pier. Most could still walk. A few were being carried or dragged by their shipmates. The worst cases showed up in an old rattletrap taxi that pulled out onto the tarmac and deposited its passengers unceremoniously onto the pavement. During one of the taxi's visits, there was a scuffle and a string of foul oaths as the cabbie tried to collect his fare. During another there was the thud of a poorly timed punch.

I climbed down the sailboat's companionway, turned off the cabin lights, and slipped into my bunk, waiting for my crew to return. The relentless pounding of the electric bass continued to vibrate through the hull. The sounds of screeching rubber and the voices of returning fishermen punctuated the night. I slept in fits and starts, waking each time the ship's clock sounded another hour. Finally, just as the light began to grow in the east, I heard the sound of boots thumping on the sailboat's deck—a burst of laughter—another sound of boots—a chorus of familiar voices.

They're back, I thought with a certain relief. Then I rolled over and squeezed my eyes closed, trying to catch one last hour of sleep before *Brendan* would need to put to sea again.

Chapter 9

Williamsport

DAWN BROKE SUNDAY under a wild northern sky. The fishing boat, *Island Voyager*, fired up her diesels just as the sun appeared above the rim of the hills to the east. As the engines rumbled to life, Derrick Day stepped to the door of his wheelhouse, announcing that he and his brothers were ready to leave the pier.

I started the sailboat's engine, ducked my head below, called for my crew. Moments later, I watched with a certain amusement as first Amanda, then Nat, then Liz step onto the deck and move gingerly past me, shielding their eyes and squinting with obvious pain into the clean morning light. On the fishing boat, two of Day's brothers emerged from the fo'castle wearing the same agonized expressions. Somehow, these five managed to disentangle *Brendan's* mooring lines and shove the boats clear of one another.

As the sailboat pulled out into the harbor, I began to wonder about Richard. Where was he? Had he come back to the boat—or had his shipmates left him ashore under a tree somewhere to sleep off the effects of the evening's festivities? I was about to pull the engine out of gear and initiate a boat-wide search when I glanced down to see a haggard face, gray as a corpse, emerging from the cabin. "Feeling . . . a little . . . sick," Richard muttered, staggering toward the rail. I averted my eyes and tried not to listen as he deposited his entire portion of the Kin Barsok into St. Anthony harbor.

The seas were choppy beyond the harbor mouth and the northeast breeze was cold. Richard finished his business at the rail and retreated into the cabin without another word. The others managed to hoist the mainsail and the working jibs before they, too, asked if they might return to their bunks. Amanda was the only one who remained on deck—and only for a few moments. "I'll give a holler if I need you," I lied, steering her toward her cabin.

I jammed my cap down around my ears as the sailboat pulled out of St. Anthony Bight, and I zipped up the collar of my foul weather jacket. The truth was that I was not at all disappointed to be left on my own up here today. I had known, ever since Derrick Day had started talking about the party, what sort of condition my shipmates were likely to be in this morning. But like Day, I didn't care. For I realized I had sixty miles to sail today—just as he realized he had a hundred and thirty miles to steam. For both of us, this translated into one of those experiences that we went to sea to find: a solitude, an interlude between here and there, a segment of time that didn't need to be justified or tallied or accounted for.

The passage south from St. Anthony began with a transit across the mouth of Hare Bay, a distance of about seven miles, followed by an easy run along a series of skerries and pinnacle rocks: Little Cormorandier, Massacre Rock, Great Cormorandier, Great Verdon, Fichot Island. A few miles beyond these, at Saint Julien Harbor, the coast became bold and steep-to, with deep water of fifty fathoms (three hundred feet) and more right up to the shore. With the wind moderating and backing into the north, the sailboat was able to run along this coast barely half a mile from the rock, and I was treated to a profusion of form and texture, shadow and light, crowned by a sky so clear and empty that it appeared almost black.

As I sat behind the helm watching the shore and guiding the boat across gray-green seas, I found myself thinking about some of the people I had met in the past few weeks, some of the lives that had intersected, however briefly, with my own. Every one of them— fisherman or no—had seen his life affected in profound and indelible ways by the cod collapse—this was something I had expected from the outset. But a surprising number—especially here on the Great Northern Peninsula—had also seen their lives affected by this new fishery, the northern shrimp. Jock Gardener and his sons David and Michael were out there right now in the Hawkes Channel, dragging for their share of the new quotas. Derrick Day and his brothers were steaming north, about to do the same. Donna Whalen, Calvin and Mabel's daughter, was back at work in a shrimp processing plant that had recently opened in a community near Flowers Cove. Bern Bromley was in the midst of negotiating a deal to bring a new shrimp plant to his community—and thus to save it, at least for a few more years, from economic ruin.

I felt myself in something of a dilemma this morning as I thought about these people—friends, many of them, good people, hard working people. I found myself hoping against hope that they had found a solution—that they weren't just making the same mistake that so many had made with the cod—that somehow, this time, the voices of reason and good judgment would prevail. Yet in light of what I'd seen and heard in the past few weeks, I couldn't help wondering: was it wise, the way this new fishery was being pursued? Did it make sense for so many to be entering all at once? Was the fishery sustainable? Would it be the salvation of northern Newfoundland, as some were claiming? Or was it just another chapter in the same tragic story—another instance, like the northern cod, of thinking for the short term, ignoring warning signs, disrupting ecosystems, driving yet another species to the brink of collapse?

One of the people that I thought might be able to answer such questions when I had talked with him last winter was DFO fisheries manager Don Parsons, for he was the man at the Northwest Atlantic Fisheries Centre in St. John's who was in charge of putting together stock assessment data and of issuing stock status reports for northern shrimp for the entire east coast of Newfoundland and Labrador. Surprisingly, however, even Parsons seemed to be at a loss for answers.

"The shrimp fishery in the Hawkes Channel area is essentially new," he explained, "with very little historical data for establishing baselines and making comparisons. DFO scientists have only done one full scale stock assessment—during a pair of multi-species research surveys in 1995-96. There isn't another full survey planned until early next century. In the mean time, all we have to go on are reports from the fishermen themselves, estimates of fishing effort, actual tonnages being landed, that sort of thing."

When I asked him about the sustainability of this fishery over the long term, Parsons remained similarly tentative. "Right now, there's a lot of shrimp. We think the current quota of eighty-four million pounds is well within the limit for sustainable yield—probably less than ten percent of the total biomass. The question is, how long will the high abundance last? There are indications, for instance, that the survival rate for shrimp larvae on the Labrador shelf was particularly high during the cold conditions of the late 1980s and early 1990s—but that it may have dropped off during the middle years of this decade. In this case, with a species that takes about six years to mature, we may be looking at a significant reduction in shrimp populations some time in the not-too-distant future.

"If you want to know my own personal feelings," said Parsons with a look of concern on his lean, bearded face, "I'm worried about the amount of capital outlay that has been taking place in this fishery—both by the fishermen and by the communities. There are a lot of people out there spending a lot of money gearing up for this thing—money that many of them can't afford. I guess I find myself hoping, along with everybody else, that their optimism turns out to be well-founded."

"But aren't you—or your department—a big part of the reason for that optimism?"

"Read our stock assessment report for last year. It's all there, everything I've just told you—the short history of the fishery, the sparsity of the survey data, the uncertainty of our measurements, the difficulty of predicting what's going to happen next. Believe it or not, fisheries managers have learned something important since the collapse of the cod. We've learned to talk about our uncertainties— to include them in our forecasts, not just sweep them under the table and pretend they're not there."

"But you've doubled the quotas on northern shrimp—twice in the last two years. Doesn't that fact alone serve as an invitation for everybody who can to jump on board?"

The fisheries manager closed his eyes and drew a long, slow breath. "We set the quotas where we think they belong. That's our job—we just try to do it the best we can."

"And if you find out later that the stocks are not as large as you thought . . .?"

"If we find out the stocks are smaller, we reduce the quotas."

"What if that means that hundreds of fishermen and small communities get squeezed out of the picture again . . .?"

"I don't like to think about that. It's a situation nobody needs to. . . a situation nobody wants to contemplate right now."

"So you just ignore it?"

"You do your job."

"And hope that you're right?"

"Yes. And hope to merciful God that you're right."

As the sailboat traveled south past Croc Harbor, Cape Rouge, Conche, Boutitou Rock, Englee, Canada Head, the coast became progressively higher and steeper. Palisades rose seven hundred, a thousand, twelve hundred feet straight out of the sea, interrupted every few miles by narrow, steep-sided fiords that sliced like knife-wounds into the interior.

By late afternoon—just as my crew began to show some signs of life below—we drew abeam of one such fiord whose name, according to the chart, was Fourche Harbor. A pair of bold capes guarded the mouth. A small group of humpback whales rolled and blew in the approaches. A pair of eagles rode a column of rising air above the southern cape, while in the darkness beyond, a series of waterfalls perforated the fiord walls, glistening like silver thread against the rock.

Amanda appeared on deck just as the sailboat moved under the shadow of the land, followed a few moments later by Nat and Richard and Liz. After a brief series of greetings, all four set to work helping to jibe the mainsail and stow the jibs. They worked without talking. Their eyes, however, betrayed the surprise that all must have felt as they tried to comprehend the cavernous vista that opened in the rock before them.

As the sailboat moved into the fiord, the wind fell strangely silent. Odd currents swirled in unpredictable eddies under the keel. A swell entering from the sea hissed against the base of the rock, while overhead, clouds of seabirds rose from their nests to cry out their displeasure at the trespassers below.

Two miles inland, the sheer granite walls continued to soar to almost a thousand feet. As the distance between them narrowed, the shadows at their base grew darker and the surface of the water became inky black.

For an instant, this place began to feel like an alien world, so empty and inhospitable that it was hard to imagine another human being having ever set foot here. A few moments later, however, this illusion was shattered as a narrow cove opened on the right, revealing the broken fishing stages and the crumbling buildings of a deserted outport.

I turned the sailboat into the cove, looking for a place to anchor, while the others dropped and stowed the mainsail. The closer we approached this village, however, the more desolate it appeared. Most of the buildings had been stripped of their doors and windows. Several of the roofs had collapsed. The church—or what was left of it—had no belfry. The churchyard was a jumble of broken fences and toppled grave markers. The waterfront was lined with disman- tled piers and fishing stores, and in a meadow beyond, a row of wooden dories lay like rotting corpses, their bones exposed to the empty sky.

I felt the hair begin to tingle at the base of my neck as I wheeled the sailboat around and pointed her bows back out into the fiord, looking for a happier setting somewhere ahead to anchor for the evening. No sooner had we left this cove, however, than we were confronted with a scene of even greater devastation. For around the next bend, scattered along the banks of a small river delta, were the remains of what could almost have been a bombed-out city: a jumble of ruined tanks, ruptured towers, toppled corrugated roofs, and broken machinery that seemed so out of place that for a moment I was unable to imagine what it was.

"Looks like some kind of abandoned industrial site," said Nat as the sailboat moved past.

Suddenly a synapse closed in my brain, and I realized exactly what it was and what sad and ill-fated place my crew and I had stumbled upon.

"Williamsport," I muttered.

"Say again?"

"Williamsport. . . it has to be. The chart calls this place Fourche Harbor, but that's just the old French name. Williamsport is what modern Newfoundlanders call it. I've read about what happened here—I've listened to people's stories."

"Then what is this ruin we're looking at?" asked Nat.

I paused, staring at the mass of broken, twisted metal, decom- posing with a slow, cold fire, returning, imperceptibly, to a state of equilibrium with the huge, impersonal landscapes that surrounded it.

"It's the ruin of Newfoundland . . . or one of them. It's the ruin of the human enterprise."

Once the sailboat was anchored for the evening, about a mile to the west of the ruined commercial site, Amanda and the others launched the rubber boat in preparation for a late afternoon foray ashore. Nat and I were eager to return to the ruin—a place that I explained had once been a whaling station, then a factory for manufacturing liquefied fish. The others, less curious perhaps, or simply more in need of physical exercise after their recent misadventures, opted for an hour's hike along the stream bed at the western end of the fiord.

Nat and I deposited our shipmates at the mouth of the stream, then turned back down the fiord. I steered the rubber boat toward the center of the ruin and drove ashore on a steep, sandy beach. Nat scurried up the incline and tied the boat's painter to a piece of half-buried metal, and I followed, checking his handiwork to assure myself that the boat was secure. No sooner had I given him the thumbs-up than he mounted an iron catwalk, moved around a row of rusted tanks, and climbed to the top of a huge iron boiler. He gestured for me to follow, but I declined, preferring to investigate this place at a more conservative pace.

I turned and moved slowly along the beach, picking my way among the wreckage, listening to the crunch of boot against sand. From this close range, I had no doubt that this mass of rubble was indeed the old whaling station that I had read about—nor did I doubt that the toppled buildings a mile across the fiord were the remains of the old outport of Williamsport. At the end of the beach I climbed to the top of a rusted platform and gazed across the fiord, pondering the sad story of this place and of the people who strived—and ultimately failed—here.

It is likely that no one still living remembers exactly when the village was first settled—historical records were seldom kept for this part of the French Shore, and, except for summer drying stations, permanent settlements of any type were considered illegal until the French withdrew their claim to this coast in the treaty of 1904. Suffice it to say that by the early part of the twentieth century there was a village here, and that soon after the treaty had taken effect, it became known by its English name of Williamsport.

For the next few decades, the village was merely the home of a few simple fishermen and their families. In the early 1930s, however, a Norwegian entrepreneur, Captain Olaf Olsen, arrived to establish the first of a series of commercial ventures on the large, flat river delta on the far side of the fiord. Olsen's venture was a whaling station, operated for almost twenty years under the auspices of one of his subsidiary organizations, the Olsen Whaling and Sealing Company. Early in this venture, Olsen took on a partner, Chesley (Ches) Crosbie, the heir of one of Newfoundland's wealthiest merchant dynasties (and the father of present-day politician and former fisheries minister John Crosbie). Together, these two operated a slaughtering and manufacturing facility that, for a time, produced a quality-grade whale oil that was transported to markets worldwide and that generated a handsome profit.

After Olsen's death in 1945, Ches Crosbie became sole owner of the Olsen Whaling and Sealing Company. Despite the advancing age of the facilities at Williamsport, he continued to operate the whaling factory here. During the next several summers, in fact, he decided to use this place as a training ground for the young men of his family— his eldest son, John, his future son-in-law, Gene Shinkle, and his youngest son, Andrew—to give them a slice of real world experience as they learned about the Crosbie business empire.

John, the future politician, was sent to sea for a pair of summers to work as a catcher on board one of the whaling ships. "Shink," as the son-in-law was called, was put to work in Williamsport on the slip—the place where the whales were drawn up onto the shore to be butchered. Fifteen-year old Andrew, meanwhile, was assigned to labor in one of the try works—a job that almost cost him his life when a furnace where he was working blew up, boiling his skin and hair and burning the flesh on one of his arms down to the bone. A ship was recalled from the whaling ground to take the boy to a hospital in Montreal, where he spent the rest of the summer in the burn unit in intensive care.

By the late 1940s, Ches Crosbie realized that if his factory in Williamsport was going to remain profitable, it was going to require major modernization, a process that was made possible by means of a loan guarantee from Joey Smallwood's new provincial government in 1952. It seems, however, that just as the renovations were being completed, a new product was introduced to the world marketplace: vegetable oil. Practically overnight, whale and fish oils became obsolete and the bottom dropped out of Ches Crosbie's whaling business.

Something needed to be done at Williamsport—fast—to

somehow make use of the newly renovated facility. The idea that Crosbie came up with was a new product that he had already experimented with in one of his factories in St. John's—liquefied caplin—for use as a fertilizer and animal feed additive. The new process had proved to be profitable in St. John's—but from the beginning, the conversion of the facility at Williamsport was filled with problems.

First came the logistical dilemma of providing a steady supply of caplin to the north coast facility when most of Newfoundland's caplin fishery was located elsewhere. Ches and his brother Bill eventually solved this problem by contracting for several ships to steam north to Williamsport loaded to the gunnels with caplin, only to discover when they got there that the plant was not ready for them. It seemed that before the fish could be "digested," they needed to be processed in a huge cooker that had not yet arrived from the manufacturer. The Crosbies, knowing that the fish would soon begin decomposing in the ships, decided to try placing uncooked caplin directly into the steam boilers, where it should have been forced by 140 inch-pounds of steam pressure down into the digesters. The uncooked and decomposing fish began producing ammonia gas, however, and eventually the reverse pressure from this gas forced the fish back out of the digesters and into the boilers again, where thousands of pounds of product were ruined. Shortly afterwards, untold of tons of rotting fish started doing the same thing in the ships out in the harbor, creating a foul ammonia gas that drove the crews out of their cabins, turned knives and forks black, and began peeling paint off the bulkheads. Finally, the Crosbies were forced to dispatch the ships to another of their fishmeal plants in western Newfoundland before the ships were literally consumed by their own cargoes.

Soon after this episode, the doors on the plant at Williamsport were closed, and although the Crosbie family operated the plant on a limited basis for several more years, their business activities here were effectively ended. Indeed, the facility itself would probably have been abandoned for good at this juncture if it had not been for a period of renewed whaling activity in Newfoundland led by the Japanese during the late 1960s.

In the summer of 1966 a large Japanese fishing conglomerate, Taiyo Suisat, along with its Nova Scotia-based partner, Fishery Products Company, acquired the facility at Williamsport from the

Crosbie family for a try at yet another whaling venture. This time the product was not to be whale oil, however, but whale meat—to be used as a protein source for human consumption. To this end, a shipment of new equipment was installed at the Williamsport factory and a converted Great Lakes steamship was towed to the site and moored out in the fiord for use as a giant meat freezer. The plan itself appeared workable, yet the actual whaling operation, which began in the summer of 1967, was plagued almost from the beginning with frustration and disappointment.

The first setback for the Japanese whalers came at the hands of the Canadian Department of Fisheries and Oceans, which refused to grant them an export permit. According to the DFO, the product that was to be shipped back to Japan was not fish but meat, and as such it would require inspection by the much more strictly regulated Department of Agriculture.

A series of high level negotiations ensued between whaling company representatives and Canadian government officials, culminating in an on-site meeting at the Williamsport factory. This meeting, however, ended in tragedy, as one of the chartered airplanes was lost on the return flight from Williamsport, killing the pilot and all five passengers. (The Department of Agriculture, meanwhile, continued to enforce stringent inspection and permitting standards for the export of whale meat, causing "tremendous problems" for the Japanese whalers.)

As if these troubles weren't enough, tragedy struck once again at the Williamsport factory in the early 1970s when fire broke out on the freezer ship that was anchored out in the fiord, threatening to destroy the store of frozen whale meat that was already on board and to jeopardize the entire season's whaling activity. In an attempt to salvage what was left of their summer, Japanese company officials commandeered freezer space in small fish plants in several nearby communities—a tactic that angered fish plant managers and rekindled prejudices that were already smoldering.

The ultimate frustration came for the whalers of Taiyo Suisat in the summer of 1972, when the government of Canada ratified the International Whaling Commission's worldwide ban on commercial whaling, effectively closing the door on all further activity at Williamsport. This time there was no alternative. Managers collected company records and personal belongings. Workers packed up machinery that could be salvaged and loaded it aboard a company ship for transport back to Japan. The commercial site, like the village across the way, was abandoned to the long, purple shadows of the fiord and the inevitable ravages of time.

The sound of footsteps in the sand startled me out of my reverie. I turned around to watch Nat as he made his way across a dry creek bed, then climbed onto the platform where I stood. He was carrying several items: a small metal saw blade, a handful of broken potsherds, a coffee mug, an old wooden barrel stave. He approached without a word, and for a time we stood shoulder to shoulder, staring out across the fiord.

"It's eerie," Nat said, kicking at a piece of broken glass at his feet. "Eerie being out here alone. There used to be so many people—it's obvious as you walk around this place.

"Here, for instance. Here's somebody's morning coffee." He handed me the old tin mug. "And here's some hungry fellow's broken dinner plate. Here's the saw that the carpenter used to build the dormitory roof. . . and here, a piece of an old barrel with the whaling company's name on it."

He thrust the barrel stave toward me. I took it and held it up to the light, trying to decipher the faded letters that were branded into the grain. "Olsen. . . Whal. . .ing. . . and. . . Seal . . . ," I read aloud. "Why look, Nat, you've found a piece of history. It's a relic from the original whaling factory—from back in the 1930s or 1940s—when they were boiling down the blubber of giant blue whales out here."

"It makes me think of a poem I once read in school," said Nat, "about an inscription carved into a piece of stone in the desert. 'I am Ozymandias, king of kings,' the inscription reads. 'Look upon my works, ye Mighty, and despair.' Only there's nothing left for anybody to look upon, only wreck and decay and empty desert as far as the eye can see."

"Shelley," I said.

"Huh?"

"The poem. It's by Percy Bysshe Shelley."

"I don't think I've ever really understood that poem before," said Nat. "But I think I do now. I think it's about places like this—about the arrogance of the people who build them."

Silence. I handed back the barrel stave. I was about to turn and start back down the beach when my shipmate stopped me with his hand. "What about the people in the village?" he asked. "I understand why the whalers had to leave—with so many economic setbacks, then with Canada's ratification of the whaling ban. But why did the people in the village leave? Were they also involved in the whaling operation? Were they employees at the factory?"

I explained that this was one part of the story for which I'd never found a satisfactory answer. "Common sense would seem to suggest that while the factory was operating, some members of the local community must have worked here. Indeed, during the heyday of the operation, the entire village may have been dependent in indirect ways on the commercial operation. Then, in the late 1950s, the Crosbies closed their doors. And by the time the Japanese arrived seven years later, Williamsport was empty—the houses were boarded up—the people were gone."

Nat looked across the fiord again at the ruined village. He seemed about to ask another question—then turned away, as if he'd had enough of talking. I, too, fell silent, humbled by the impermanence of this place, saddened by its emptiness, embarrassed by the ease with which it was decomposing and returning into dust.

For Nat, the ruins of Williamsport spoke of toppled kings and crumbling empires. For me, at that moment, they spoke of our collective inability to come to an appropriate balance with the natural systems that we depend upon for our survival. The whaling ban, like the cod moratorium, was a response to a long and relentless pattern of overexploitation of particular species—a pattern whose results were not simply the commercial extinction of those species, but also the collapse of the entire social and economic order of the people who had depended upon them.

Could the devastation here be a kind of warning signal, I wondered, for what might be about to happen in modern Newfoundland in the wake of the cod collapse? Might this same scene be repeated in a few more years in Cow Head or Port au Choix or Flowers Cove or St. Anthony? The events leading up to the two crises were dissimilar in several important respects—and the willingness of the Canadian government to subsidize the former cod fishermen was also different—yet this place bore mute witness to the unpredictability of ecosystems and the tenuousness of the human enterprise.

I glanced across at the village, then down at the sailboat,

anchored a mile to the west. I was about to begin the long trek back down the beach when a noise stopped me: a rush of air, shrill and insistent, somewhere close at hand. I stopped where I stood and looked around to see the black forehead and blowhole of a humpback whale, crowned by a cloud of watery mist, barely a hundred yards away. The rush of air was followed by another, as a second whale surfaced a few yards beyond the first—then by the guttural rumble of inhale echoing against the rock.

A pair of twin-lobed tails rose in unison, and as they stood suspended over the black surface of the water, I thought about the irony of this moment. For now, barely thirty years after this fiord had been abandoned by its human inhabitants, the whales had returned. Once again they blew and sounded and fed in its inky depths, just as they had done for countless thousands of years. Once again they were the stewards of this place—and it was only the human beings who had disappeared.

Chapter 10

La Scie

THE SUN HAD NOT YET BROKEN the rim of the horizon next morning as a series of catabatic winds plummeted down the walls of the fiord. The surface of the water turned white as the sailboat was hit by the battering gusts, first from the right, then from the left. The falling winds—called "blow me downs" by Newfoundlanders—howled in the rigging and stripped the decks of everything that was not tied down. The boat staggered as if she had collided with a solid object.

Moments later, like a tornado passing, the winds subsided. In the calm that followed, a seabird from somewhere far above the masthead expelled a long, solitary cry.

Between repeated onslaughts from the blow-me-downs, my crew and I were forced to spend the entire morning retrieving *Brendan's* anchors and making her ready for sea. From inside the fiord, I had no way of knowing what the day might be like out beyond the entrance. The radios were dead, their antennas rendered useless by the walls of rock that surrounded us. There was no horizon to search for approaching weather, and the tiny patch of sky overhead revealed almost nothing.

It was close to noon by the time *Brendan* passed under the shadow of Granite Point at the mouth of the fiord and pointed her bows seaward. As I'd feared, the wind had backed during the night and was now blowing strong from the southwest. With a mountainous coast and a fetch of more than fifty miles in that direction, the seas were steep and irregular. The sky to the south was filled with half a dozen dark areas of rain, and the wind accelerated along the shore in squally gusts.

Originally, I had hoped to sail down into White Bay, to visit some of the outports there and to explore the dramatic coastline at Orange Bay, Little Harbor Deep, Great Cat Arm, Sop's Arm, Riverhead Bay. But today had become one of those times when a sailor must practice the lessons of patience and forbearance that the sea teaches and accept what is offered. Under the present conditions, and with the anchorage at Williamsport now rendered untenable, there was only one reasonable alternative: to put the wind on the beam and sail eastward toward the north-facing harbors of the Bay Verte Peninsula.

The day grew darker. Silhouettes of icebergs perforated the horizon. With each passing rain squall, the wind backed a few more degrees into the south, forcing the sailboat farther and farther east, until there was only one remaining harbor for her to fetch upon before being forced into a maelstrom of wind and current at Cape St. John. La Scie ("The Saw") was the last safe haven on the old French Shore—a circular, almost landlocked harbor lying under the loom of jagged hills just five miles inside the cape—and it was here that *Brendan* finally closed with the coast again and pulled up under the shelter of the land.

Like many ports around this island, La Scie was a harbor I had visited before. The first time I'd called here was nearly a decade ago during a circumnavigation of Newfoundland in 1989. My crew and I had been befriended that summer, in fact, by one of the community's leading citizens, a construction engineer and avid cruising mariner named Gid Sacrey.

Gid was close to seventy years old the summer I'd first met him (which meant he must have been almost eighty by now). At the time he was still hard at work in his construction business, although he'd been "trying to cut back," as he'd said, in order to spend more time cruising aboard his Grand Banks trawler yacht with his wife Maysie. He was living at the time in a small, white frame bungalow on a hillside overlooking La Scie harbor. In front of this house was a flagpole, and atop the flagpole was a large British Union Jack, announcing to all the world his near-fanatical allegiance to the colonial motherland and his emphatic disapproval of all things Canadian.

"That pack of thieves in Ottawa," he'd muttered the day I'd first met him. "They've been making deals, selling our birthright to foreigners, sucking the lifeblood out of this island ever since that bastard Joey Smallwood talked us into Confederation with Canada some forty years ago."

Gid's trawler yacht and private pier were located on the west side of the harbor, just past the fish plant. As soon as he'd spotted *Brendan's Isle* steaming through the narrows that summer, he had hollered for her to come alongside and moor on the outboard face. He'd flashed a huge grin when he discovered that I and my crew of American sailors had just come down from the Labrador coast, for he and Maysie had recently returned from a summer cruise to the same area, and he was eager to swap stories and learn about our travels.

Gid was tall and slender, well tanned from his summer's adventures, with sharp, chiseled features, thinning hair, a prominent nose, creased where the bridge of his glasses sat against his skin. His smile was an almost permanent part of his expression, and his laugh—which seemed to punctuate every sentence—was infectious. He insisted that I make use of the amenities on his pier—fresh water, electric power—then suggested that I come to his house that evening to meet Maysie and join them for a whiskey and a meal.

I found Gid's house several hours later without difficulty, for all I needed to do was look for the flagpole and the huge blue, red, and white Union Jack that graced his front yard. The house itself was plain and unpretentious—almost indistinguishable from the others in his village. Everywhere inside, however, were the indicators of a long and successful career in business. The rugs were deep-piled, the chairs and sofas were covered with satins and velours, the dining room table was rubbed mahogany. On a shelf in the living room was Maysie's collection of crystal bowls and goblets. On the end-tables were photographs of Gid and Maysie and their two adopted sons, set in silver frames.

The evening was every bit as pleasant as Gid had promised. The whiskey was a twelve year-old single malt from the western isles of Scotland. The dinner was a fresh sirloin steak, smothered in mushroom gravy. The talk was spirited, full of stories about the beautiful places each of us had sailed and the pleasant people we had met. There was no premonition that evening of the crisis looming, no mention of the pall that was already beginning to overspread this little community. For one more night, at least, we acted as if this town were still healthy and prosperous, as if the future were bright, as if this place were exactly the way it had always been.

The south wind shivered in the rigging and the sky was spitting rain as *Brendan* drew up under the shadow of the land and steamed into the narrows at the mouth of La Scie harbor. From a distance, the village looked little different than it had a decade earlier. On the right was the fish plant, fronted by a stone breakwater and mooring basin, with several small draggers rafted together inside. On the left was another public pier, a paved work area, and a community launch ramp. Around the rest of the waterfront were several dozen fishing stages, a few with dories moored alongside. Beyond these, the buildings of the town were arranged in concentric circles, one above the next, cradled within a perfect bowl of rock.

Once past the fish plant, I searched along the shore to the west for Gid Sacrey's pier, hoping there would be an empty berth. The pier itself was still there, freshly painted, marked on its outboard face with a pair of "Private" signs, guarded at the far end with a wooden gate. There was no trawler yacht anywhere in sight, however, but only a small, open fishing skiff moored along the inboard face.

As the sailboat drew closer to the pier, I spotted a man in a checkered shirt and paint-spattered coveralls with his head buried shoulder-deep in the engine compartment of the fishing skiff. He didn't seem to notice our approach until the sailboat was actually made fast to the pier. Once she was secure, I stepped below to shed my foul weather gear. When I re-emerged, the fellow was seated on the wooden planks of the pier, only a few feet from *Brendan's* cockpit.

"Friend of Gid's?" he asked.

"Yes, from a long time ago," I said.

"Shame about what happened, ain't it."

I stared at the man, uncertain how to respond. "Did he . . . I mean is he . . ."

"Oh he ain't dead, if that's what you're thinking. Just sick. Been down in St. John's in the hospital these past five months. Just come home three days ago."

The fellow, who introduced himself as Max Ryan, was also a friend of Gid's ("As who isn't in this community?" Max said. "Give you the shirt off his back, would old Gid. Give you his last nickel.") Ever since the old man's health problems, Max explained, the trawler yacht had been de-commissioned, laid up in the local shipyard, and Max had been given a berth for his fishing boat at Gid's pier. "I'm kind of watching the place until Gid gets better. Keeping the riff-raff away, I s'pose you'd say." He laughed.

Max, I soon learned, was a retired commercial fisherman, a father of four, whose grandparents had emigrated from southern Ireland in the middle of the last century to work in the copper mines at the nearby community of Tilt Cove. "I've been here for the whole show," said Max, tipping his paint-spattered baseball cap onto his forehead and scratching his black, curly beard. "I was here when the caplin used to arrive on this coast in the billions and the cod was so thick you couldn't pull your traps for the sheer weight of the fish inside. And I was here when the seals and whales and birds was starving because there wasn't a fish for any one of them to eat—let alone for a man to catch for his supper. I've seen h'it all, from the feast to the famine, and let me tell you, h'it ain't been a very pretty sight."

Max offered to walk up to his house and telephone Gid—to let him know about the sailboat at his pier and to request permission for her to remain for the night. I asked if I might follow, for I wanted to speak personally with the old man. I also wanted to spend more time getting to know this talkative, paint-spattered fellow next to me, for I had a suspicion that he might have a few useful observations to make about the fisheries and about life in his community here.

"Come ahead," said Max. "You can phone Gid while I brew us a cup of tea." He jumped to his feet, pulled his baseball cap down across his brow, wiped his grease-stained hands on the bib of his coveralls. I noticed that his shirt was mis-buttoned, forcing one section of his collar to curl up under his chin. At the crotch of his coveralls, an errant shirttail was caught in the zipper of his fly.

Max talked loudly—gesticulating with his arms and adding an aspirant "h" to each of his opening vowels. Even when his topic was the fishery, his enthusiasm seemed boundless. "You want to know why there's no more fish?" he asked rhetorically as we scurried along a paved roadway, heading toward the village. "One of the reasons is so obvious, h'it's a surprise anyone even asks. For in the last years of the fishery, late 'eighties, early 'nineties, nearly every dragger on this coast started fishing the spawning grounds. Department of Fisheries was going to cut the quotas as soon as landed tonnages began to drop—all the fellas knew. So to keep filling their nets, they went to the last places where the cod was still plentiful—the places the fish was trying to reproduce."

I followed Max into a gravel lane and up a steep incline. "Didn't the fisheries managers realize what was going on?"

"Oh the managers realized, all right. But they didn't care. According to their policy, there was no scientific evidence to prove that fishing on the spawning grounds had any effect on reproduction." The fisherman shook his head. "Imagine. Thousands of tons of spawning fish caught right in the act, and the government says there's no evidence of any harm. Well the evidence was right before their eyes, I say. The evidence was as obvious as the nose on their face."

Next moment my guide suddenly stopped in front of a double-story clapboard house, climbed a set of wooden steps, and pushed open a large green door. "Here's home," he said, stepping into a darkened hallway. "Come in. Take off your shoes. Gid's number is in the book, telephone's over there on the wall."

He filled a teapot with tap water and set it on the kitchen stove while I dialed the telephone. Almost immediately I heard Maysie's voice. "Yes, yes, ten years ago, I remember," she said. "Gid's been sick—just home from the hospital. He's sleeping now, but I'll tell him when he wakes up. He'll like to know you're staying at his pier."

By the time I finished my call, Max had brewed a mug of tea for each of us and was waiting for me at the kitchen table. I took a seat across from him and cupped my hands around the steaming mug. We talked for a time about the ordinary circumstances of our lives. Max told me about his wife Vera, his four grown children, his sixty years of living and working on the Bay Verte Peninsula, his ancestral ties to Ireland and England. I told of my own wife and children, my somewhat peripatetic life as a sailor and writer, my own family's more recent roots in southern Massachusetts.

Finally, inevitably, the conversation turned to the fishery again. I admitted that I'd heard about this business of fishing the spawning grounds, for Jock Gardener had once described it to me in rather vivid detail, explaining how the cod would gather in dense aggregations during their spawning rituals—almost as if they were inviting the fishermen to spread their nets and take as many as possible.

"Used to be difficult for a fisherman to locate the spawning grounds back in the days before Loran and GPS and electronic fish finders," said Max. "But as soon as the new electronics come along, the fish was like sitting ducks. Everybody could find them."

"Maybe some of the skippers didn't realize the fish were spawning."

"Not hardly, Cap. If you ever seen an otter trawl come up on deck after dragging through cod spawn, you'd never mistake it for anything else again. Fish and nets come up covered in milky white goo. Decks get so slippery, a man can barely walk across them. Pretty soon everything is covered with spawn—booms, winches, bulwarks. Oh, there's no mistaking when you're dragging on the spawning grounds."

"Then why?" I asked.

"Why?"

"Why would an honest, intelligent man—a man whose life depended every year upon these fish—go out and drag through the last of the breeding stocks?"

"I told you, government was going to cut the quotas as soon as the tonnages started to drop."

"But you—they—were taking the last of the fish . . . ."

Max stared at me, and I realized that I must have sounded smug and judgmental, perched upon some kind of moral high horse. He didn't become defensive, however. He just grew silent for a time, gazing at me from beneath his paint-spattered baseball cap.

"Where is it you said your family come from?" he asked at last.

"Massachusetts."

"Ah yes. . . Massachusetts. Now let me see. Seems I remember a place on the coast down there, a large, sandy point of land, juts out fifty miles or so from the mainland, surrounded by fishing banks."

"Cape Cod?"

"Yes, that's it, Cape Cod. Well now, from the name of that place, sounds like you might've had a few codfish down there too, once upon a time."

"Yes," I admitted. "We did. Once upon a time."

"Well I don't know much about how your people used to catch their fish down in Cape Cod. I guess you was just too 'honest and intelligent,' was you, to drag for your fish on the spawning grounds? Yes, you was just too careful . . . saving the cod for your sons and grandsons. . . .

. . . That is, until you finally fished them all out."

The sky to the south had turned black and the rain was falling in a solid wall as I said goodbye to Max an hour later. During our mug of tea, we'd managed to talk through half a dozen issues central to the fishery collapse. Yet somehow, as I made my way back down through the village, I kept returning in my mind to his comment about "my people" and the part they had played in the destruction of the fishery in the waters surrounding Cape Cod—for that remark had touched a sensitive nerve.

Not that any members of my immediate family had been commercial fishermen—for they had not. But the collapse of the ground fisheries along the northeastern coast of the United States is only one recent example of the pattern of commercial exploitation that has characterized America's centuries-old relationship with the natural world—and I knew that "my people" had been participants in that exploitation for many generations.

On my father's side, the most successful of my progenitors had always been miners. From the bog iron pits of eastern Massachusetts to the coal fields of Pennsylvania to the silver mines of Colorado, they had tunneled under mountains and stripped the living cover from the Earth in order to claim its riches for their own. And just in case this paternal legacy weren't enough, I was also descended on my mother's side from a nineteenth century "harvester of trees" named Langdon Hubbard, an indomitable woodsman and ruthless entrepreneur who had contrived almost single-handedly to cut or burn down more than forty thousand acres of virgin Michigan forest.

The point for me in all of this is that, fishermen or not, "my people" have been charter members of the fraternity that has pillaged America's natural systems. Like the fishermen of Cape Cod, like the hundreds of thousands of others who have made their fortunes from nature's riches, my people, too, have justified their actions by telling themselves that the commodities they sought were endless, that no matter how many trees might be cut down or how many tons of ore might be removed from the earth or how many fish might be caught, the supply would never run out. And indeed, for a time, they appeared to be correct—as if nature really were an inexhaustible cornucopia of material wealth and humanity were its rightful heir.

I remember the first time I learned that this formula was flawed. I was fifteen years-old, traveling with my father back in the mid-1950s, during one of his frequent business trips to the open pit mines of the Mesabi Range in northern Minnesota. As we stood on the rim of the great Hull-Rust-Mahoning Pit, the largest hole that human beings had ever carved into the Earth, my father turned and stared at me with a pained expression. "When your great grandfather first came up here in the 1890s, people thought the reserves of iron ore on this range were inexhaustible—enough to last the North American steel industry for hundreds of years. In his generation it was easy to believe that kind of talk—especially after they'd seen the estimates of reserves, after they'd witnessed the scale of these mines.

"But now we know. As long as the ore was being taken at a rate of a few million tons a year, there was no problem. But over the next few decades that number grew—first to fifty million tons, then to eighty million, then to a hundred million—until the reserves of high grade ore were all but mined out. A decade from now, low grade taconite ore will be all that's left. And by the end of this century, we'll be lucky if there's much of that."

Ours is the generation, it seems, that has finally been forced up against the limits. Our burgeoning human population, recently risen past six billion, coupled with centuries of industrialization and rising standards of living, have combined to stress the Earth's natural systems on a planetary scale. Once-massive reserves of essential commodities have been decimated. Thousands of species have become extinct. Entire regions have been stripped of their natural cover. Ground water has been contaminated. Water tables have dropped. Topsoils have eroded into the rivers. Large areas of the oceans have been fished to exhaustion. For other generations in other settings, such occurrences have taken place on local scales. For ours, they have finally started to take place on global scales.

Maybe the miners and foresters and fishermen of earlier generations just didn't know any better. Maybe they really were "honest and intelligent" people who were simply never required to face up to the long term impacts of their actions. But what about now—when the impacts of our extractive industries extend to every corner of the planet and when the long term effects are increasingly apparent for everyone to see? Are we, like lemmings, doomed to follow those who came before us to the same inevitable ends? Or might we somehow learn to reconform the way we act, to curb our appetites, to treat the Earth and the oceans with a different kind of caring . . .?

A long, shrill whistle called the first shift to work at the fish plant next morning just as the sun's upper limb appeared on the horizon to the east. Overhead, swirls of dappled cirrus cloud swept across the dome of the sky while rows of gray cumulonimbus formed like smoke above the western hills. The sky spoke of approaching weather. But the wind had dropped—and I realized it was time to leave this harbor and try to double the cape to the east before conditions became unruly once again. I knew that we must not sail, however, until I had paid a visit to Gid and had thanked him in person for the use of his facility.

I pulled on a jacket and climbed to the deck of the sailboat. I was about to step onto the narrow pier when a white Ford sedan pulled into the gravel parking area beyond the gate. I watched as a figure emerged from the automobile, stepped toward the wooden door, and fumbled with a key. Moments later the gate swung open, and I realized it was Gid himself come for a visit.

The old man moved down the pier with a shuffling gait. His cheeks were hollow, his complexion was hospital-white, his hair was grayer and thinner than I remembered. But he moved with a purposefulness that made it clear that he would not accept another's help, and he didn't carry a cane. When he recognized me, he squared his shoulders and flashed the old familiar grin.

We exchanged greetings, and I said how sorry I was to hear that he'd been sick. He dismissed my remark with a wave of his hand. "She's beautiful," he said, gazing at the green hull and the maze of spars and rigging before him. "Beautiful . . . just as I remember her."

I asked how soon it might be before he'd be able to launch his own boat.

"Soon," he said without conviction. "Or as soon, anyhow, as an old man can pull himself back together again after the doctors down in St. John's have tried their damndest to take him apart." He propped himself against a piling and rubbed his eyes with a handkerchief. "It's been hard, m'son, since last you was here. Hard for La Scie, for Newfoundland. Hard for a man at the end of his days, watching the unraveling of everything he's ever known.

"Look around this village, what do you see? Businesses closed. Houses boarded up. Young people moving away like rats deserting a sinking ship. The only ones left are those few that have gone back into the fishery now that the plant has reopened—fishing for snow crab and turbot this time. And now the managers at DFO telling us that the turbot, too, may soon be in trouble."

He stared at me with an expression of utter exasperation. "It's the politicians in Ottawa done this to us. They traded away our fish—traded it for a wheat contract in Saskatchewan, for a Toyota factory in Ontario. They traded it to the special interests—same as they did with our lumber and pulpwood—same as they'll soon be doing with our oil. Oh they knew what they was doing, all right— and they knew it was wrong. They did it for paybacks and short term jobs. They did it for votes, for political favors.

"Damn Canadians," he said, clenching his teeth and dropping his voice to a whisper. "If only the English was still here, for they'd never have let such a thing happen. The English are gentlemen—and gentlemen don't steal what isn't theirs. Gentlemen would never treat the people of Newfoundland the way these bastards have done."

I stood in silence before the old man, wishing that things were really as simple as he imagined, wishing I could somehow find a way to ease his pain.

"Damn Canadians," he whispered again, breaking into a long, wheezing cough and gazing stone-faced at the empty piers across the harbor.

Chapter 11

Fortune Harbor

CAPE ST. JOHN, at the eastern extremity of the Bay Verte Peninsula, marks a boundary both political and geographic. To the north are the bold, forbidding coasts of the old French shore; to the south and east are the protected bays and the wooded islands and thoroughfares of a region recognized traditionally as English-speaking Newfoundland.

The political boundary no longer counts for much, for the entire island of Newfoundland was officially united under English colonial rule just after the turn of the twentieth century, then combined with the territory of Labrador in an island-wide referendum forty-five years later (1949) to become the tenth province of Canada. The geographical boundary persists, however, for the physical shapes of the land and sea have not changed. The headlands and coastal palisades rise just as steeply from the water's surface; the ledges and bottom contours are just as abrupt; the rocks and boulders remain where they were deposited at the end of the last ice age, ten thousand years ago.

North of Cape St. John, the inshore branch of the Labrador Current follows a deep trench that parallels the coastal contour only a few miles from the shore. The water is frigid, covered with huge, floating slabs of sea ice from December until May, dotted with icebergs and bergy bits for most of the rest of the year. Because of the influence of this current, the outer coast remains empty of vegetation, giving it the look and feel of an Arctic landscape, and winds have an icy bite to them, even in mid-summer.

South and west of the cape all these features begin to moderate. As the Labrador current flows up against the Bay Verte Peninsula, it is forced to alter course. Most of it swings east toward Twillingate and Fogo Island, following the contours of the coastal trench and carrying the migrating ice and frigid temperatures with it. Meanwhile, a series of deep, island-studded arms and thoroughfares perforate the land to the west in a region known collectively as Notre Dame Bay. The prevailing westerly winds blow off the land here in summertime, heating the surface waters of the bay, warming the air, helping to dissipate the fogs that are so frequent over the colder regions farther north and east.

Cape St. John is thus a climatic interface—a boundary zone between sub-arctic and boreal coasts—and like many such boundaries, it invites a kind of meteorological chaos. Currents swirl and collide here, creating eddies and overfalls. Winds accelerate on the headlands. Wave-trains generated on opposite sides of the cape mount and cross in unpredictable patterns, steepening and changing their shapes in the shoal water close to the shore. Blow-me-downs stumble like invisible tornadoes down the faces of the cape's three promontories and slam into the surface of the sea.

On the morning *Brendan's Isle* set out from La Scie, the weather and sea conditions appeared peaceful at first. But within a few miles of the harbor a gusty southeast wind began to build. Soon the boat was driving into a steepening head sea, buffeted by the sudden gusts that fell from the nearby headlands. I asked Amanda if she thought it might be time to tie in a reef. Even as I was framing my question another gust hit the boat, and we both grabbed for something solid to hang on to. Richard struggled to hold down the helm as the boat rolled onto her side, dragging her boom and mainsail in the water.

"Reef? Who needs a reef?" yelled Amanda, battling to fasten her harness and fix her tether to the jack line at her feet. "A few more knockdowns like that one and the mainsail will be in shreds!"

During a brief lull, Richard drove the boat off, placing her in a defensive attitude so that Amanda and I could move forward to a pair of work stations at the mast. We lowered the mainsail to the first set of reefing points, fastened it at either end, and tied the unused portion into a furl along the boom. Several minutes later, as the wind and seas continued to build, Richard drove the boat off again so that we could repeat this procedure, tying in the second reef and changing down to the smallest jib.

When the bows came up to the wind again, the sailboat was properly canvassed and ready at last for the challenge that lay before her. During the reefing maneuvers she had fallen off several miles from the coast and had moved into an area of confused seas. Green water mounted over the bows and sluiced down both decks. But this time she was able to stand up to the wind and move ahead with slow but steady progress. Nat and Liz emerged from the companionway, clipped on to the jack line, and joined Amanda and me at the windward rail. We arranged ourselves in a row, squinting into the spray, howling with delight each time the boat leapt into a wave, prepared at last to pay the cape its inevitable toll.

I had been hopeful as *Brendan* left La Scie that we might be able to double Cape St. John early in the day before conditions became too difficult, then sail across the mouth of Notre Dame Bay, a distance of about forty miles, to the village of Twillingate. It was nearly noon, however, by the time the sailboat had actually clawed her way past the last of the off-lying ledges and had born off toward the south, clear of the cape at last. In deference to the late hour and the strengthening southeast wind, I decided to follow a more circuitous route down into the inner reaches of the bay, there to work our way south and east through a maze of islands and thoroughfares.

By late afternoon, after traversing a series of broad, open channels, we pulled up under a headland at the northern end of a wooded peninsula. For a time it appeared that even following this longer route we might be able to make Twillingate before dark. But just north of this headland, the wind suddenly dropped and the boat slowed almost to a halt. Happily, my chart showed an area of landlocked fiords only a few miles to the east—a place called Fortune Harbor—that beckoned with the promise of dozens of safe, protected anchorages.

The sun broke out from behind a cloud just as *Brendan* pulled abreast of an opening in the rock and passed into a narrow, steep-sided channel. The afternoon light blazed russet and gold against the land and the wind fell to a whisper. Half a mile inland, dense stands of spruce covered the hillsides. A grove of birches crowned an island ahead—deciduous trees, the first we'd seen in many weeks.

The channel swung to the left and opened into a bay surrounded by meadows and rolling hills. In a valley on the far side of this bay, a stone church with a white wooden steeple stood framed against green fields. Scattered about the valley were a dozen fishermen's houses, many with wooden stages, well maintained, and dories moored in front. To the east were several commercial buildings, all newly painted, and beyond these was a fish processing plant. The area behind the plant was filled with automobiles and pickup trucks; the shipping bays were stacked with boxes and nets and plastic barrels; the piers were lined with small, open fishing boats.

What was this place? It looked like some kind of illustrator's fantasy—an advertisement for the local chamber of commerce, a scene from a travel magazine. The single clear note of a church bell echoed off the hills as *Brendan* made her way across the bay in the dying breeze. I wondered, as we turned up into a narrow arm to the west of the village, whether we were still in Newfoundland at all— or whether we had somehow been transported into some kind of magical Never-never land.

The sun dropped behind the western hills and shadows grew long across the surface of the harbor. Suddenly, as the sailboat moved around the end of another island, a series of dark shapes appeared in the water ahead. Floating barrels, it seemed—row upon row of them—connected by long sections of heavy polypropylene rope and fastened with anchors to either shore.

I felt a mix of emotions as Richard slowed the boat and turned her up into the wind, for almost immediately I recognized the apparatus in the water and realized that it must be associated with some kind of aquafarming operation. One part of me (the sailor) felt upset, for the arm we were about to enter had been closed to navigation. Yet at the same time, I felt oddly excited, for it seemed that we had just happened upon the final piece of the puzzle: the missing ingredient that had transformed the village here from a welfare ghetto on the brink of economic collapse into a picture of peace and prosperity. I told myself that tomorrow, as soon as my crew had started on their morning chores, I would head ashore, seek out the aquafarm's proprietor, and try to learn what had been happening in this place.

"Go ahead," said the woman. "Try the mussel salad. It's made with vinegar, sugar, onions, red peppers. It's no good just looking at it. Go ahead, eat!"

I lifted the plastic salad plate, pried off the throw-away lid, and slipped a spoon under a bed of marinated mussels smothered in a vinaigrette dressing and swimming in a slurry of chopped vegetables. The mussels literally melted in my mouth, and I made a series of unintelligible noises as I chewed and swallowed.

"More?" the woman asked.

"Mmmm."

"Here. I'll get another plate—you can have as many as you'd like."

As she stepped over to the refrigerator, I cast my eyes around the wood-paneled room where I was seated. It was a large, multi-purpose space, part kitchen, part dining room, part sitting area with a wood stove and comfortable, overstuffed furniture. Although the construction was in the style of a traditional chinklog cabin, the building was almost new.

It was the home of Joe Wiseman, the manager of the local aquafarm, and his wife Valerie. Fortunately, I'd found them both at home this morning when I'd knocked on their door, and Joe had immediately invited me in for a coffee. It was Valerie, however, who had come up with the idea of offering me a "free sample" of the farm's cultured mussel salad.

Joe sat across the table from me as I finished the first platter of salad, stroking the head of a large, black Newfoundland puppy. Both he and the dog watched with attention as Valerie delivered the next platter of salad.

"We're a young business," said Joe, "still growing, still trying to develop markets. The mussel salad is what we call a 'value added' product—aimed at the high end consumers. Last week we shipped a hundred cases to Sobey's, a big Canadian grocery store chain down in Nova Scotia. We're also shipping cooked meats to a smokehouse in Bonavista Bay. The retail markets sell them as smoked mussels—I'm told they're doing well."

Joe was a native of Fortune Harbor—although he didn't really look the part. His sallow complexion, wire rim glasses, and nearly bald head gave him the appearance of a cleric or a college don—and he spoke without a noticeable accent. Yet, as he was quick to emphasize, his roots in this community were long and deep.

He'd been born here fifty-two years ago, the son of the village dry goods merchant, and he'd grown up in a house that had once stood only a few yards from the site of this present building. He was only thirteen when he'd left to go away to school, then to attend the university in St. John's. When he'd come back, he had taken a job as the village school teacher in a tiny, two room schoolhouse on the hill behind the church—a role he'd performed in this community for over twenty years. Finally, a year and a half ago, he'd been asked to become manager of the local aquaculture operation—a mussel farm owned by a St. John's firm: Atlantic Ocean Farms, Limited.

"A new job to go along with a new marriage," said Joe, glancing at Valerie with a playful smile. "It's the second time around for both of us. Put that together with a new house and a new dog . . . I guess you might say we're at the cutting edge of the new Newfoundland."

The aquafarming venture, Joe explained, had been operating in Fortune Harbor for fifteen years, although for many of those years it hadn't appeared to be much more than a risky experiment. At first, people in the area thought the idea was crazy. Most of them didn't even eat mussels—some refused to let them be boiled in their houses because of what they called the "bad smell."

"People just assumed that this was another government make-work project, that it wouldn't last a year. Even the government had trouble taking it seriously at first. But the company's founder, a fellow from western Canada named Joe Walsh, wouldn't take no for an answer. He started with an idea—a dream really—and he wouldn't let go. He and his partners worked through all the early problems, finding proper growing sites, developing techniques for collecting spat, learning how to harvest under the ice. Finally, nearly two decades later, the result is what you see: a fine little business, almost two miles of growing sites up in the Northwest Arm, three hundred thousand pounds of mussels shipped out last year, maybe four hundred thousand this year, sold to markets all over the world."

I asked about the impact of the aquafarm on the people living here.

"Jobs—simple as that. Twenty five or thirty good, steady jobs. The fact is, the farm has become the life blood of this community. Before it started, Fortune Harbor was depopulating, like hundreds of outports all over Newfoundland. At its peak a century ago, this was a shipbuilding and fishing center for the Labrador fishery, with seven, maybe eight hundred people living here. Then, as that fishery declined, people started leaving. Fortune Harbor was just too far up the bay, too far from the local fishing grounds, to support a large fishery. By the early 1980s, the population had dwindled to less than a hundred.

"Finally, when the aquafarm started, the numbers began to stabilize. Now we're holding steady at about ninety people, with a job for anybody who wants one. Every family, I think, has somebody on the payroll at the mussel farm. As far as I know, there isn't a person in Fortune Harbor living on TAGS payments—or even taking TAGS retraining. It's been a real life-saver—maybe the reason this place is still on the map at all."

I finished the last of the mussel salad and handed Valerie the empty platter. Joe stepped over to a window where he could look out at the harbor. A pair of small, open fishing vessels—the type Newfoundlanders call trap skiffs—moved past, heading toward the farm site.

"Are they going out to harvest mussels?" I asked.

"Not today. There are still plenty in the refrigerators down at the plant. Those men are going out to do some water tests this morning, then to check on the microscopic mussel larvae—the 'spat,' we call them—that attached themselves to our collectors about two weeks ago. If all goes well, those larvae will become our future harvest in about two, two and a half years from now."

Joe was a walking encyclopedia about both the business and the biology of farming mussels, and he was eager to share his knowledge. During the next half hour, I asked him dozens of questions, and he did his best to provide answers. Suddenly, however, he stopped in mid-sentence and stared at a clock on the wall.

"Sorry," he said, holding up his hands in a gesture of surrender. "Just look at the time. I need to get down to the plant this morning. But I have an idea. I've started a little side business—a picnic boat that I run as a kind of tourist attraction. We sail every afternoon at three o'clock for a trip out to the Northwest Arm. During the trip I give a talk about the aquafarm, cook up some mussels, tell people about the history of this place. It gives me a chance to be a teacher again.

"How about it?—why don't you and your crew come along this afternoon? Then we can finish all this business over a couple of beers and a mess of steamed Newfoundland mussels."

"Three o'clock, you say?"
"Down at the pier in front of the processing plant."
"We'll be there."

Last evening, as *Brendan's Isle* had entered Fortune Harbor, I'd been as surprised as any of my shipmates at suddenly finding ourselves surrounded by a commercial aquafarm. For in spite of the growing importance of aquaculture in fisheries worldwide, it is a still a relative newcomer to Newfoundland. And for reasons that are obvious to anyone who has experienced this region's harsh winters, most of the successful growing sites around this island have been located along the more temperate and ice-free southern coasts.

It was in 1987 during *Brendan's* first visit to Newfoundland, in fact, that I and another group of young sailors first happened upon an experimental aquafarm in a nearly deserted fiord called Roti Bay down on the southwest coast. The operators of that farm, a couple of local fishermen from the nearby village of St. Alban's, were experimenting with various species of finfish—Atlantic salmon, steelhead trout, Arctic char—in an attempt to learn which might adapt most readily to local climate and water conditions and which might prove most profitable when they were brought to market.

At that early stage, almost every aspect of the operation involved risks and unknowns. Would the fish survive the harsh climate? Would the bay "flush" adequately with tidal action to preclude the buildup of toxins, chemicals from the fish feed, fecal waste from the fish themselves? Would the floating pens withstand the pressure of local shorefast ice that formed each winter in the bay? Would the operators be able to access the farm site to feed the fish during the icy season—or during storms and gales?

The answer to most of these questions, at least for the short term, has been yes, and the development of aquaculture sites along the southwest coast—for both finfish and shellfish—has proceeded vigorously during the past decade. The farm at Roti Bay has grown from a small experimental station into a major production site, with harvests of salmon and steelhead trout currently approaching two thousand tons annually. Other smaller operators have established aquafarm sites for the production of char, rainbow trout, speckled trout. And more recently, several former cod fishermen have organized family "crews" to try their hands at producing farm-raised Atlantic cod. These fish are caught in the spring in specially licensed cod traps, fed with high protein fish food all summer, and shipped to market as "high end" fish fillets in the fall.

In addition to finfish farming, there have also been a number of shellfish sites established along the south and southwest coasts for the production of oysters, scallops, sea urchins, mussels. In our conversation this morning, Joe cited official statistics indicating that the province had issued over one hundred licenses for the production of mussels alone. Among these, some thirty or forty were what he described as "serious growers," in direct competition with his own company, Atlantic Ocean Farms.

"But we're responding to the challenge," said Joe. "Our company is developing a new site right now, also down on the southwest coast, in a place called Miller's Passage. It's a beautiful place—several times larger than Fortune Bay but otherwise quite similar. When the Miller's Passage site is producing at full capacity, we'll be able to harvest a million pounds of mussels a year from that one facility alone."

For growers like Joe Wiseman, the promise of aquaculture must feel heady and intoxicating, for production forecasts seem to point toward a future of almost limitless growth. Indeed, fishing industry analysts, commenting on the dramatic increase of aquaculture almost everywhere in the world, have often characterized it as the technological cure-all, the miracle that is poised to resolve the growing crisis in the wild fishery for the twenty-first century.

A look at world production statistics for the last several decades would seem, at least at first glance, to support this optimism. In 1977, for instance, aquaculture accounted for only about two million tons—or approximately three percent—of all fish, crustaceans, and mollusks consumed by human beings worldwide. By 1987 this number had risen to nine million tons and ten percent of total human consumption, and by 1997 it had climbed to twenty-eight million tons and twenty percent of consumption. By the year 2010, according to United Nations projections, world production of farm-raised sea foods may rise to as much as forty million tons and thirty-three percent of all the seafood consumed by human beings worldwide.

Statistics are a funny business, however, and numbers such as these can be made to tell a variety of different stories, depending on the intention of the person who uses them. As regards these particular numbers, it bears pointing out that over half the reported world growth in aquaculture since the late 1970s has taken place in non-marine (freshwater) settings, most of these in mainland China— and that over two-thirds of the projected growth for the coming decade will also take place in China, on small farms and coopera- tives where fish and seaweed aquaculture is being coordinated in environmentally benign settings with other farming activities. The real "miracle" of aquaculture, it seems, is thus taking place in a single Asian nation and as an integral part of its government's efforts to stimulate sustainable forms of food production. Without the Chinese experience to skew the numbers, the world statistics for the growth of aquaculture appear far less impressive—and in fact conform more closely to the experience of growers in Newfoundland and much of the rest of North America: modest growth (on the order of two to four percent per year) limited by large capital require- ments, unpredictable market forces, and several kinds of environ- mental constraints.

Unlike entry into the wild fishery, which at its simplest level requires nothing more than a hook, some bait, and a few hundred feet of fish line, commercial aquafarming is an expensive proposi- tion. With finfish farming, the expenses begin with the construction of hatcheries or with the collection of immature fish from wild settings. Next come the costs of nets, floating pens, platforms, and mooring gear for the growing sites, shoreside storage facilities, and vessels and other vehicles for accessing the sites. Added to these are the substantial costs of feeding the fish for several years (usually with a combination of fish meal, soybean meal, and grain-based feed) and for treating the fish and the water at the growing site with antibiotics and other chemical additives.

In the case of shellfish farming, certain of these costs do not apply. Hatcheries are not necessary, as the larval "spat" are normally collected on simple apparatus near the growing sites. Feeding is also unnecessary, as bivalve mollusks occupy a niche low on the food chain and live on plankton and other microorganisms already present in the water. Otherwise, however, both forms of aquaculture share the economic risks associated with the long wait between "planting" and "harvesting" (typically on the order of two to three years), during which time the growers' capital is tied up, equipment depreciates, and market conditions change. (The wholesale price that Joe's company was able to command for its Newfoundland mussels, for example, plummeted from $2.26 per pound in 1996 to $1.07 per pound in 1997, reducing by more than fifty percent the value of a crop that had been planted in Fortune Harbor two and a half years earlier.)

As Joe is quick to point out, commercial aquaculture is no get-rich-quick scheme. Like all farming ventures, it faces continual economic risks and uncertainties. Moreover, it also carries with it significant environmental costs—some of them vastly more harmful than others.

Perhaps the most benign form of aquaculture is the type that is being practiced (and has been practiced for centuries) by small farmers in China. At the beginning of the growing season, local ponds are flooded and stocked with carp, tilapia, and other freshwater species. During the next several months, the fish are fed on farm residues and wastes from the farm animals. The animals, in turn, are fed on aquatic plants grown in the ponds. Later, during the dry season, the fish are harvested and the ponds emptied so the water can be used to help irrigate crops. The nutrient-rich bottom sediments created by the fish droppings are removed and spread on nearby fields. In this way, the circle is closed and the organic cycle completed.

In contrast, most western forms of aquaculture are intensive, single species ventures that are organically discontinuous with the settings in which they take place. Mollusk aquafarms such as the one at Fortune Harbor are arguably the least harmful of these, as they require no specialized feeds, almost no chemical additives, and no major alterations to the physical setting. Finfish farms that raise carnivorous species such as salmon and steelhead trout are among the most harmful, for not only do they require large quantities of feed and other additives but they also produce large amounts of fecal wastes that collect beneath the fish pens and can quickly degrade the surrounding area. (Researchers have determined that each ton of cultivated fish requires about eight tons of clean water and produces up to a ton of waste material.) Sites that do not have strong flushing action from either tide or moving current can quickly become toxified, making them uninhabitable both for the farmed stocks and for nearby wild populations.

The most environmentally damaging form of commercial aquaculture involves neither shellfish nor finfish, however, but cultured shrimp. Global production of tiger prawns, for example, has grown more than six hundred percent in the past ten years, to three and a half million tons, and has become a major, multi-billion dollar export industry in dozens of tropical third world nations. The shrimp are grown in flooded coastal wetlands and bulldozed mangrove forests, where eighty to ninety percent of tropical fish species used to spend at least some part of their life cycles. Although exact figures are difficult to obtain, it has been estimated that in the past two decades, more than two and a half million acres of coastal habitat have been destroyed to make way for commercial shrimp ponds. The Philippines have lost over half a million acres—two-thirds of their coastal mangrove forests. Thailand has lost an equal amount. Ecuador has lost 160 square miles—one fifth of its coastal mangroves.

The environmental cost of this kind of commercial aquafarming is twofold. First, for every acre of coastal wetland that is transferred to shrimp production, the wild fish catch drops by nearly seven hundred pounds a year. This has decimated local coastal fisheries, where the residents used to derive large portions of their protein from the oceans. Second, intensive shrimp farming leads to the same kinds of environmental degradation as intensive finfish farming. To protect overcrowded stocks from predators and disease, the shrimp are dosed with antibiotics and pesticides. These substances, in combination with shrimp excrement and partially eaten fishmeal, then enter the surrounding environment, altering its chemistry, contaminating bottom sediments, poisoning groundwater. Three to five years of intensive shrimp aquaculture is all it takes to transform a once-productive wetland ecosystem into a highly saline "mud desert" in which neither shrimp nor fish nor most other indigenous organisms can survive.

Clearly, the impacts of aquaculture vary dramatically from place to place and species to species. Some forms can be safely integrated into the natural systems that surround them; others cause extensive and often irreversible environmental damage. Some, like Chinese pond farming, add to the total amount of protein available for human consumption; others, like marine finfish farming, require several times more protein in the form of grains and fish meal feeds than they will ever produce. Some types, like oyster or mussel farming, result in far larger and healthier crops than would occur in natural ecosystems; others, like shrimp farming, actually degrade once-productive wetlands and destroy the wild fisheries they were intended to augment.

For those who posit aquaculture as the miracle solution to collapsing world fisheries, the message has to be: look again. Except in a few limited cases, the farming of cultured species, like the farming of cattle or pigs or chickens, carries significant costs. Wealthy consumers seem willing to pay such costs—at least in the short term—which is one reason the fish markets of North America are still full of produce. But as wild fisheries continue to be stressed, other questions loom. Can aquaculture fill the "protein gap" that is almost certain to occur as we attempt to feed the next several billion human mouths to be added to the Earth's population in the coming decades? Can seafood farmers learn to duplicate the almost incomprehensible productivity of the oceans? Can they develop technologies to replace the efficiency of natural ecosystems— without destroying those systems in the process?

It was just a few minutes past three o'clock as Joe Wiseman lifted the cover of his old twenty-five horse Johnson outboard and fiddled with the carburetor. He wrapped a piece of clothesline around the flywheel, gave a pull, and watched with satisfaction as the engine sputtered to life.

In front of him, seated on a pair of facing benches, were his passengers: Amanda and Nat and Liz and me on one side, an elderly American couple, Pat and Audrey Norris, and their ten-year old grandson, Graham, on the other side. We were assembled on a large floating platform, rectangular in shape, surrounded by a metal railing and fastened to a pair of aluminum pontoons. On the deck next to Joe was a guitar case, a tub of ice and soft drinks and beer, and several five-pound bags of mussels. We were about to head off to the Northwest Arm for a picnic, Newfoundland style.

Joe was obviously in high spirits as he threw the old outboard into reverse and backed the pontoon-boat away from the pier. As he pointed the bows down the harbor, he talked with the American couple about their common ancestry—for, coincidentally, both they and he had roots in southern Ireland. His own grandfather, he told them, had been impressed on an English warship during the late decades of the last century. He had jumped ship in St. John's, then had made his way up the coast to Fortune Harbor during the heyday of the Labrador fishery. Here he had fallen in love and married the merchant's daughter, a happy turn of events that had established the young Irishman firmly within the local community and had defined his family's economic future for several generations.

The pontoon boat swung wide around an area of shoal water and moved past a long, narrow cove behind Gillespie Island where *Brendan* lay at anchor. Just west of the island, the boat swung wide again and entered the aquafarm.

"This harbor was once filled with schooners," said Joe, as he maneuvered his way past the first several rows of floating mussel sets. "They were local boats, built here, operated by the men and boys of Fortune Harbor. Each spring, as they were fitting out for fishing down the Labrador, my grandfather would sell them boots, clothing, blankets, flour, salt, kerosene, hemp rope, marlin twine. He wouldn't get paid with a share of the fish, though, until the fall— and then only if the schooner came back—if the fishing had been successful and the little ship's holds were filled with salt cod."

Joe cut the throttle to idle speed and picked up a wooden pole with a hook on the end. "That was then," he said, as he thrust the pole down into the water. He felt around with the hook for several seconds, then pulled up a large sack of tubular netting covered with thousands of mussels.

"And this is now."

The journey through the mussel farm continued as the pontoon boat made its way slowly into the farthest reaches of the Northwest Arm, to a wooded cul-de-sac surrounded by high hills. During all this time, Joe provided a running commentary on the business and biology of mollusk farming. He talked about the importance of finding good growing sites—places with plenty of nutrients, proper salinity and water temperature, adequate tidal flow, good flushing action. He talked about the problems of drift ice, disease, pollution. He described the life cycle of the Atlantic blue mussel—even called the organism by its scientific name, *Mytilus edulis*—and he emphasized the importance, for growers, of understanding its biological timetable. He described various items of equipment that Joe Walsh and others had developed as they had worked out ways to grow and harvest mussels on an icy coast at fifty degrees north latitude.

At one point, as we were preparing for an interlude ashore to boil up a few pounds of mussels and sing some old Newfie folk songs, I asked Joe his opinion about what the future might hold. Could this kind of operation eventually provide large groups of people with jobs and income in the absence of the wild fisheries? Might *Brendan* and crew return to Newfoundland in a few more years to find the entire island girded by seafood farms?

"You hear people tossing around all kinds of numbers," said Joe. "In the mussel business, for instance, I know that this year New-foundland growers will produce a total of something like two million pounds. In two or three years, early next century, people are talking about production up around ten million pounds, with maybe twenty million pounds possible somewhere down the road."

"Do you think these numbers are realistic?"

"Honestly—I can't say. But there's one thing I can tell you—the whole thing is going to be limited by the number of good growing sites. It's not easy to find places like Fortune Harbor—good clean places, protected from weather and moving ice, with deep water, plenty of circulation, plenty of plankton for the mussels to feed on. Why this very operation is a case in point. When Joe Walsh and his partners first came out here nearly twenty years ago, they set up the original farm in an area a few miles down the peninsula called Winter Tickle. Only things didn't work out down there. There was too much ice—not enough flushing action. The whole situation just turned out to be too risky."

Joe nudged the bow of the pontoon boat onto a narrow strip of beach that lay under the shadow of wooded hills. "I suppose if you're asking whether aquafarms like this one represent the future of Newfoundland, I'd have to say no, probably not. In many ways this place is unique—one in a thousand. Most of the small bays and coves on this island simply won't work for sustainable aquafarming.

"But if you're asking whether this particular aquafarm repre-sents the future of Fortune Harbor, well that's another story. This farm represents the present and the future both. It has put this community back on the map."

He tilted the outboard engine up so that its propeller was out of the water, grabbed his guitar, and handed me a string bag full of plump black mussels. "Now let's stop talking about these tasty little fellas," he said with a grin as wide as his face, "and let's start to eat."

Chapter 12

Seldom Come By

MOST OF US WHO LIVE in the high speed, high-tech world of urban North America have forgotten what it means to feel personally connected with the geographical settings that surround us. A deep and enduring experience of place—as an integral component of one's identity—disappeared for most modern urbanites several generations ago along with the village common and the family farm. Following the job market, moving to the newest housing development, climbing the corporate ladder, the average citizen in the United States now changes his address once every four and one half years; the average citizen in Canada does the same once every six years. Almost none of us, it seems, live in the places we were born any longer.

Perhaps this pervasive experience of rootlessness is one of the reasons visitors "from away" often have such a hard time understanding the inhabitants of Newfoundland's outports—for here, in settlements that have been occupied by the same families for a dozen generations, the relationship between the people and the places they live is as fundamental and self-defining as the relationship between a group of siblings and their parents.

There are many ways in which this personal relationship with one's geography is expressed in outport life. Natural landmarks and navigational features are identified with the names of local personalities: Sam Hitches Harbor, Joe Batt's Arm, Mary's Tickle, Kate's Head, Christopher Island, Lost Children's Ledge. Favored fishing berths are passed from father to son, some of them remaining within the same family for hundreds of years. Garden plots, grave sites, building lots become indelibly connected with particular kinship groups, not through legal, written records but through the unspoken forces of custom and physical presence. Finally, after generations of such presence, an almost seamless thread of connectiveness binds geography and community, community and family, family and the individual.

Of all the ways that Newfoundland outporters have expressed their relationship with their geographical settings, perhaps none are so revealing as the sentimental, often whimsical names they have given to the places they live: Heart's Content, Come by Chance, Happy Adventure, Paradise, Goobies, Heart's Delight, Sunnyside, Ferryland, Harbor Grace. I had called at many such communities in the seven summers that *Brendan* and I had sailed these coasts, and I'd always found them to live up to the promise of their names. There was another such place that I had never visited, however, on the south side of Fogo Island—a setting somewhat off the beaten track where I'd always wanted to go, if for no other reason that to experience the poetry and gentle humor of a village called Seldom Come By.

The morning *Brendan* set sail from Fortune Harbor, I had already made the decision to bypass the busy commercial center of Twillingate and head directly for Fogo Island and the little outport of Seldom. The day was warm and dry, the winds were gentle, and the air was filled with the late summer aromas of meadow grass and wild flowers. The sea beyond the harbor mouth was smooth and brilliant blue. Even the icebergs that lay grounded on the nearby headlands seemed to deny their harsh beginnings, glittering like gemstones against the pastel greens and ochres of the land.

It was early afternoon by the time *Brendan* completed the forty mile passage, rounded the lighted buoy at Cann Island, and drew up into the approaches to Seldom harbor. A church set high on a hillside marked the harbor entrance. White frame buildings, in various stages of repair, circled the waterfront. A fish plant with a long, narrow facing pier was situated just inside the headland to the left, while the rusted hulk of an old iron barge lay beached in the mud at the northwest end of the harbor.

Two small trap skiffs laden with stacks of wire baskets were moored along the fish plant pier. I was about to maneuver the sailboat between them and ask permission to lie alongside when I heard a small female voice calling from an adjacent pier several hundred yards down the harbor. I turned around to see the figure of a young woman, dressed in a T-shirt and denim overalls, balancing on top of a wooden piling and waving her arms. Behind her stood a pair of warehouse buildings, one sheathed in white clapboard, the other covered with red shingles. On the front of the farthest building was a sign with large block lettering: *Fishermen's Union Trading Company, Ltd.*

The young woman waved and called again. I wheeled *Brendan* in a semi-circle and approached the pier where she was standing. In another minute she had taken the sailboat's mooring lines and had made them fast to a pair of wooden cleats. "Electric hookup is over there," she said, gesturing toward a decorative wooden lamppost near the corner of the pier. "Fresh water, showers, bathrooms are all up at the general store."

. At this close range, our hostess seemed barely older than a child. She was short and slender, with pretty, sculptured features and dark auburn hair, clipped in the style of a page boy. She was a student, she said, just finished her first year at Memorial University in St. John's. She was working here at the Fishermen's Union Trading Company restoration as a summer guide—her family lived only a few hundred yards down the road. Her name, she said, was Shawna Payne.

My surprise at being greeted by this pretty young woman was exceeded only by my surprise at finding a marina pier and historical restoration in Seldom Come By at all. The facility, Shawna explained, was new—built by the Fogo Island Cooperative with the aid of a half million dollar government grant. The white building on the right had once been a general store, she said, operated by the local fish merchant. The red-shingle building on the left had been used as a cod liver oil factory.

I asked if the marina charged a dockage fee.

"Fifteen dollars a night. Flat rate."

"Seems reasonable," I said, thinking that a similar facility back in the United States would probably be charging five or six times this amount. "And how many boats have stopped here for the night so far this summer?"

"You're the fourteenth—with most of August still to go."

After doing a little mental arithmetic, I decided that the Fogo Island Cooperative was fortunate to have secured its half million dollar government grant, for nobody, it seemed, was likely to be getting rich soon on the income from Seldom's new marina.

I paid the dockage fee as my crew gathered shower kits and towels and headed up to the general store in search of fresh hot water. Shawna excused herself to wait with several other guides in the front foyer of the store building—but not before announcing that the sailboat's crew was "hers" and that she would be our "official interpreter" when we were ready to visit the two historic buildings. "The tour takes about an hour," she said. "Anybody who wants to come, just meet me at four o'clock in front of the cod liver oil factory."

The afternoon shadows were just beginning to lengthen as Amanda and Liz and I climbed to the deck of the marina pier and crossed a gravel promenade. Shawna stood braced against a set of wooden steps in front of the red-shingled warehouse. She waited at half-attention with her lips pursed, her mouth set in an inscrutable smile. She seemed to be trying to compose herself into some kind of public persona, I thought—trying to overcome the nervousness she was feeling, perhaps, as she prepared for her talk.

Both Amanda and Liz attempted to engage her in conversation while we waited for Nat and Richard, but with little success. She seemed distracted, as if she simply wasn't ready to deal with us yet. The one exception occurred as Liz asked her about her coursework at the university and her plans for the future. "Some day I'd like to become a doctor—maybe even a psychiatrist," Shawna said, laughing self-consciously. "Half the people in this village are going crazy anyhow. So I'm sure I'll have plenty of customers."

After the others had arrived, Shawna led us through a wooden door and into a long, narrow room. At the near end of the room was an ungainly apparatus that looked like a giant cider press—the cod liver oil machine that had given the building its name. Scattered about the rest of the room was a collection of traditional tools and artifacts: barrows and sledges, shovels and forks, jigs, floats, traps, knives, tubs of caulking, reels of twine. The collection was notable for its sheer size and variety. But just as with her remarks about the cod liver oil machine, Shawna's description of these tools and of the fishery they had served seemed dull and emotionless. As she talked, I got the feeling that she may have memorized every word.

On the second floor of the building, Shawna stopped in front of a photograph of a small fishing boat poised on a boatyard slipway. Here she told the story of the Fogo Island Cooperative, an organization formed in the late 1960s in response to a government plan to close several of Fogo's outports and move the inhabitants into large economic centers. Rather than complying with the government's plan, however, the citizens of Fogo had held a series of island-wide meetings and had formed their own economic union, pledging to work together to operate their fisheries and fish plants on a cooperative basis and to make their communities economically self-sufficient.

As Shawna told this tale—still in a monotone that sounded as if she were reading from a prepared text—I found myself thinking about the historical context of the events she was describing—events that still live in infamy in the minds of thousands of rural Newfoundlanders.

In the middle 1960s, Newfoundland Premier Joey Smallwood had devised a scheme to modernize his province's economy by "relocating" the inhabitants of the small, isolated coastal communities. These outports, Smallwood argued, were costly and inefficient—too small to have their own schools, medical facilities, and other basic services—too geographically diverse to be connected with the rest of the island by road. If outporters were ever to become economically competitive with the rest of Canada, the Premier argued, they would need to abandon their traditional ways, leave their homes, and move to large mainland "growth centers" where they could join the modern labor force and become productive participants in a new industrialized Newfoundland.

During the next decade, dozens of outports were either abandoned or severely reduced in size and thousands of their inhabitants were relocated in accordance with the dictates of this program. In a diaspora that saw Newfoundlanders moving to the far corners of the North American continent, an entire generation was scattered to the wind. Some managed to join the modern labor force and become integrated into mainstream urban life. Many others did not. Lonely, emotionally dislocated, and without marketable skills or formal education, these became a generation of wanderers, marginalized in a society that did not seem to need or want them.

No matter what eventually happened to the people affected by Smallwood's relocation program, almost all remained emotionally attached to the geographical settings that had formed such a huge part of their identities. Over the years, many decided to return and take up residence again in the villages of their youth, reaching out for family and friends, seeking the security of whatever was left of home. Others, unable to return on a permanent basis, were drawn back to family reunions and homecoming celebrations, a pattern that persisted even when there was nothing left of the old village sites but crumbling, deserted buildings and empty fields.

For most outporters, "relocation" became a synonym for being cheated, lied to, and forcibly driven from their homes, and the name Joey Smallwood became a curse. Farley Mowat, in his book *The New Founde Land*, describes the anguish of the men and women victimized by this social dislocation. One of the fishermen in Mowat's book complains about the way he and his family had been forced to leave their village. "We was drove," he cries in a moment of anger and frustration. "Aye, Jesus, Jesus God, but we was drove!"

I mentioned this dark page in Newfoundland's recent past to Shawna, suggesting that her neighbors here in Fogo may have been among the lucky ones. "Here people seemed to have found a way to stay in their villages and keep their homes," I said, "at a time when so many others were being forced out."

Shawna became quiet for a time. "Maybe it don't matter," she said at last, "Maybe it would've been better if everybody'd just left Seldom thirty years ago." A dark look crossed her face, and I thought for a moment that she was going to cry. Several seconds later, however, she had composed herself and had turned once again to the rest of the group.

She led us through a doorway, down a staircase, and across a wooden deck, stopping at the entrance to the general store. Here she began to talk about the merchants who had once owned these premises and the generations of fishermen who had come here to trade their fish for flour and sugar, blankets and ammunition, fish hooks and twine. Once again, however, her words seemed flat and emotionless, and I found myself wondering whether her presentation might have been scripted by the local chamber of commerce, edited so as not to rekindle painful memories among the local populace or to offend the sensibilities of innocent tourists.

"You're talking about the merchant system as if it had been a pleasant thing," I said. "Somehow I can't believe you mean that. The merchants here were still operating a monopoly, weren't they? Which meant the fishermen were powerless to change things. They had to participate or starve."

Once again Shawna stopped speaking. Her silence became uncomfortable, almost painful. Finally she turned to me with a look of utter consternation. "I'm nineteen years old—twenty next month. I've lived in Fogo all my life. Don't you think I know about the merchant system, how unfair it was? Don't you think I know how my grandfather had to struggle to make a go, how my father was forced to…"

"My question was wrong, I'm sorry. I didn't mean to suggest . . . ."

"Don't apologize. You've no need to apologize. For the system was unfair, just as you say. The merchants had the final say on everything. The fishermen had no other choice but to go along with the merchants' rules.

"Funny thing, as far as I can see, the system still works the same way today. There are still people out there setting prices, opening this fishery, closing that one, making all the rules. Only now they aren't just the local merchants from Seldom or Fogo or Twillingate. Now they're politicians and business executives in the highest office buildings and the biggest cities in the world—Ottawa, New York, London, Tokyo."

She gazed from face to face at the little group before her, as if she were sizing up each one in turn. When she spoke again, her voice had an intensity that I had not heard before.

"My father is a fisherman—been a fisherman all his life. Before the moratorium he was fishing cod traps, doing well. My parents had a nice house in the village that they'd built themselves. Then, when the fishery closed, the government wanted to buy my father's license back. They offered him money to learn a 'trade,' they called it, laying bricks or running a bulldozer or operating a printing press. But what's the point of that? There's no job in Seldom for a printer or a brick layer and nobody owns a bulldozer. Only way to get a job like that would be to move someplace else. But how is a man fifty-eight years old going to say goodbye to his family and friends, sell the house that he's built with his own hands, move to a place where nobody knows him, look for a job he's never done?"

She set her jaws in a defiant grimace. "Have you ever looked at the hands of a man who has fished all his life? I mean really looked at them? Well I have. I've memorized the scars on my father's wrists and knuckles. I've counted his broken fingers. If only the politicians in Ottawa could look at my father's hands. If only they could see how hard he works—they wouldn't do this to us. They would understand how foolish their programs are—how impossible for a man like my father to stop the only life he's ever known and try to start another."

She stared across the harbor at the rooftops of her village, drawing her mouth into a frown and tugging unconsciously at the hem of her T-shirt. "For the longest time when I was growing up I tried to pretend that nothing was wrong. I was in denial, I guess you'd say, telling myself that all this trouble would pass, that our lives would go back again to the way they'd always been—telling myself that nothing had changed. And then, six months ago, I came home after my first semester at Memorial. I looked around this village, at the friends I'd grown up with, at my parents, at our neighbors, and suddenly I knew that everything had changed—that our lives were never going to be the same. People were boarding up their houses—boarding them up because they couldn't sell them. Houses that had cost a hundred thousand and a lifetime of blood and sweat and tears and nobody would give ten thousand for them now—nobody would take them even if the owners had tried to give them away.

"When the moratorium first come, my father said he wouldn't sell his license. Wouldn't take their damn money, he said, no matter how bad things got. I was proud of him for that, even when the fish plant closed. I was proud of the way he stood up to them.

"And then—a year ago last spring—the government opened up a new fishery—snow crab—opened it up to the inshore fishermen, increased the quotas to double what they'd been. My father got a quota of two hundred-fifty pounds a week, enough to make a nice profit, he said, if the price stayed good. Three, four dollars a pound he was getting last year, and for a time it seemed like he'd found a way to make a living again.

"He bought a string of pots, put some money in his boat, got all geared up. And then—without a warning—the bottom dropped out. The price of crabs fell from three and a half dollars to eighty-five cents. Eighty-five cents! It wasn't enough to pay a man to leave the harbor—wasn't enough to pay for fuel."

She stared down toward the fish plant and narrowed her eyes as if she were trying to reassemble a long-forgotten picture in her mind. "When I was a little girl, seems like my father was never home. Seems like I spent my whole life waiting on our front porch, looking down the harbor, watching every boat as it come up around Cann Island, wondering whether this one was him or that one was him, calling out to my mother when he finally come steaming around the point and up to the fish plant.

"But now when I come home, my father is always there. Father and mother both, as if they can't think of anywhere else to go. My mother cleans the house. Day after day she scrubs the walls and floors and woodwork like she's trying to make them disappear. And my father . . . my father just sits in his chair, quiet, staring at the wall. It makes me want to cry to see him like that, silent, brooding. I'd rather see him kick the table. I'd rather see him rage.

"Eighty-five cents a pound! Who in hell come up with a price like eighty-five cents a pound? Nobody in Seldom can make a profit on their crab at eighty-five cents a pound. Somebody's making money—somebody in St. John's or New York or Tokyo. But not here. Another year like this and there may not be any more fishermen in Seldom." She narrowed her eyes again and stared at the empty promenade before her. "Another year like this, may not be a village here at all."

The cry of a solitary gull echoed across Seldom harbor as the sun dropped beneath the rooftops of the village. The chatter of tiny wavelets beat a steady rhythm against the sailboat's hull. I was seated in the cockpit with a mug of coffee; my shipmates were lingering over their evening meal below. We had barely spoken together since our hour with Shawna earlier in the afternoon, for there seemed no words to express the tangle of emotions that each one was feeling.

I knew a little about the dilemma that Shawna's father faced, for during a journey to St. John's the previous winter I had met and spoken with several scientists involved with the management of the snow crab fishery. One with whom I had talked was Department of

Fisheries and Oceans marine biologist David Taylor. As a senior member of the team responsible for the preparation of annual stock status reports on the snow crab, Taylor was one of Newfoundland's most influential managers for this fishery as well as one of the scientists most directly involved in its monitoring.

According to Taylor, the snow crab fishery was one of the few bright spots in an otherwise discouraging prospect for Newfoundland fishermen. Like the northern shrimp, this fishery, too, had been expanding over the past few decades, from a total of about fifty license-holders in the late 1970s to a total of more than a thousand by the mid-1980s. During the next several years there had been a drop in landings as crab populations reacted to the increased fishing pressure. But by the early 1990s the crab began a dramatic recovery, and once again fishery managers initiated a phase of rapid expansion.

By 1995 nearly two thousand new permits had been issued, including a large number of "temporary permits" for inshore fishermen (such as Shawna's father) with boats under thirty-five feet. In 1996 and 1997 additional new permits were issued, bringing the total number of licensed enterprises in the fishery to over thirty-two hundred and the total annual landings to nearly thirty-eight thousand tons.

As Taylor looked into his scientific crystal ball, he was optimistic about the future of the snow crab fishery. "There are two reasons why we've opened this fishery to the small inshore operators. First is the good news from our research surveys. There are large populations of legal-sized male crabs distributed throughout most of the survey areas. And there are plenty of younger, sub-legal sized males ready to recruit to the fishery over the next two to three years.

"The second reason is trap design. When the males of this species reach maturity, their carapace width generally measures over a hundred millimeters, whereas when the females mature, their carapace width never gets much above eighty-five millimeters. The legal mesh size of our traps is ninety-five millimeters—a size that assures the capture of most of the larger males even as it releases virtually all the females. This way, we keep the fishery strong even as we also guarantee plenty of reproductive capacity for the future."

Another observer of the snow crab fishery with whom I was able to speak last winter was Memorial University marine biologist Richard Haedrich. In contrast to government scientists such as

David Taylor, Haedrich was notably less optimistic about both the present and the future of the crab fishery.

"The fate of the snow crab and the northern shrimp are disturbingly similar," Haedrich said, "for like the shrimp, the crab was an important component of the cod's diet. Both fisheries are examples of what scientists describe as 'fishing down the food chain.' First we move in with our trawls and traps and eliminate the predator (in this case, the cod)— then we do the same with each of its former prey. If we follow this pattern to its logical conclusion, we'll soon be licensing our fishermen to scour the banks of Newfoundland for copepods and krill."

"Okay," I said. "The down-side of this story is that the cod is gone. But what about the up-side? At least for the fishermen, it seems there might actually be a trade-off here. One fishery has disappeared—but another has come along to take its place. If the crab traps really do release the females, and if one of the crab's main predators has now been effectively eliminated from the food chain, what's to keep this fishery from becoming even larger and more lucrative than the one it replaced?"

"In a word," said Haedrich, "the DFO. The way the government managers deplete a fishery—the way they've done it time and time again—is to raise quotas, increase the number of licenses, double or triple the total allowable catch, encourage a gold rush mentality among fishermen.

"But look what eventually happens. Markets become glutted with product. Prices plummet. Fishermen have to land larger and larger numbers of fish or crab or shrimp in order to cover their costs and make a profit. The little guys are squeezed out—and eventually only the big company boats can afford to remain.

"And the worst outcome of all, at least to my way of thinking, is that without careful controls, the targeted species may finally succumb to the increased fishing pressure and collapse. Then we're left with one more chapter in the same old story—a few years of boom followed by another resounding bust, both for the fishermen and for the species they depend on for their lives."

I was still deep in thought, staring down past the fish plant, when I heard a small, almost inaudible voice coming from somewhere close behind me. "Can I come aboard? I'm about to head home—I just wanted to stop and say goodbye."

It was Shawna—although in the dropping light I hardly recognized her. She was wearing a baseball cap and a light cotton windbreaker that billowed in the breeze. Her face was nearly covered by her upturned collar and her hands were jammed deep into the pockets of her coveralls.

I invited her to step aboard and offered her a coffee. Amanda poured each of us a mug and joined us in the cockpit. We sat for several minutes in awkward silence, cradling the hot mugs in our hands, blowing steam off the tops.

"I'll be okay," said Shawna, as if someone had just asked a question. "I'm young. I'm getting an education. I'll be able to leave Seldom—make a life for myself someplace else."

"People need doctors everywhere," said Amanda.

"Especially psychiatrists," said Shawna with a little laugh. "I'll never run out of business on this island."

She gazed from face to face, then turned away with a helpless shrug. "It's not for me that I'm worried—it's for my parents. They've never been away from this village more than two days in their lives.

"It's almost funny, you know. I went with them once to St. John's to visit a cousin. We were supposed to stay there a week. But my mother started feeling a cold coming on. My father got worried about the weather. We managed to stay exactly one night before we come back home."

She blew the steam off her coffee again and took a long, slow drink. "My parents were both born in Seldom—same as their parents before them. I can't even imagine them living anyplace else. Their lives are in this village. Everything they know is in this village—everything they know how to do. I realize this may sound strange to you, coming as you do from so far away, but I'm honestly afraid it might kill them if they was ever forced to leave."

Chapter 13

Catalina

THE WEST WIND RATTLED in the treetops next morning, and the sky was filled with mares tails. I was awake before sunrise, seated at the nav-station, poring over a stack of navigational charts. The feature on the charts that I was most concerned about was a treacherous, forty-mile section of coast that lies to the east and south of Fogo Island: the infamous "Straight Shore" of Newfoundland. There are no safe harbors along this shore. The off-lying banks are dotted with low, reef-strewn islands. The waters close to the beach are shoal and filled with uncharted dangers. And at Cape Freels, at the far eastern end, there lies an area of shallow ledges and unpredictable currents so foul and uninviting that it has earned an equally foul and uninviting name from local mariners: the Stinking Banks.

The winds for the past several days had been light. The latest weather forecast, however, called for increasing westerlies, strengthening and backing into the southwest by midday, then strengthening again and increasing to southwest gales by afternoon. Ordinarily, such a forecast would be ample cause for a little sailboat like ours to remain in harbor for the rest of the day, tucked up under the lee of the land and moored securely to a strong pier. On this particular morning, however, the forecast gales seemed an advantage rather than a threat, for if the forecasters were correct (I reasoned), the wind would blow directly off the land, transforming the Straight Shore into a sheltered area of slight seas and fast, dry sailing for its entire forty-mile length.

As soon as breakfast was over and the morning chores completed, my shipmates and I cast off *Brendan's* mooring lines and pointed her bows seaward, heading south and east toward the Straight Shore and the bays of eastern Newfoundland. For the first six hours of this passage, the weather conditions developed almost exactly as the forecasters had predicted, and my decision to sail seemed a good one. The day was clear, and the wind, gusting across the land, was warm. All this began to change, however, as soon as the boat sailed clear of Cape Freels and entered the area of shoal water that extends for nearly ten miles to the east.

Here, at the gaping mouth of Bonavista Bay, the wind accelerated along the shore, gusting to well above forecast velocities. The air and water temperatures plummeted as the boat drew away from the land, and soon a cold mist streamed past the rigging, obscuring the horizon and limiting the visibility to less than a mile.

Earlier in the day, while *Brendan* was still sailing under the lee of the Straight Shore, I had asked Amanda and Richard to help me reduce the rig to a fully-reefed mainsail and spitfire jib. But now even this small amount of sail began to overpower the boat in the gusts that swirled up out of the gloom. I took over the helm as we drew abeam of the whistle buoy at Charge Rock, and I struggled to drive the boat a few more degrees to windward. Just over two miles ahead were the Stinking Banks. To the west and south of these was Bonavista Bay itself, with dozens of safe harbors at Valleyfield, Indian Bay, Deer Island, St. Brendan's, Lockers Bay, Sand Cove, and a maze of islands and thoroughfares beyond.

For an hour I battled with the helm—unwilling to admit that I had made a mistake in ignoring the morning's forecast. I tried to force the sailboat into breaking seas and keep her head to wind—but she simply would not respond. She heeled over, spilling the wind out of her sails, making more leeway than headway, and the Stinking Banks remained an obstacle that she could not surmount.

"I get a feeling we might soon be spending the night out here," hollered Amanda as the boat hobby-horsed across crooked seas.

"Might be better than breaking the rig," cried Nat.

"Or breaking ourselves," I added, realizing that the only sensible alternative at this point was to place the boat in a defensive attitude and heave-to in the mouth of Bonavista Bay.

Often during a gale at sea, a sailor must learn how to go with the flow. As the wind increases and the seas grow more chaotic, you must learn how to set aside your own agenda and surrender to the agenda that nature has prepared for you, seeking a safe compromise with the conditions at hand.

Some sailboats manage best under such conditions when they are brought head-to-wind, with a drogue or sea-anchor fastened to the bows. Others ride most comfortably when they are left to "lie ahull," as sailors say, drifting on their own in the trough of the swell with all the sails removed. And still others are best served when they're allowed to run off, powered by a tiny patch of sail to maintain steerage, dragging warps from astern to keep from running too fast down breaking seas and tripping over their own bows.

Once I had made the decision to stop and place the boat in a defensive attitude, I had little doubt about which of these tactics would serve best, for *Brendan* was a boat that could ride to a following sea better than any I had ever sailed. I asked Nat to steer downwind and put the seas on the quarter while Amanda and I went forward to rig the storm trysail. Almost immediately the boat stopped laboring. The spray that had been driving across the bows suddenly ceased. The noise of the wind dropped. The crash of waves sluicing down the decks was replaced by the hissing sound of water flowing past the taffrail. When I realized that we were still moving too fast, I asked Richard to deploy a three-hundred foot coil of spare anchor line and fasten it to a pair of cleats astern. Once this final piece of gear was in place, the boat moved off on an easy reach, slipping down the backs of seas, making her way slowly south and east.

The next twelve hours served as a break in the progression of the journey—a hiatus in which there was nothing else to do but hunker down and wait for the gale to moderate. Beginning with Nat, each member of the crew agreed to take an hour's trick at the helm. Meanwhile I remained below, on-call in case of emergency, but otherwise confined to the solitude of the cabins and the safety of my own bunk.

For hour after hour I lay pinned against the leeboard, listening to the creak of the steering cable and the rush of water along the hull, banished to the prison of my own thoughts. As I lay there, pondering the events of recent weeks, I realized that more and more often lately I had been falling into a dark mood—one that had become both more acute and more persistent as the weeks had passed. It had started, innocently enough, as a kind of vague and undifferentiated sadness—a response, I told myself, that was understandable, given the gravity of the crisis that had fallen upon this place. So many of the people I had met here were trying to cope with the same tragic occurrences in their lives: the loss of jobs, the breakup of families, the unraveling of communities, the disappearance of the single resource that had made their living possible.

Then, as the weeks had passed, this mood began to deepen. Perhaps the change had started the day I'd met with Bern Bromley in the newspaper office at St. Anthony—or the afternoon I had wandered with Nat among the ruins at Williamsport—or the morning I had talked with old Gid Sacrey on the pier at La Scie. But wherever it had started, I now found myself trying to cope with something far more painful than mere melancholy. Now, each time I visited another depopulating village or heard another tale of struggle and disappointment, I felt increasingly helpless—incapable of relieving even the smallest dimension of the human crisis that was occurring all around me. I began to feel inadequate, frustrated, angry—and with nowhere else to direct these feelings, I began to direct them inward—onto myself. I started questioning my purpose here—wondering about my motives for making this journey at all. Was there a point to all these miles—or were they like the chorus of some dark and melancholy song, full of storm and rage, repeating the same sad circumstances to no apparent end?

This was the mood I had found myself in last night after Shawna had left for home—the same mood I'd still been struggling with earlier this morning after I'd finished my breakfast and was waiting in the cockpit for my crew to complete their morning chores.

Shawna had already arrived for work at the marina as I'd stepped from the sailboat's deck and onto the gravel promenade. She was standing in front of the general store, brushing off the wooden steps with a cornstraw broom. She seemed oddly subdued, however—as if she no longer knew me—as if our meeting the previous afternoon had never taken place.

Even from a distance I could feel her discomfort, and I imagined that I could understand its cause. Yesterday for a few brief moments, she had let down her guard. She had allowed herself to reveal something deeply personal about the dislocations in her life, even as she must have realized there was nothing any of us could do to alter the circumstances that had caused them. No wonder she felt uncomfortable this morning, for now our very presence here had become a confirmation of her own vulnerability, a reminder of her pain, a challenge to her pride and self-esteem.

I wanted to say something—to assure her that the situation in Seldom wasn't as desperate as she imagined. But I knew my words would sound empty. I was a traveler, after all—a visitor from away. She and her family would remain in Seldom, at least for the near term; I and my crew would move on. She would be left to manage with a seemingly impossible dilemma. We would cast off our mooring lines and sail away.

As I stood this morning on the pier in front of the sailboat, I felt wave after wave of frustration and anger that I realized had been building in me for several weeks. I began to feel like some kind of voyeur . . . aloof . . . isolated from the realities of this place. What right did I have to be here anyway? Who had asked me to come? What was I trying to prove? I felt like a stranger, trapped in this voyeur's role that I had somehow fallen into . . . or else had fashioned for myself. Perhaps I should just give up on this voyage, I thought, return home to the States, try to forget what I had witnessed here. . . .

I was so distracted by these thoughts that I didn't even notice Shawna as she put down her broom and started moving across the pier toward me. She approached until she was standing on the edge of the wooden deck only a few feet away.

"Amanda tells me you're going to write a book," she said. The sound of her voice was so close it made me jump.

"Book? Oh well I . . . well maybe . . . ."

"Only maybe? It needs to be more than maybe . . . ."

I assured her that yes . . . yes certainly I was going to write a book. I had been thinking about it, planning it, working toward it for many years.

She smiled. "Be sure to write about Seldom in your book. Write about me, my mother, my dad. Tell people what has happened here. Tell them the good things as well as the bad. Maybe it will make a difference. Maybe somewhere, our story will help."

I gazed across the pier at the childlike figure before me and I nearly laughed out loud—for I realized that she had just turned the tables on me. Ever since yesterday I had been trying to find a way to help relieve her pain. Instead, ironically, she had just found a way to help relieve my own.

"Thank you," I said.

"For what?"

"Well . . . let's just say for being a good psychiatrist."

She looked puzzled. "Are you like the others—about to go crazy too?"

"Isn't everybody?"

We both laughed.

Shortly after midnight the fog began to lift and the wind veered into the northwest. Richard called out from the helmsman's station that he had just spotted a light flashing on the horizon far off to starboard. I climbed out of my bunk, pulled on my boots and jacket, and mounted the steps of the companionway.

The wind still whined in the rigging and the seas were still steep and confused, but the air had turned colder, and a gibbous moon had emerged from behind ragged clouds to light the decks with an eerie silver glow. The flashing light on the horizon, I explained to Richard, was the lighthouse at Cape Bonavista, a bold headland that marked the boundary between Bonavista Bay to the north and Trinity Bay to the south. If we bore off, keeping the wind on our quarter and the lighthouse on our starboard bow, we should close with the cape by sunrise. Then, with luck, we might fetch up under its lee and find safe harbor somewhere along the Trinity shore.

The night advanced through the setting of the moon and the ponderous rotation of the dipper around the northern star. Amanda followed Richard at the helm. Liz followed Amanda. The dawn crept into the eastern sky, and the shape of the land grew on the horizon like a grizzled beast emerging from the sea. The wind eased back as the sailboat doubled Cape Bonavista, then eased again as she passed a series of small headlands at Spillar's Point, Cape L'Argent, Flowers Point, North Head. Finally, as she drew abreast of a fairway buoy at Poor Shoal, the high land to the north closed in behind her and the wind dropped in earnest.

To the east, a trio of humpback whales rolled in lazy circles and blew in the scarlet dawn. To the west a set of range lights marked the entrance to Catalina harbor, a landlocked bay that provided the most secure anchorage on this coast for a dozen miles in either direction. I fired up the diesel and followed a fishing boat into a buoyed channel that led between a pair of rocky headlands to a small village. I hardly noticed the men who stood clustered on the government pier or the rafts of fishing vessels moored on either side, so eager was I to conclude this long and difficult night. I guided the sailboat into an empty berth, made a cursory check of the mooring lines, and headed below for a few hours of deep and dreamless sleep.

"Watch them boxes. Watch now, you fellas. Stay clear the truck while she's backing up!"

The voice barked orders like the sergeant of a combat platoon. I awoke to the staccato commands, punctuated by the roar of a truck engine and the hissing of air brakes. Moments later I heard a deafening crash that sounded as if the entire pier had just been buried in a landslide.

"Stand aside there. Stand clear."

I rolled out of my bunk and climbed to the sailboat's deck. A few dozen feet down the pier, a dump truck was pulling away from a mound of shaved ice that had just been deposited in the center of the pavement. Next to the ice was a blue Ford Contour, its door ajar. Inside the car, seated behind the steering wheel, was a heavyset man with large, fleshy jowls and curly black hair.

"Shovels now," the man hollered. "Make it quick. We ain't got all afternoon."

I stopped at the top of the companionway and peered about, trying to make sense of the scene before me. To my right was the man in the automobile, dressed in tan chino trousers and an orange windbreaker. To my left, just beyond the mound of shaved ice, were half a dozen others, all wearing tall rubber boots and waterproof slickers. Two of these men were offloading boxes of snow crab from a trio of skiffs that lay rafted together just ahead of the sailboat. The other four were shoveling ice into the boxes and carrying them to a refrigeration truck that was waiting a few yards farther down the pier.

The man in the automobile was obviously the job foreman. He sat spread-eagled in the driver's seat, one foot on the floor of the vehicle, one foot on the pavement. In his lap was a clipboard, filled with a stack of greasy papers. Tucked behind one ear was a large felt-tipped pen.

Amanda stood near the open door of the car, peering over the man's shoulder. The man, when he wasn't calling out orders to his crew, seemed intent on talking to her. He spoke in rapid bursts over the sounds of the loading operation, his words punctuating the evening like the quick report of rifle fire.

I stepped across the bridge deck and onto the pier. I did not move toward the car, however, for there was something about this fellow that I simply did not care to deal with this evening. Perhaps it was the way he sprawled in the automobile seat—or the way he barked his commands at the men on the pier. Perhaps it was the story that I imagined he was telling Amanda—a familiar story that I was afraid I may have heard too many times. Or perhaps it was just me—my mood, left over from the evening before. Whatever the reason, however, I decided to let my shipmate listen to the foreman's tale on her own.

I moved past the car, around the mound of shaved ice, past the men loading the crab into the waiting refrigeration truck, and down the wharf to a paved roadway that led toward the center of town. Part way up a small hill I came to an abandoned house. I sat on a broken concrete step and looked back down toward the waterfront.

There, on the right, was the government pier, surrounded by trap skiffs and cod dories, their open cockpits laden with stacks of snow crab pots. On the left was the old fish plant, abandoned now and lined with broken piers and rotting pilings. Between the two, moored stern-to along a narrow promenade, lay a row of shrimp draggers, their booms hoisted skyward, with a damaged shrimp trawl spread out on the roadway beyond.

It seemed as if the whole terrible story was here—the dilemma that my shipmates and I had learned about, episode by episode, as we had made our way around this island. The only elements not here, it seemed, were the solutions—and I suddenly found myself longing for solutions. I didn't want to have to witness another tale of loss and collapse—I wanted to learn what could be done—or was *being* done—to turn this situation around. I wanted to take a broader look at the context of this crisis—at other fisheries in other parts of the world that had faced similar difficulties—and I wanted to learn some of the strategies that people had devised to solve them.

As chance would have it, there was a place barely sixty sea miles from here where I hoped some of these solutions might be found, a place that had been at the center of the cod story for more than four hundred years and that could still be said to own that distinction: Newfoundland's provincial capital city of St. John's.

Long before this voyage had started, I had been in contact with dozens of people who lived and worked in St. John's: community leaders, fisheries managers, lawyers, scientists, politicians. Two with whom I had kept in contact during the voyage were men who had already played large roles in the unfolding drama of the cod story: retired politician and former federal fisheries minister, John Crosbie, and Memorial University marine biologist Richard Haedrich.

Crosbie, whose grandfather had founded one of the great merchant dynasties in Newfoundland, was a well known figure in island politics. He had served both the provincial and federal governments as a career politician for twenty-seven years. Near the end of this career, in April 1991, Canada's then-Prime Minister Brian Mulroney had appointed him Federal Minister of Fisheries and Oceans, a job he had held for the two critical years leading up to and following the imposition of the cod fishing moratorium. As a politician, Crosbie had always fashioned himself a friend of the fisherman ("fish don't vote; fishermen do"), yet in the end he'd become the messenger whose terrible job it had been to tell the people of Newfoundland that their fisheries had collapsed.

In contrast, Richard Haedrich was a scientist with virtually no ties to the Canadian government or to the Department of Fisheries and Oceans. He was a New Englander who had emigrated with his family to Newfoundland fifteen years earlier to teach marine biology and to pursue fisheries research at Newfoundland's Memorial University. Known by his peers as a near-fanatical champion of the fish ("My colleagues tell me that I care more about fish than people"), he was a researcher who had been studying the interactions of human and fish communities and the health and future of ocean fisheries not just in Newfoundland but all over the world.

I had corresponded with both men during this journey and had arranged to meet with each of them as soon as *Brendan* arrived in St. John's. Now, with the sailboat lying in Catalina, we were less than sixty miles from the capital city, an easy day's run. As I sat staring down at the waterfront, I made up my mind to contact both Crosbie and Haedrich that very evening. Then, on the first fair wind, I promised myself that my crew and I would sail for St. John's.

Chapter 14

St. John's

TO THE SOUTH AND WEST of Catalina harbor, the coast of Newfoundland presents itself as a series of mountainous promontories formed roughly in the shape of an "H" and connected to the rest of the island by a narrow isthmus: the Avalon peninsula. Except for a few tenacious hills that at their narrowest point measure barely two miles across, this entire land mass might have been a separate island, a kind of Newfoundland in miniature, jutting out into the north Atlantic like some gnarled carbuncle.

In fact, in many ways the Avalon peninsula *is* a separate island. Along with the nearby coasts of Trinity Bay, this is the area of Newfoundland that the earliest European visitors first explored. For numerous reasons, it is also the region that they first settled. The climate here is more temperate than in other parts of the island. The bays are long and narrow and well protected. The coasts are deeply crenellated, containing hundreds of small harbors and coves. The land, advancing southeastward into the Atlantic, is closer than any other in Newfoundland to the vast fishing grounds of the southern and eastern Grand Banks. Today nearly two thirds of Newfoundland's population, or about 350,000 people, live on the Avalon peninsula, with about 250,000 of these residing in the capital city of St. John's.

The route southward from Catalina to the Avalon peninsula takes a small vessel twenty miles across the mouth of Fortune Bay, then another twenty miles across Conception Bay to Cape St. Francis and the easternmost coast of the Avalon. A hundred years ago this would have been a busy stretch of water. In early spring the horizon would have been filled with silhouettes of sealing schooners and slab-sided factory ships as they steamed north from St. John's, heading for the great whelping patches of northeastern Newfoundland. A month later, after the pack ice had started to break up, the sealers would have been followed by hundreds of local schooners heading toward Battle Harbor and points north for a summer of fishing on the Labrador. In July and August the near shore waters would have been filled with small dories and fishing smacks working the shallow banks and headlands with their jigs and nets. And at almost any time during the navigation season, an observant mariner might have spotted the masts and billowing sails of one of the great Grand Bankers as it proceeded to the offshore ground from its home port in Lunenburg or Gloucester, Lisbon or Cadiz, Brittany or the Devon coast.

Perhaps not surprisingly, on the morning *Brendan* made this passage a century later, there was almost no traffic. A few crabbers accompanied the sailboat out of Catalina harbor before turning east and steaming out over the horizon. A whale-watching boat circled slowly under the cliffs of Baccalieu Island. Another whale-watcher circled just south of Cape St. Francis. And a few miles farther on, near the village of Torbay, a sailing yacht drove past—rail down and going fast—the first we'd seen for several weeks.

Even as *Brendan* made her final approach to St. John's, there was only the funnel of a single ship far off on the eastern horizon to signal the proximity of the largest city in Newfoundland. The coast here was bold, fronted by palisades that rose several hundred feet straight out of the sea. On their seaward face the cliffs were empty of vegetation. At their base the sea hissed and roiled, while above them a wisp of smoke, a stone tower, a cluster of antennas provided the only visible signs that less than a mile inland more than a quarter million people lived and worked.

The sailboat ran close along the shore until a lighthouse and an abandoned set of concrete gun emplacements appeared part way up the granite face. Within moments, a slender gash opened like a window in the rock. A pair of buoys appeared, marking a narrow channel. *Brendan* wheeled up between them, dropped her sails, and steamed into a large oval basin.

In another moment she found herself immersed in a confusion of shape and color and sound, surrounded by tier upon tier of warehouses and church spires, offices and public buildings: the modern-day city of St. John's.

It was eighteen hours later as I stepped off the sailboat and started walking north along the harborfront, headed for the luncheon meeting that I had arranged with the Honorable John C. Crosbie. *Brendan* was moored at the southern end of St. John's harbor, next to a large container pier, in an area where the local draggers used to lie. There were no longer any fishing boats at this end of the harbor, only an old steel sailing yacht and a handful of sightseeing boats. Several hundred yards to the north, a Cuban factory trawler lay moored against the concrete quay, her hull and superstructure rusted and tattered, the number 217 barely readable on her bow. Beyond the Cuban, a black Japanese factory ship, *Sinu Maru*, was moored at the foot of Ayre's Cove Road, under the shadow of the Scotia Centre building, where Crosbie now had his law offices.

I was admittedly anxious about this encounter with Crosbie, for I had learned of his reputation as a man with a blunt manner and a sharp, sometimes caustic tongue. We had been introduced by letter the winter before and had spoken several times on the telephone, but I'd not yet met the man in person. I had been anticipating this encounter for some time, however, and had tried to learn what I could about him, both from mutual acquaintances and from the written record, including Crosbie's own political memoirs, published just a few months earlier.

As I scurried down Harbor Drive toward the office building, I found myself trying to conjure an image of what this place must have looked like a hundred years ago when Crosbie's grandfather, Sir John Chalker Crosbie, had first come here as a young upstart businessman, intent upon breaking into the "powerful convoy of privilege" that was the fish marketing cartel in Newfoundland. In those days, neither the concrete promenade that I was walking on nor the road that paralleled it had yet been constructed. Both had been built many years later on an area of landfill that, in the elder Crosbie's days, had been host to a maze of wooden piers and warehouses and merchants' offices.

Here, perhaps in the very place I was walking, had once stood the premises of the old Duder Company, one of the largest fish merchants in Newfoundland. After the great bank crash of 1894, this company had fallen onto hard times. A few years later, after the owners had been forced into bankruptcy, young John Chalker Crosbie had acquired the premises and had founded a new enterprise, Crosbie and Company (later the Newfoundland Produce Company), that would eventually catapult him and his family into both financial and political prominence.

"Sir John" (as he preferred to be called in his later years) was one of the architects of that peculiar marriage of entrepreneurial chutzpah and political favoritism that would characterize both business and politics in Newfoundland for much of the next century. His successes as a fish merchant, ship builder, insurance broker, and shipping fleet owner elevated him into a celebrity status in which he could run for and win political office. And his influence in the political arena could then pave the way for favors that might lead to future business opportunities.

After Sir John's untimely death in 1932, his eldest son Chesley (Ches) took over the leadership of the Crosbie companies and ushered them through the tumultuous years of the Great Depression, the Second World War, the Confederation with Canada, and the first decade of the political leadership of "King Joey" Smallwood. By the time Ches died in 1961 and passed the family leadership on to his sons, the Crosbie name was associated with more than forty commercial ventures, the Crosbie payroll totaled ten million dollars and extended to some thirteen-hundred employees, and the Crosbie influence permeated the halls of power of Newfoundland.

Thus it was that young John Carnell Crosbie was born into a world of privilege that elevated him into a kind of instant renown among his fellow Newfoundlanders. The fact that the family businesses suffered several major setbacks in the decades after his father's death was not John's fault, for the business side of the family legacy had been left to the care of his younger brother, Andrew, while John chose to pursue a career in local (and eventually national) politics. Andrew, meanwhile, tried to fulfill the expectations of his famous father and shepherd the Crosbie business empire through the next several decades. By the early 1980s, however, he had managed to squander much of it through poor business decisions and risky speculations, then to lose even more through costly legal skirmishes for tax evasion and other questionable business practices. Only Andrew's death from cancer in 1991 had saved him from having to face additional charges on thirty-eight counts of theft and fraud that had been pending at the time in the Newfoundland courts.

John Crosbie appears to have had no hand in his brother's economic misadventures, nor was his political career ever seriously damaged because of the seamy side of his family's rise to (and fall from) financial prominence. He did manage to hurt *himself* any number of times during his political career, however, especially during his abortive attempt to become Prime Minister of Canada in 1983. With his quick temper and propensity to make insensitive remarks about sensitive political issues, he was constantly putting his foot in his mouth. Michael Harris, author of the official biography of the Crosbie family, describes him as "an administrative Clydesdale" who had a habit of "flattening toes of those closest to him." Joey Smallwood, who never made a secret of his dislike for John Crosbie, once called him "the most pig-headed, determined, self-willed, self-opinionated, prodigious worker I have ever met."

Especially in Newfoundland, John Crosbie's twenty-seven year political career was well documented. He had gone on record countless times to elaborate his political views, justify his actions, air his predictions about the future. His political memoirs, all five hundred pages of them, were currently being displayed on the front checkout counter of every bookstore on the island. There was a sense in which my meeting with him was certain to be redundant—for there was almost nothing about Crosbie that had not already been ferreted out by the local press, satirized by the pundits, chewed over by the general population.

Yet despite his notoriety, I wanted very much to meet this man: the heir to one of the great Newfoundland fishing fortunes, the career politician, the self-styled champion of the little guy, the bearer of the bad news, and now the private citizen who just might have more to gain (or lose) by what happened next on this island than any other person in Newfoundland.

The chrome-bordered elevator emitted a nearly imperceptible hum as it decelerated at the tenth floor of the Scotia Centre building. The doors slid open, and I stepped into a plush foyer, decorated with potted ferns and paintings of old sailing ships. A young woman dressed a tailored suit sat at a receptionist's desk beneath a gold-lettered sign: *Patterson Palmer Hunt Murphy, Atlantic Canada Lawyers.*

I approached the desk and gave the woman my name. She glanced at me with a mannequin smile. "Mister Crosbie has been expecting you," she said, gesturing toward a large mahogany door that stood ajar behind her.

I moved past the woman, knocked on the door, and stepped across the threshold and into the room. The husky, white-haired Crosbie was seated in a padded swivel chair behind a rectangular wooden desk. A pair of books were arranged side by side in front of him. One, I could see, was a copy of his recently published memoirs, *No Holds Barred.* The other was a paperback volume that looked like it might have been a scientific treatise of some sort.

"Mustn't shake hands," said Crosbie. "I have a terrible cold." He withdrew a pen from the inside pocket of his gray pinstripe suit, scribbled a signature on the title page of his memoirs, and handed me the book. "Sit down," he said, staring at a blemish on the wall behind me. "Tell me what can I do for you."

I began by trying to describe the purpose of my recent travels and to enumerate a few of the concerns that had brought me here. But Crosbie, it seemed, was already aware of the concerns that had brought me here—aware, too, that I was a writer, and that there might be a book somewhere in the offing in which he might be slated to play a part.

"The story's all there," he said, pointing at the volume in my hand. "Read my chapter on the collapse of the fishery and my years as fisheries minister. I was a victim of sloppy science—the whole department was."

I explained that I wasn't interested in dredging up the past. Everybody had made mistakes. What was done was done. I was more interested in what might be about to happen next.

Crosbie, however, seemed not to have heard me. "The scientists had a model for how the fish stocks were supposed to respond to various catch levels. They also had a commitment to rebuild the stocks—and the pressure was on to do just that. They had a lot at stake—their own reputations, their professional credibility. So when their research surveys were ambiguous—as they often were—they just selected the numbers that agreed with whatever they wanted the model to tell them."

"Are you saying that the scientists lied to you?"

"Not lied, exactly. It was more complicated than that." He picked up the second volume on the table before him and thrust it toward me. It was a book called *Fishing for the Truth*, written by Memorial University sociologist Alan Christopher Finlayson.

"Here's the best explanation I've found for what was going on with DFO science during the years leading up to the moratorium."

"I've read it."

"Then you know Finlayson's argument."

"If I remember correctly, it's a kind of sweeping indictment of the entire scientific method. He argues that there's really no such thing as unbiased scientific 'truth'—that it's always distorted by the various social and economic pressures that come to bear on the scientists themselves."

"Exactly. And when you understand that, then you'll understand the situation the Department of Fisheries was up against in the late 1980s—when our entire science branch decided to change their minds. For years they'd been assuring Ottawa that there was plenty of fish. Then, all of a sudden, they told us they'd been wrong. From a quota of 266,000 tons in 1988, they suddenly proposed a new quota of 125,000 tons in 1989. Tom Siddon was fisheries minister at the time—I was Minister of Transport. But I stood behind Tom's decision to leave the quotas essentially where they were—at least for another year."

Crosbie placed his hands in his lap and swung around in his chair until he was facing the opposite wall. "It would have been political suicide for an elected official to make a cut that large all at once. We were dealing with thousands of human beings—people with wives and families, people who live and breathe and eat and need jobs. If we'd suddenly cut the quotas in half, we'd have forced the collapse of the entire inshore fishery—or else we'd have closed the offshore and driven two of the largest seafood companies in Newfoundland into bankruptcy."

"Two years later it was far worse."

"Yes, as things turned out, that's true—but at least two years later Ottawa had had time to put together a package—something I could offer the fishermen in return. If I hadn't, I promise you, there'd have been rioting in the streets in every village in Newfoundland."

I tried to meet the former minister's gaze, but somehow he managed to keep his eyes averted.

"Now the package has ended," I said. "What happens now?"

"What happens now," said Crosbie, clearing his throat and swallowing painfully, "is that we stop all this talk about fish and take a walk down Water Street. I've made reservations in one of the best restaurants in St. John's—a place called Bianca's. My wife Jane is planning to meet us there for lunch—we're probably late already."

A quarter-hour later I followed Crosbie through a set of tinted glass doors and into a darkened dining room. A waiter dressed in beige livery greeted us at the maître d's stand and led us toward a table near the rear wall. Seated on the far side was a trim, silver-haired woman dressed in a print blouse and dark blue tailored suit. On the table in front of her was a soup tureen and a trio of china bowls.

The woman stood as we approached and flashed an easy smile. "Jane Crosbie," she said, extending her hand. "I'm so pleased to meet the intrepid American sailor at last." She leaned across the table and kissed her husband on the forehead. "You were late, John, so I ordered the cold vichyssoise and the Romanian Chardonnay. I hope you don't mind."

"I've a cold," grumbled Crosbie, massaging his throat. He cocked his head toward the waiter, who was still standing at attention behind him. "Bring me a double Scotch, ice cubes, no water."

Jane chatted amiably while the waiter hurried off to the bar. She had been shopping all morning, she said, buying clothes for a trip with her husband the following week. "John will be giving a speech to a group of Canadian businessmen about the future of Atlantic Canada. I suppose we'll need to look presentable."

I turned to the former minister just as the waiter returned with his Scotch. "I'm curious . . . just what do you think *is* the future of Atlantic Canada? Do you think there's a rejuvenated cod fishery somewhere out there? Do you think the fish will ever recover to their former numbers?"

"I'd like to say yes," said Crosbie. "But the prospects don't look good—certainly not for the next few decades—maybe not ever."

I mentioned several of the places I had visited during the past weeks: Cow Head, Port au Choix, Flowers Cove, St. Anthony, La Scie, Seldom Come By. What was going to happen in villages like these, I asked. What were the people going to do if the cod didn't recover?

"Most of the places you mention—the outports—have been in trouble for a long time. Rural Newfoundland has been living on the dole for twenty years. People there weren't able to make it even when the fish were plentiful. Now, for most of them, it's time to retrain, relocate, join the new economy . . . ."

"The new economy?"

"This province hasn't been standing still during the troubles we've had in the fishery. Take Hibernia, for example—the new oil field out on the Grand Banks. That prospect alone is projected to produce a hundred fifty thousand barrels a day when it's fully up and running. And the Terra Nova field—almost as large. And the Whiterose and the Hebron and five or six others. There's more than a billion barrels in total reserves out there, the fourth largest oil field ever discovered in Canada."

I found myself thinking about Tobias Foley, Calvin Whalen, Derrick Day, Gid Sacrey, Max Ryan. I found myself thinking about Shawna's father—sitting at home, brooding, staring at the wall. "How is Hibernia going to help the people of the outports—the little people who've been forced out by this thing?"

"Hibernia won't solve everybody's problems—that's obvious. But the oil will generate royalties for the province, new tax monies, hundreds, maybe thousands of new jobs. It's almost impossible to project the ripple effect that an industry like this can have on a place like Newfoundland."

"John is the one who kept the Hibernia project alive," said Jane, "when Ottawa was ready to abandon it. He's very proud of his record on that."

Her husband grimaced, finished his drink, signaled to the waiter to bring him another. I wanted to ask him about the dangers of exploring for offshore oil in the midst of one of the largest and most prolific ocean ecosystems in the world. I wanted to ask about the impacts of seismic testing, the noise and concussion of underwater drilling, the danger of icebergs moving through the oil fields and leading to the possibility, at least, of a lethal spill that might effect thousands of square miles of ocean habitat.

But I didn't ask about any of these things—for I realized all of a sudden that I knew what the answers were going to be. The Crosbie family's long financial involvement in the Hibernia project was, after all, a matter of public record. John's brother Andrew had been one of the founders and principal investors in Crosbie Offshore Services Ltd., the first large service company to run material and supplies out to the drill rigs. His maternal grandfather had purchased a huge tract of land at Freshwater Bay back in the early 1980s, in the expectation that some day it might become the site of a massive supply base to the Hibernia project. His sons, Ches and Michael, were both St. John's lawyers with clients whose businesses and professional activities were dependent in various ways upon the oil patch. His family's financial future—as well as his own political past—was intimately tied to the growth and development of offshore oil in Newfoundland.

Seeking a way to make polite conversation, I turned to my hostess as she poured each of us a glass of Romanian Chardonnay. "It seems Hibernia may turn out to be the crowning achievement in your husband's political career."

"Yes, isn't it wonderful," she said, passing me a bowl of cold vichyssoise. "We have such promising times to look forward to. I think John should be so proud of what he has accomplished, don't you?"

The afternoon was overcast and the sky was spitting rain as I said goodbye to the Crosbies half an hour later in front of the restaurant and started walking north along Water Street. My original plan had been to travel on foot up the mile or so of steep, winding streets that led to the university—to give my body time to digest the meal I had just eaten and to give my brain a chance to process the hour I had spent with the former fisheries minister. As the rain began to fall harder, however, I waved down a taxi. Several minutes later I found myself pulling up in front of a small, unadorned brick building at number Four Clark Place—the headquarters of Memorial University's Eco Research Program and the offices of Professor Richard Haedrich.

I paid the cabbie, scurried across the weed-filled yard, and knocked on the front door. When I saw that it was ajar, I stepped into a hallway cluttered with file chests and boxes of books and papers. In a small room on the left sat two young women working over a pair of computer terminals. In a doorway at the end of the hall stood a man wearing an open collar shirt, gray down vest, and faded chino trousers. He was slender, with an athletic build, light blue eyes, and close-cropped, sandy blond hair, flecked with gray. In spite of the tortoise shell reading glasses perched part way down his nose, his face had a boyish look to it, and he exuded a youthful energy that I'm certain would have rivaled that of most of his students.

He stepped around a carton of books and grabbed my elbow. "Take a look at this," he said, as if we'd been interrupted in the midst of an ongoing conversation. He held up a graph printed on a sheet of cardboard that he had clutched in his hand. FISHERIES EVOLVE, the title read, AS THE FISH COMMUNITY IS CHANGED. "It's the simplest idea in the world when you think about it—the way the fish and the fishermen interact. Trouble is. . . most of us never bother to think about it."

Thus began one of the most frenetic, exhilarating, disturbing encounters I'd experienced all summer. Haedrich, whom I had met only briefly during a visit to St. John's the previous winter, was a man on a mission. His mind seemed always to be several moves ahead of his tongue, and he often appeared slightly out of breath, so eager was he to share whatever he was thinking.

I was aware of his interest in the relationships between human and fish communities, for I had read several of his papers on the subject. Much like his colleague Jon Lien (the Whale Man), Haedrich understood that human beings were powerful predators who were often the cause of profound dislocations in the natural systems in which they participated. He also knew that we had a habit of making exceptions of ourselves—of envisioning our behavior as being somehow above or beyond or outside the rest of nature.

"The hunter who thinks of himself as disconnected from the natural world will never understand when the number of his prey begins to decrease," said Haedrich. "It will always seem a mystery . . . a 'natural cycle' that he is helpless to control. It's a mindset, you see . . . a kind of convenient amnesia. If you forget that you're a part of the larger system, then you needn't feel responsible for your actions. When one population of prey collapses, you just move on to the next . . . ."

Two of the fisheries I had discussed with Haedrich during the previous winter were the northern shrimp and the snow crab. Both were examples of the concept illustrated in his graph: the "downward" shift in fish populations (and thus of fisheries) once the top predator has been removed. "The scary thing," he said as he led me along the cluttered hallway, "is that nothing fundamental has changed. These two emergent fisheries are being 'managed' in many of the same ways as the northern cod. 'Exploited' might be more to the point. It's going on ten years after the cod collapse, and the people at DFO don't seem to have learned a damn thing."

Haedrich rolled his eyes when I told him I had just finished having lunch with John Crosbie. "I'm not sure whether you're aware," I said, "but Crosbie blames the scientists for many of the troubles he had when he was fisheries chief. He claims they were unwilling—or unable—to provide his managers with accurate estimates of the remaining cod stocks."

Haedrich turned without speaking to a file cabinet behind him and withdrew a printout of an article from a prestigious Canadian scientific publication, the *Canadian Journal of Fisheries and Aquatic Sciences*. "Have you read this?" he asked, thrusting the article toward me. "It's an editorial piece that a young biologist named Jeff Hutchings and I collaborated on about a year ago. Probably one of the few things I've ever written in which I actually agree with John Crosbie."

I indicated that I had not read the piece—although I did know Jeff Hutchings. I also knew of Jeff's battle with the DFO several years back over a paper he had written about seals and cod.

"Jeff is an excellent fisheries biologist—one of the best we have. He left the DFO when he finally realized that he simply couldn't *do* science in that kind of setting. Too often he was a dissenting voice— and in the government system, dissenting voices were not acknowledged. The managers there practiced what they called 'consensus science'—only the majority voice was counted, and only one set of advice went forward to the minister.

"Crosbie was right, you see—or at least he was right as regards his own scientists. There was tremendous pressure within his department for consensus. Science thrives on controversy—but at the DFO, controversy was a no-no. The dissenting voices—like Jeff's—were either silenced or drummed out of the corps, and only the party line was allowed to be heard."

I continued, following Haedrich's line of reasoning. "So when the party line was in error, there was no mechanism to correct it. The error was permitted to grow until it became dangerously large . . ."

large enough, finally, to cause scientists there to miss the collapse of an entire species."

"Incredible, isn't it," said Haedrich. "Even now it seems hard to believe."

He frowned and turned away. I waited in a kind of embarrassed silence while he fidgeted with a bronze paperweight on his desk.

"What can people do now?" I asked at last. "What changes do we need to make so that the same sequence of events won't simply repeat itself again and again, fishery after fishery, until there's nothing left?"

Haedrich squeezed his eyes closed and rubbed his temples with his thumbs. "One obvious place to start is to do what Jeff and I and others have suggested—remove the scientists from the government payroll—establish an independent scientific advisory board for the fisheries managers to answer to.

"There are other ideas, too—good ones. We could set up seasonal fisheries and no-fish zones to protect known spawning areas. We could establish individual quotas to discourage wasteful competition on the fishing ground. We could crack down on hi-grading, impose large fines for the dumping of by-catch, restrict the use of otter trawls and other destructive fishing technologies . . . ."

He looked at me with a pained smile. "Trouble is, even in a place like Newfoundland where we've experienced the problem first hand, people are only paying lip service to ideas like these. In reality, very little is changing.

"Listen to the way people talk—fishermen, scientists, managers, almost everybody who works in the fisheries. We talk about *fish stocks*—not species or populations but *stocks*, as if the fish were a commodity reserved for our own private consumption—as if we might 'stockpile' them until we need them—as if, after they're gone, we might simply 'restock' and start all over.

"Or listen again: we don't just talk about catching fish, we talk about *harvesting* them—as if the fish had somehow been 'planted,' like corn or cotton, and now we were simply gathering in what was rightfully ours.

"Or how about *by-catch*, the term used almost universally to describe the unwanted species that collect in a fisherman's nets. *By-kill* would seem to be a lot closer to the truth—for all but a few are dead or dying by the time they've been dumped back into the sea."

He turned and stared out the window at the rain. "Do you

understand what I'm talking about? I'm not complaining about habits of speech. I'm talking about something much more basic, something cultural perhaps, embedded deep in our collective mindset. The words give us away. They signal something fundamental about how we think about ourselves and our relationship with the fish.

"Can we change?"

"Well that's the million dollar question, isn't it? I've been investigating fisheries all over the world . . . in North America, Europe, Africa, South America, Asia, the Pacific archipelagos. I wish I could tell you that there's good news, that people have learned from what's been happening in places like Newfoundland. But the truth is, with very few exceptions, the story's the same almost everywhere you look. Coastal fisheries decimated. Massive populations of forage fish ground into fertilizer and animal feed. Newly discovered deep demersal species like orange roughy and Peruvian sea bass depleted so fast that scientists can't even learn the fish's biology before the species is fished out.

"Can we change? I don't know. We have the ability, I know that much. We're one of the most adaptable creatures on earth. We're what biologists call a 'red queen' species—like geese or cod— capable of altering our behavior dramatically in response to changing circumstances, once we perceive the need. *But at what point will we finally perceive the need?*—that's the real question. And will it be in time to reverse the damage we've done—or will the natural systems that we've exploited be so indelibly altered as to be beyond retrieval?"

The rain had stopped and the light was almost gone from the sky as Haedrich and I stepped out onto the front doorstep of his office building several hours later. We had talked most of the afternoon, circling around a set of questions that neither wished to leave unanswered, searching for solutions that, in the end, eluded both of us.

He pulled the door closed behind him and fiddled with a key. "I'd offer you a lift to the harbor," he said, "but I only have my bicycle—and I'm afraid the passenger seat's a little small."

I laughed, thanked him for the hours he had spent with me,

explained that I'd rather walk to the harbor anyhow. It was all downhill, I said, and I needed a chance to clear my brain and try to organize all the pieces of this strange, unsettling day. Haedrich mounted his bicycle, waved, and rode off into the darkness. I waited until he had disappeared around a corner, then set off on foot in the opposite direction.

For a time I simply followed my nose. Whenever I came to an intersection, I merely chose the direction that led downhill, for I knew that the harbor was somewhere below. I passed through neighborhoods that mimicked the tumultuous history of this city: a stately promenade of mansions, a public park, a street of wooden row houses, a line of tumbledown shops and boarded storefronts. At last I came to a darkened alley with steep stone steps, then to a street lined with offices and souvenir shops, and finally, down one last block, to the harbor itself.

I crossed the road that paralleled the harborfront, stepped to the edge of the concrete promenade, and stared out at the dark surface of the water. Was this the end of my search, then? Had I finally arrived at the political and economic and scientific center of the cod story, only to discover that the answers I had been seeking were still as elusive as ever? This afternoon I had been confronted by two utterly dissimilar personalities: one the career politician, calloused, opportunistic, informed by three generations of economic self-interest; and the other the scientist and academician, objective, self-effacing, steeped in the idealism of the enlightenment, stalked by the ever-present specter of despair.

Crosbie, for one, had come as no surprise. With the family that had nurtured him and the social setting in which he had been raised, how could he have been otherwise? For nearly a hundred years his father and grandfather had pursued the entrepreneurial dream. From salt cod to seal pelts, from whale oil to fish meal pellets, the Crosbie companies had always managed to stay one step ahead of the island's dwindling resource base. Now that the cod was gone, what could be more sensible than to turn one's attention to the hottest new commodity in the province and get involved in the oil patch?

In reality, Crosbie was little different than the rest of us. He was simply living by the rules that the majority of people in western society live by. He may have started with a few more advantages than most—a famous name, a bit of inherited wealth, a position of social prominence—but otherwise he was simply trying to maximize his gain and look out for his own. Like many of the fishermen who had once formed the basis of his political constituency, he was gearing up for the next windfall, making sure that when the time came to head back out to the banks, he would be in line to bring back his share of the "catch."

In contrast, the afternoon that I'd spent with Dick Haedrich had been far less predictable, far more unsettling. I liked Haedrich. He was intelligent and eager and disarmingly honest. His concern for the fish was both extreme and uncompromising—and thereby open to all manner of misinterpretation. Yet to understand it, one had merely to understand that it was rooted in an even deeper concern for the people who had once depended on the fish—and who were now faced with the terrible consequences of their disappearance.

For my own part, I was convinced that Haedrich was on the right track—that if we were ever to turn this thing around, we would need to change ourselves—and indeed our entire society—in profound and indelible ways. Yet I also sensed how preposterous such a notion was, at least in the near term. I wanted to think of Haedrich as a voice of reason who might help to guide the rest of us toward solutions. Instead I feared that he might simply be a voice in the wilderness, a Quixotic tilter at windmills, brandishing his words against the dragons in our midst before riding off ineffectually into the night.

I gazed out into the black waters of the harbor, fighting off the temptation to surrender to cynicism or despair. The solutions, when they came, were not going to be simple—no one had ever suggested that they were. Newfoundland's debt for the pillaging of the northern cod was not going to be paid in six short years. Indeed, it might not be paid in six times six years—perhaps not even in the lifetimes of every person living on this island.

I had thought this visit to St. John's might provide a conclusion to this summer's journey. I had thought my meetings with Crosbie and Haedrich might resolve a few of the questions that had followed me around these coasts and effect some kind of closure. But now, as I stared out at the darkened harbor, I understood that there would be no such closure, no such neat tying-up of loose ends.

I would find no easy solutions to the crisis in Newfoundland— this much was now clear. But perhaps, I thought, I might still find a means to complete this voyage in another way—by closing the circle and concluding the geographical journey I had set out to make. I might sail again to La Poile, the village my crew and I had visited when we'd first come to this island many years before, and I might try again to locate the old fisherman, Henry Coyne.

I'd recently learned that the cod fishery had been reopened in La Poile on an experimental basis. What this meant, despite the controversy still raging in scientific circles, is that the villagers would be fishing again. Even now, Henry would be out somewhere in the broad reaches of La Poile Bay. He would be setting his trawls and filling his dory with fish—just as he'd been doing when I'd first met him eleven years ago—and I suddenly realized that before I left this island, I wanted to witness this simple act again.

I looked down the harbor along the concrete pier to the hulking form of the Japanese factory ship. A quarter mile past the ship, I could just make out the familiar shape of *Brendan's* mast and rigging, framed against the flickering lights of the city. Tomorrow, I decided, we would put to sea again, *Brendan* and her crew and I, to sail three hundred miles, double three stormy capes, and complete the circumnavigation that I had promised we would make. We would not sail this time in search of solutions—for I had learned that these would not be forthcoming—but to close a circle, fulfill a pledge, and pay our respects to an old friend.

Chapter 15

La Poile

THE FOG LAY DRAPED in a soft gray blanket over the surface of the sea. Moisture dripped from the sailboat's rigging. The dawn crept into the still morning, rising in increments like footlights rising over a darkened stage. Aboard the boat, the only sounds were the hissing of the bow wave and the swirl of water tailing off the stern, while close ahead a fog whistle moaned its lonely message, insistent and forlorn.

Brendan's Isle had been underway for two and a half days. The first day had been a nasty slog into head seas and gale force winds. At Cape Race the wind had eased and backed into the south, and the sailboat had reached off toward the Burin Peninsula and the French islands of St. Pierre and Miquelon. Finally the wind had dropped in earnest, and she had crept for a long foggy night across the St. Pierre and Burgeo Banks toward the bold southwest coast of Newfoundland.

The fog whistle sounded again, close on the starboard bow. On the radar screen I could just make out the shape of Ireland Island, marking the entrance to La Poile Bay. But close at hand, in the area where the whistle buoy should have been, I saw only fleeting apparitions—half a dozen vague images, appearing and disappearing on the screen, as if the bay were being guarded by a flotilla of ghosts.

I was just about to send a lookout to the bow when the nearest of the radar images materialized out of the gloom. It was a dory, rising and falling in the oily swell. Seated on the center thwart was a man in yellow oilskins, hauling hand over hand on a long baited line. Behind him was another, similarly dressed, pulling a large cod off one of the hooks. Both men waved as the sailboat passed. The man on the center thwart flashed a toothy grin and pointed down into the belly of the dory. It was filled to the tops of his boots with fish.

The fog began to lift as *Brendan* made her way past the lighthouse at Ireland Island. Slowly the shape of the land appeared—the white curl of surf, the abrupt shape of boulders along the shore, the loom of dark hills beyond—and as it did so, I was treated to a spectacle that I had not seen all summer. The bay, from shore to shore, was filled with working fishing boats. A trap skiff with a small home-built cuddy was steaming south just beyond the ledges at the Naked Man. An open dory was setting its trawls near the mouth of La Plante Harbor. Two more were working under Eastern Point, while another was traveling north toward Christmas Head and the village of La Poile.

I will not say that I was taken by surprise by all this fishing activity, for I had been told about the experimental ground fishery that had been opened along this coast. Yet the experience of actually seeing the boats—after nearly two months of deserted bays and empty seas—came as a shock. The wind drew ahead, the fog lifted in earnest, and I stared dumbfounded at the scene before me. Perhaps I'd just passed through some kind of time warp, I thought, and the calendar had somehow been set back a dozen years. Or perhaps this whole experience of the disappearing fish had never happened—perhaps I'd been asleep, like some nautical Rip Van Winkle, and was just now waking from a terrible dream.

A hazy circle of sun emerged from behind a layer of cloud as Amanda and Nat and Liz finished securing the sailboat to an empty pier across from the village on the south side of La Poile harbor. The scene at the fish plant, several hundred yards to the north, was chaotic. At any given moment half a dozen dories jostled for position in front of the plant while another two or three lay moored along the pier face. In each of the moored boats a man stood in the bows, throwing fish onto the deck of the pier. Others gathered the stiffened carcasses and carried them over to a long stainless steel table, where a row of rubber-suited filleters split and gutted them, then slid them down a chute toward a group of women and boys who iced and packed them in large, flat plastic boxes.

It seemed as if the entire village had gathered at the fish plant this morning. Half of those assembled appeared to have some sort of assigned job, while the other half stood clustered about in small groups, watching the mayhem. Even from a few hundred yards away, the feeling of excitement was palpable. Each time another dory approached the pier, there was a murmur of anticipation. Children clapped and danced and tugged at their mothers' skirts. Teenage boys posed self-consciously, trying to look as if they were the ones who had caught the fish. Elderly men clambered up on boxes and craned their necks to see how deeply each boat was laden.

For a time I watched this scene with the same feeling of excitement, for it was like watching a large family gathered to open gifts on Christmas morning. But slowly, inevitably, I was overtaken by a different response: a deep, almost inexpressible feeling of foreboding. I had been communicating for many months with fisheries scientists—both those who were being paid by the Canadian government and those who were not—and I knew about their concerns. As one might expect, most government scientists were "guardedly optimistic" about the reopening of this coast, as they were, after all, the ones who had collectively authorized it. The non-government scientists, however, were almost unanimously opposed.

Ram Myers, who until recently had been one of the DFO's senior marine biologists, described himself as "shocked" when he'd learned of the government's decision to reopen this coast. "There is no evidence that I've seen indicating that the fish stocks have rebounded," he said. "In fact, there are many signs that point the other direction." He then added, "As far as I can see, nobody up there [at the Department of Fisheries] has learned anything."

Jeff Hutchings, now a colleague of Myers at Dalhousie University, shared the older scientist's concern. "Let's not forget that Mifflin [the current federal fisheries minister] made the decision to reopen this coast just ten days before the election call. Was it a political move? Mifflin claims it wasn't, but it's hard to imagine that it could have been otherwise, especially as there was so little hard evidence to justify his decision."

Perhaps the most outspoken opponent of the reopening with whom I had spoken was Dick Haedrich. In a recent paper, he had raised questions about the actions of government fisheries managers, arguing that based on existing models, their recommended quota for this coast was several times higher than a prudent "precautionary approach" would support.

In conversation, Haedrich explained the reasons for his concern. "The DFO never did any formal risk analysis—they just estimated the cod's total biomass, then set the quota at twenty percent. The problem, as anybody who has studied cod biology can tell you, is that these fish reproduce at an average annual rate of about eighteen and a half percent. What this means—based on the DFO's own projections—is that people out there are actually fishing the local cod populations *down* again. And if government estimates of total biomass are too high, as many of us fear, then the fish may be heading for another collapse—perhaps their last."

As I stood on *Brendan's* foredeck, staring across at the fish plant and contemplating the scientists' dire predictions, I failed to notice a dory emerging from behind a headland at the harbor mouth. With all the noise and activity at the plant, I didn't hear the rumble of her outboard, either, as she proceeded down the narrow cove toward the sailboat. Moments later the dory pulled alongside, and I felt an odd sensation of someone staring at me. I turned, and with a start I found myself gazing down into a grizzled face framed in a gray beard and a shock of steel gray hair. "Henry," I said. "Henry Coyne!"

The old man leered up at me with a mischievous grin. "You like fish, Cap?" he said. Then with the same careless gesture that he'd used as he had greeted me and *Brendan* a dozen years ago, he grabbed a fat cod from the heap at his feet and tossed it over the gunwale and onto the sailboat's deck. I laughed, thanked him, told him what a lovely fish it was, promised we would make a meal of it that very evening.

"Take as many as you wish," he said with a swagger in his voice. "There's plenty where this one come from."

I thought at first that the old man might be in a hurry to get over to the plant and offload his morning's catch. But he seemed content just to stand knee-deep in fish and visit for a time. "Fish plant can wait," he said, shutting down his outboard engine and accepting the mug of coffee that Amanda poured for him.

We talked about all the predictable topics: the weather, his family, the voyage that *Brendan* and her crew had made this past summer. But most of all we talked about the fish. The coast had been open since June, he said. It was a kind of fishing free-for-all, with a single quota for the whole region. When the quota was filled, the region was closed—no more fishing until the following month.

In response to my question about the quantity of cod that he and the others had been finding out in the bay, he cast his eyes down into his dory. "Plenty of fish, as anybody can see . . . though to be truthful, Cap, there was more in June than in July . . . more in July than in August . . . ."

"Some scientists are saying there may not be enough cod out there to sustain this fishery—even for only a few days a month."

He stood for several seconds in silence, pursing his lips and rubbing his hands on the front of his coveralls. "You wasn't in La Poile during all the years when the fish was gone. You didn't see the people, walking around like they was half-dead, going through the motions, acting like there wasn't any point to it all. But now . . . just look at them now. Even though it's only a few days . . . it's like somebody give this community a new chance at life. . . ."

The old fisherman turned toward the sailboat again and leaned against the gunwale. He folded his fingers, one across the other, in a gesture of supplication. "We only needs a little. Only takes a few fish to keep a community like this going. Maybe fifty, maybe a hundred ton. A single dragger can take that much in a week. Surely there's enough fish to keep a few small dories working in this bay. Surely there's enough to give the people here another chance."

In the early evening as the light was dropping in the west, the men of the village began appearing on the wharves again, for now was time to bait the trawls and set them out in the bay for the night. I had just finished my supper and was sitting alone in *Brendan's* cockpit, sipping on a cup of coffee, listening to the sound of voices, watching the shadows grow across the harbor.

All day my shipmates and I had been over in the village. We had taken the rubber boat across to join the crowd of onlookers as Henry offloaded his fish, then to visit with him for an hour up in the kitchen of his little cottage. We had talked with his neighbors, visited with his daughter at the dry goods store where she worked, played a game of catch with a group of children on the government wharf.

Now, as the shadows grew longer and darkness settled over the village, I felt the spell that such a place can often weave—a spell in which the present seems to lose its hold and ordinary time becomes distorted. In spite of the small generating station that supplied electric power to the village, most of the buildings remained dark. The silhouettes of dories moving across the harbor and the shadowy figures of men working on their decks stood out in sharp relief against the glassy surface of the water. Except for the occasional rattle of an outboard engine, this might have been a scene from a hundred or two hundred or even three hundred years ago. I squeezed my eyes closed, trying to imagine it so.

And then I looked again. And what I saw was so fragile and so rooted in the present moment that it almost stopped my breath: a tiny village at the edge of a windswept island, perched on the brink of a catastrophe. Would this village—or any of the others like it around the vast, rugged perimeter of this island—be able to survive another year, I wondered? Would it be able to survive another ten? Would the fish that remained next winter somehow manage to replenish themselves? Would they run up the bay again next spring, and again the spring after that? Would the children clap and dance and would the old men clamber up on boxes and crane their necks to watch the boats come in? And would the boats be laden up to the tops of the fishermen's boots with beautiful fat fish?

I looked again at the darkened wharves and the murky shapes of men and dories moving about the harbor. And I squeezed my eyes closed, trying to imagine it so.

Epilogue

FIVE FISHING SEASONS HAVE COME AND GONE since *Brendan's Isle* and her crew and I have concluded our circumnavigation of Newfoundland and returned safely home. In the interim, although I have not traveled back to the island, I have continued to correspond with friends in Newfoundland, peruse the scientific literature, and follow the fate of the northern cod. And finally I have also completed this second, infinitely more difficult circumnavigation, putting pen to paper to conclude the written voyage which has become this book.

For many such literary journeys, a hiatus of several years might find the issues clouded, the cast of characters displaced, the warnings passé, the ideas blunted and stale. Would that this were so. Would that I could report at the conclusion of this narrative that the fish were on the rebound, that the village economies had been rejuvenated, that the big fish companies had learned restraint, that the fishermen had gained a new respect for the needs of the species they hunted, that the government scientists and fisheries managers, having learned from their mistakes, were now instituting conservation measures that would protect and sustain fish populations into the future.

Sadly, none of these events has come to pass. In many ways both the plight of the people of Newfoundland and the crisis in their fisheries have only worsened since the new century began. After a series of limited (politically motivated?) re-openings of the cod fishery along various portions of the Newfoundland coast between 1998 and 2002, and in response to continuing bad news from official stock surveys, the DFO decided once again to close the northern, western, and eastern coasts of Newfoundland to all forms of cod fishing in April 2003. That same spring, at a meeting of the Committee on the Status of Endangered Wildlife in Canada (or COSEWIC) in Whitehorse, Yukon, the northern cod was officially designated an "endangered species" ("a species facing imminent extirpation or extinction")—the first time in Canadian history that a major population of saltwater fish has been so designated. At the same meeting several other breeding populations of Atlantic cod were also adjudged to be seriously at risk. The so-called Laurentian North population (or Gulf cod) was assessed as "threatened," while both the Arctic cod and the Maritime (or Scotian shelf) cod were assessed as being "of special concern." In all three of the latter fisheries the remnant cod populations have been estimated to stand at between five and ten percent of their original, pre-industrial fishing biomass. The remnant population of the northern cod has been estimated to stand at less than one half of one percent of its original, pre industrial fishing biomass.

For the most part, the ongoing story of the people of the outports has been equally discouraging. After several summers of limited inshore "hook and line" fishing, the dories and trap skiffs of La Poile (including Henry Coyne's) were once again confined to their moorings during the summer of 2003. There was no cod shipped out of the fish plant that year, no self-conscious posturing of teenage boys, no clapping and dancing of little children, no craning of necks by the old men as the boats came in.

In Flowers Cove Jock Gardiner considered himself lucky to have found part time work as an electrician after he stopped running the *Craig and Dianne* out to the shrimping grounds in 2002. His sons David and Michael took over the boat in the summer of 2003, only to find themselves tied up to a pier for eight straight weeks during the height of the summer fishery. The reason for the stoppage was simple: the wholesale price for northern shrimp had dropped so low that none of the draggers from Flowers Cove or the Belle Isle Strait area could afford the fuel to steam out to the fishing grounds.

According to Bern Bromley (now retired), the shrimp processing plant in St. Anthony has found itself in similar trouble. In all the east coast fishing zones, the catch limits for northern shrimp have been raised repeatedly by the DFO. The resulting increase in landed product, combined with a mysterious drop in the average size of the shrimp and a new import tariff imposed by the European Economic Union, have led to the price collapse that curtailed openings of the plant throughout 2003. As the plant lay idle, complaints of "overcapacity" in the processing sector fueled an impassioned debate and called into question the recent construction of similar plants all over Newfoundland.

The news from the snow crab fishery is marginally better. Shawna Payne's father, still living in Seldom, has returned to landing his two-hundred-forty pounds per week, although at an average two dollars a pound, he is just barely able to pay his overheads and show a slim profit. According to recent DFO stock status reports, the favorable conditions that have supported this price are projected to hold up, at least for the near term. Such forecasts, tentative as they may be, are nevertheless reassuring, for with no cod quotas for the foreseeable future, small boat operators such as Shawna's father will be dependent on the snow crab for virtually all their commercial fishing income.

In the world of fisheries science, an event of major importance took place in the spring of 2003 when marine biologist Ram Myers, along with colleague and co-author Boris Worm, published a study in the journal *Nature* about the catastrophic decline in the biomass of virtually every one of the world's large ocean species since the beginning of modern commercial fishing. Readers may recall that Myers began his career working as a research scientist for the DFO in St. John's. Then, after leaving his government post, he spent much of the decade of the 1990s critiquing his old employer, debunking DFO science, and placing the blame for the collapse of the northern cod directly upon the policies and actions of DFO management.

"In the past several years my focus has become more global," says Myers. "I've come to understand that the collapse of the Grand Banks fisheries is only one part of the picture. It's just the tip of the iceberg really. Our new research took a decade just to gather all the numbers. We used catch records and survey data collected by governments and fishing companies going back fifty years and more—records that had been all but lost to the scientific record."

What Myers and his colleague discovered in their data was that fully ninety percent of the biomass of all large ocean species, including cod, halibut, marlin, tuna, swordfish, and many large sharks, have disappeared from the world's oceans in recent decades. In every ocean in the world, in every major ocean fishery, the story has been the same. Once industrialized fishing interests have moved in to a new area, the fish biomass of targeted species has typically been reduced by eighty percent within the first fifteen years of fishing effort. Under the pressure of continued fishing, most populations have declined another ten percent, while others (like the northern cod) have disappeared to the point of extinction, belying the ocean's long-held reputation of being a renewable resource of nearly infinite proportions.

Part of the problem, argues Myers, is the matter of "shifting baselines," in which managers and fishermen alike keep on redefining "normal" as they adapt to increasingly degraded ecosystems. "Collectively, we succumb to a kind of global memory loss," says Myers, "forgetting just how many fish once roamed the sea and how large they once were. What this means is that fishing's impact on ocean ecosystems has been continually underestimated, so that even our best restoration efforts have been using targets that are way too low.

"One of our aims with this study," Myers adds, "has been to find the missing baseline—the *real* baseline—so that scientists, conservationists, government commissions, fisheries managers can recalibrate the models they've been using and begin to comprehend the true magnitude of the destruction that's taken place."

A fishery nearer home that has undergone the sort of degradation Myers is talking about is the American east coast ground fishery in the Gulf of Maine and the Georges Bank. Like the Newfoundland fisheries, like fisheries everywhere, the shelf waters and offshore banks of New England have been literally decimated in the last several decades, as first the foreign factory trawlers and then a new fleet of American built super-trawlers have scoured the fishing grounds, leaving only remnant populations of pollock and haddock and cod and a desperate industry that has retreated in numbers and shrunken in size, just as the fish have done.

While Myers has been documenting the global scale of the crisis, another scientist who has become familiar to readers of these pages, Jeff Hutchings, has been concentrating on factors that may influence recovery.

"It's not time to throw up our hands in surrender," says Hutchings, "—not yet anyhow.

"The first steps toward solutions involve raising consciousness, getting fishermen and scientists, politicians and ordinary citizens to realize that there are some very serious problems out there and that they affect us all. The second step is to do what Ram and others have been trying to do: to step back, take longer view, recalibrate our measuring sticks so as to become aware of the true extent of the destruction. The third step, the one I've been focused on for the last few years, has to do with trying to understand the specific factors that lead to a fishery's collapse and the strategies that can be employed to control or repair the damage."

In enumerating such strategies, Hutchings talks about the need for setting realistic recovery targets and well-informed time frames. He focuses on the Canadian experience and he emphasizes the practical, yet he also joins a chorus of scientific and environmental voices around the globe who are beginning to call for a "new ocean ethic," a paradigm shift in which the world ocean becomes transformed, in the words of American fisheries administrator Andrew Rosenberg, "from a place that we use to a place that we care for."

If there is one insight that I, as a citizen of this planet, have taken home from my journeys to Newfoundland, it is that the events that have taken place there are not unique. Their roots and analogues are everywhere around us, and the same crisis threatens virtually every nation and every major population center on the planet.

In a very real sense we are all Newfoundlanders. Their dilemma is our own. Their frustration is our own. The difficult choices that they face as they try to resolve the crisis in their fisheries are the choices we all face as we try to determine how to live sustainably on a planet that is fragile and finite and surprisingly small. We can choose to ignore these events and pay the inevitable price of our ignorance—or we can decide to pay attention, internalize the lessons that they teach, and strive together to become custodians of a world ocean that may one day become whole again.

Notes and Sources

Prologue

p. 8 *The fish had been growing*: The term "fisher" has become the generally accepted form among scientists and sociologists in recent decades for describing the men and women who work in the world fisheries. This term has the advantage of including all such workers rather than those of only one sex, and has thus gained currency in the scientific and professional literature. For most Newfoundlanders, however, a "fisher" is a kind of weasel (*mustela pennanti*), a relative of minks and otters, formerly valued for its fur. The people who go to sea to catch fish for a living (both men and women) still conceive of themselves almost universally as "fishermen."

As this book is in part a work of oral history, I have chosen to remain with the common usage throughout. It was a woman from the little village of La Scie, let it be noted, who once famously proclaimed: "I won't be referred to as a fisher by no damn bureaucrats or politicians from Ottawa. I'm a fisherman and proud of it."

p. 8 *Crosbie's voice droned on*: Canadian news coverage of the protest by fishermen in the Radisson hotel lobby was extensive, appearing the following morning in both video and print media all over the country. For one such report, see "Anger Greets Two-Year Ban on Cod Fishing," Ottawa *Citizen*, July 3, 1992, p. 1, final edition.

Chapter 1

p. 21 *Many of the local fishermen*: Michael Harris describes Cabot Martin as "the poet laureate of the inshore fishery" in his exposé of the seamy politics surrounding the cod collapse, *Lament for an Ocean: The Collapse of the Atlantic Cod Fishery: A True Crime Story*, McClelland & Stewart Inc., Toronto, 1998, p.150.

p. 21 *I first came to know*: reference in this paragraph is to Cabot Martin, *No Fish and Our Lives: Some Survival Notes for Newfoundland*,

Creative Publishers, St. John's, Newfoundland, 1992. This book contains columns and editorials published in the weekly St. John's *Sunday Express* between March 1989 and May 1991.

p. 22 *One reason for the*: Personal communications with Cabot Martin in this and following paragraphs took place during an interview with the author on February 4, 1999.

p. 22 *"The tiger retreats*: Cabot Martin, "Scientists Voice Fear for the Barren Seabed," St. John's *Sunday Express*, May 19, 1991, as reprinted in Martin, op. cit., p. 28.

p. 23 *A little over a year*: Cabot Martin, personal communication, as p. 22.

p. 23 *"Next time you are down*: Cabot Martin, "Should We Let the Draggers at the Cod Again?" in St. John's *Evening Telegram*, Sept. 27. 1998, p. 11.

p. 23 *I spoke with Martin*: Cabot Martin, personal communication, as p. 22.

Chapter 2

p. 32 *It is easy when*: the history of the European settlement of Newfoundland that follows derives primarily from two sources: D.W. Prowse, *History of Newfoundland from the English Colonial and Foreign Records*, Macmillan and Co., London, 1895 (hereinafter "Prowse"), and Frederick W. Rowe, *A History of Newfoundland and Labrador*, McGraw-Hill Ryerson Limited, Toronto, 1980 (hereinafter "Rowe").

p. 33 *The huge numbers of cod*: Early names and references to Newfoundland are from Farley Mowat, *The New Founde Land: A Personal Voyage of Discovery*, McClelland & Stewart, Toronto, 1989, p. 65.

p. 34 *Slowly, however, patterns*: for "winter crews," Prowse, p. xvii.

p. 34 *By the beginning of*: for numbers of European ships pursuing the ship fishery, Rowe, pp. 95-97. For Cartier and the French presence, Prowse, p. 45.

p. 35 *Seasonal ship fishing*: for the "vexing problems" of governing a colony, the Newfoundland Act of 1699, and the fishing admirals, Rowe, p. 115 ff.

p. 36 *The reason that stands*: In his Introduction, Prowse complains: "Our treatment by the British Government has been so stupid, cruel, and barbarous that it requires the actual perusal of the

State Papers to convince us that such a policy was ever carried out." Prowse, p. xix.

p. 36 *One of the most obvious*: Many historians and commentators on the settlement of the Newfoundland outports have remarked on the unusual site choices made by the early settlers. One of the latest to do so is Pol Chantraine, who writes about accessibility to the fishing banks as the "essential criterion" for choosing a village site. Pol Chantraine, *The Last Cod Fish: Life and Death of the Newfoundland Way of Life*, Jespersen Press Limited, St. John's, Newfoundland, 1993, pp. 28-29.

Chapter 3

p. 42 *The first of the compensation*: for a discussion of The Atlantic Ground fish Strategy (TAGS) and other compensation and retraining packages initiated by the Canadian federal government in the years following the cod collapse, see Michael Harris, op. cit., Chapter 9, "The Bailout Blues," pp. 205-220.

p. 47 *Historically, the hunting of seals*: unless otherwise noted, details in this and following paragraphs about the early history of sealing in Newfoundland are from Farley Mowat, *The New Founde Land*, pp. 103-155, and Farley Mowat, *Sea of Slaughter*, The Atlantic Monthly Press, Boston, 1984, pp. 345-362.

p. 48 *The first widespread awareness*: Mowat, *Sea of Slaughter*, pp. 371-72.

p. 49 *Eyewitness descriptions of*: the reference in this paragraph is to Silver Donald Cameron, "Seals and Sinners: Over the Bloodied Ice, a Haze of Mixed Moralities," The St. John's *Evening Telegram Weekend Magazine*, v. 26, n.22, May 29, 1976, p. 8.

p. 49 *The media campaign succeeded*: Mowat, *Sea of Slaughter*, pp. 394-403.

p. 51 *In December 1987*: statistics on the seal fishery in this and the following paragraph are from two Canadian Department of Fisheries and Oceans publications: "1999 Seal Facts," p. 2 ff., and "Atlantic Seal Hunt 1999 Management Plan," pp. 6-7.

p. 52 *Seals eat cod*: for DFO estimates of the magnitude of harp seal predation, see "1999 Seal Facts," p. 4. For IFAW estimates, see International Marine Mammal Association Technical Briefing No. 93-01, 1993, "Cod Crisis: Are Seals Part of the Problem?" pp. 5-7.

p. 52 *One of the people I talked*: Personal communications with Dr. Jeffrey Hutchings in this and following paragraphs took place during two interviews, both at Dalhousie University, Halifax, Nova Scotia, the first on August 25, 1997, and the second on December 13, 1998.

p. 53 *At the conclusion of*: Stephen Thorne of the Canadian Press reports on the "gag order" issued by DFO director William Doubleday on the Hutchings paper on seal predation in "Director admits DFO scuttled seal report," Halifax *Chronicle Herald*, August 26, 1997.

Chapter 4

p. 57 *Twenty-five years ago, when:* A good general discussion of the early history of Newfoundland, including habitation by the Maritime Archaic (Red Paint), Beothuk, and early Micmac Indians appears in Rowe, pp. 23-33 and pp.166-169.

p. 58 *In more recent times*: For a discussion of the French Shore and "the French Shore problem" as presented in this and following paragraphs, see Rowe, pp. 311-325.

p. 59 *I had managed to learn a little*: For stock assessments, catch limits, and catch sizes for northern shrimp (*Pandalus borealis*) in the Gulf of St. Lawrence from 1970 through 1997, see DFO Stock Status Report C4-06 (1998), Regional Stock Assessment Office, DFO, Mt. Joli, Quebec, February 1998.

p. 60 *"Cod eat shrimp," commented*: Personal communications with Dr. Louise Savard, DFO, Mt. Joli, Quebec, quoted in this paragraph took place during an interview with the author on November 20, 1998.

Chapter 5

p. 71 *As a result, by the*: for a detailed discussion of the Great Ocean Conveyor Belt hypothesis and a brief description of its best-known proponent, Wally Broecker, see Myron Arms, *Riddle of the Ice*, Anchor Books, New York, 1998, especially pp. 118-136.

In the Epilogue of the same book, I also make brief reference to the North Atlantic Oscillation or NAO (p. 245), a climate feature that has been known for decades but that has only recently become the object of intensified study. Recent data from a new generation of submersible, remote controlled instrument platforms (called PALACES) have begun to document the interrelationship between deepwater formation in the Labrador Sea that helps to drive the

Great Ocean Conveyor Belt and patterns of oscillations of the NAO. For a useful discussion of the NAO see James W. Hurrell, "Decadal Trends in the North Atlantic Oscillation: Regional Temperatures and Precipitation," Science, v. 269, 4 August, 1995, pp. 676-679.

p. 72 *The frustration of having to turn*: Arms, op. cit pp. 1-16.

p. 73 *The first study, published in*: The "classic" scientific study on cod recruitment and salinity referenced in this and following paragraphs is entitled "Nutrient flux onto the Labrador Shelf from Hudson Strait and its biological consequences," W. H. Sutcliffe Jr., R.H. Loucks, K.F. Drinkwater, and A.R. Coote, *Canadian Journal of Fisheries and Aquatic Sciences*, v. 40, n.10, 1983, pp. 1692-1701.

p. 73 *According to this hypothesis*: For the "food chain "hypothesis," ibid, pp. 1697-1700.

p. 74 *The first serious challenge to*: The 1993 study by Drinkwater et. al. on cod recruitment and salinity is entitled "Salinity and recruitment of Atlantic Cod (Gadus morhua) in the Newfoundland Region," R.A. Myers, K.F. Drinkwater, N.J. Barrowman, and J.W. Baird, *Canadian Journal of Fisheries and Aquatic Sciences*, v. 50, n. 8, 1993, pp. 1599-1609.

p. 74 *So far, so good. But another*: For the negative correlation of phytoplankton biomass and cod recruitment, ibid, pp. 1606-1607.

p. 74 *What began as a promising idea*: for the "larval freezing hypothesis" and its inadequacies, ibid, pp. 1607-1608.

p. 74 *Given the limited application*: ibid, p. 1608.

p. 75 *For Hutchings and Myers, the*: Hutchings and Myers refute "the "environmental hypothesis" of Ken Drinkwater and others in a study "entitled "What can be learned from the collapse of a renewable resource? Atlantic cod, Gadus morhua, of Newfoundland and Labrador," Jeffrey A. Hutchings and Ransom A. Myers, *Canadian Journal of Fisheries and Aquatic Sciences*, v. 51. n. 9, 1994, pp. 2126-2146.

p. 76 *For all three of the study areas*: ibid, p. 2143.

p. 76 *When asked to comment*: Personal communications with Dr. Ransom A. Myers in this and following paragraphs took place during two interviews, the first at Dalhousie University, Halifax, Nova Scotia, on August 27, 1997, the second at the home of Sifford Pearre, Halifax, Nova Scotia, on December 13, 1998. Arguments quoted here about cold water conditions in the nineteenth and early twentieth centuries are also found in Hutchings and Myers 1994, p. 2133.

p. 76 *Hutchings elaborates*: For times and places of personal interviews with Dr. Jeffrey Hutchings, see footnote, p. 52. The arguments stated in this and following paragraphs are also found in substantially the same form in Hutchings and Myers 1994, p. 2141.

p. 77 *Ken Drinkwater, in spite of*: personal communications with Dr. Ken Drinkwater in this and following paragraphs took place during an interview with the author on March 25, 1999.

p. 77 *Perhaps because of the influence*: Ken Drinkwater, personal communication, as p. 77. Also on observed differences in growth rates between Georges Bank cod stocks and northern cod stocks, see Ken F. Drinkwater and David G. Mountain, DFO pamphlet, *Climate and Oceanography*, p. 21.

p. 79 *But by the 1980s*: it should be noted that Drinkwater's argument regarding the absence of "resilience" in a cod population weakened by overfishing (stated in a personal communication, as p. 116) is essentially the same argument as that proposed by Hutchings and Myers 1994, p. 2143. I would interpret this as an indication of the influence that Hutchings and Myers have exerted upon Drinkwater's thinking since 1994.

p. 79 *Drinkwater and others have written*: For an overview of recent climate variability on the shelf waters of eastern Canada and its connections with the NAO, K. F. Drinkwater, "Atmospheric and Oceanic Variability in the Northwest Atlantic During the 1980s and early 1990s," *Journal of Northwest Atlantic Fisheries Sciences*, v. 18, 1996, pp. 77-97. Also, K. F. Drinkwater and R.A. Myers, "Interannual Variability in the Atmospheric and Oceanographic Conditions in the Labrador Sea and their Association with the North Atlantic Oscillation," Working Paper for the ICES/GLOBEC Workshop on Prediction and Decadal-Scale Ocean Climate Fluctuations of the North Atlantic, September 1997.

p. 80 *The similarities don't end here*: According to Christopher Flavin of Worldwatch Institute, "the average global temperature for January-August 1998 was a full four tenths of a degree warmer than the average for 1997, the previous record-setting year" (C. Flavin, "The Last Tango in Buenos Aires," *World-Watch* Magazine, Nov./Dec. 1998, p. 11.)

The "tenfold" increase in violent weather events is based upon insured weather-related damages, as reported by insurance companies worldwide. Such damages reported in the single year of 1998 were greater than all similar damages reported during the entire decade of the 1980s, adjusted to 1998 dollars. (Personal communication, Lester Brown, former president of Worldwatch Institute, during the Institute's Annual Briefing, January 15, 1999.)

Chapter 7

p. 101 *It came as no surprise*: Details in this and following paragraphs about John Slade and Company and its activities in Battle Harbor are summarized from information presented in the Battle Harbor Interpretation Center, housed in the old Salmon Store, Battle Harbor, from two interviews with Michael Earle, the first on July 23, 1998, the second on August 27, 1999, and from correspondences with Joyce Yates, Battle Harbor Historic Trust, December 1999.

p. 101 *During the early decades of*: estimates of the numbers of fishermen and vessels in the Labrador fishery are from Wilfred T. Grenfell and others, *Labrador: The Country and the People*, The Macmillan Company, New York, 1910, p.315, (hereinafter "Grenfell"). It should also be noted that more recent historians have argued that Grenfell's estimate of thirty thousand men is a considerable overestimate and have revised the figure to about eighteen thousand men.

p. 102 *At least partially in*: Grenfell discusses the Labrador fish merchants of the 19th and early 20th centuries, including Baine, Johnston & Company, in Grenfell, pp. 179-183. Certain of the details in this and following paragraphs about Baine, Johnston & Company and its activities in Battle Harbor are also summarized from information presented in the Battle Harbor Interpretation Center, as p. 101.

p. 102 *Observers of the Newfoundland*: Grenfell quotes Sir W.R. Kennedy in his chapter on "The Missions," in Grenfell, p. 245.

p. 103 *Another who was similarly*: For a brief history of the "Labrador Deep-sea Mission," as summarized in this and following paragraphs, see Grenfell, pp. 236-242.

p. 103 *Even though the focus*: Grenfell's description of the truck system appears in Grenfell, p. 247. His influence upon the sealskin boot trade in Flowers Cove is described in Grenfell, p. 243.

p. 103 *Both the Grenfell Hospital*: for a thorough discussion of historical catch records for northern cod in the Labrador and Newfoundland fisheries, see Jeffrey A. Hutchings and Ransom A. Myers, "The Biological Collapse of Atlantic Cod of Newfoundland and Labrador," *Institute of Island Studies*, 1995, especially pp. 55 ff.

p. 104 *Finally in 1955 the premises*: Details about The Earle Freighting Service Limited in this and following paragraphs are summarized from information presented in the Battle Harbor Interpretation Center and from interviews with Michael Earle, as p. 101.

p. 107 *I explained to Mike that*: For Grenfell's observations about the "enterprising men" of the merchant trade, see Grenfell, p. 180 ff.

p. 107 *"It's odd," Mike said*: For a brief discussion of the influx of indentured "servants" into the Newfoundland fishery, see Rowe, pp. 212-213, and pp. 242-243. For a more thorough discussion of the usages of "servant" "and "fishing servant" in the vernaculars of Newfoundland, see "servant," in *Dictionary of Newfoundland English*, 2nd Edition, University of Toronto Press, Toronto 1990, p. 461.

Chapter 8

p. 110 *How many humpback whales were*: The estimate of "upwards of five thousand" whales is from Dr. Jon Lien, personal communication, during an interview with the author on October 30, 1999. For a more detailed discussion of humpback populations in eastern Newfoundland, their numbers, and their feeding habits as discussed in this and following paragraphs, see Sean Todd, "Acoustical Properties of Fishing Gear: Possible Relationships to Baleen Whale Entrapment," Memorial University School of Graduate Studies Master's Thesis, July 1991, p.3 ff.

p. 111 *Fifty years ago, in the*: Timetable for the hunting of Newfoundland humpbacks "into the 1960s" is from Jon Lien, personal communication, as p. 110.

p. 111 *Several factors finally conspired:* Details regarding the IWC whaling ban are from Jon Lien, personal communication, as p. 110, as well as from "The Whale Man Saves More then Just Whales," *The Evening Telegram*, June 11, 1990, p. 6.

p. 112 *Lien, the leader of*: For the genesis of the whale rescue program, see "Whale Rescue Service on the Endangered List," St. John's *Sunday Express*, April 17, 1988.

p. 112 *After that first summer*: for statistics on whale entrapments, see "Whales Get Trapped in Record Numbers," *The Evening Telegram*, August 23, 1991, p. 7.

p. 113 *"We do a whale almost every*: The first sentence of Lien's words appear here as they are quoted in *The Evening Telegram*, as p.

168. The remaining sentences of the paragraph appear as they are quoted in the Toronto *Globe and Mail,* "A Whale of an Alarm," February 6, 1993, Science Section, p. 1.

p. 113 *The second phase of Lien's program*: For the evolution of the whale alarm as it was developed for use with cod traps, see "Keeping Whales out of Trouble," St. John's *Gazette,* August 29, 1991, p. 12. Also see Toronto *Globe and Mail*, as p. 111 above.

Lien adds: "We also produced a whole variety of 'beepers' for different types of fishing gear [other than cod traps]. Some cost as little as $10 and directions were printed so fishermen could build them for themselves." Jon Lien, personal communication, as p. 110.

p. 113 *The incredible success of:* Jon Lien and others have noted that the Newfoundland humpback population has increased by some five thousand whales since 1978. The assertion that Lien's programs may have saved the lives of "one in three" of these whales is based on the assumption that of approximately one thousand freed whales, half were females that would have reproduced at least once every ten years. This (extremely conservative) multiplier would account for 1750 whales, or about one-third of the current population.

p. 114 *"Human beings cannot be treated*: Lien's words appear here as they are quoted in *The Evening Telegram*, as p. 111.

p. 114 *The official position of the*: For "irreversible changes in the structure and organization of the larger fish community," see Richard L. Haedrich and Nigel L. Merrett, "Changing Size Structure in Exploited Deep-Sea Fish Communities," ICES CM 1998/O:77, Deepwater Fish and Fisheries Poster. Also see Lawrence C. Hamilton and Richard L. Haedrich, "Fishing Down Food Webs," pp.5-7 in "Climate, Ecology, and Social Change in Fishing Communities of the North Atlantic Arc," working paper presented at the International Conference of Polar Aspects of Global Change, Tromso, Norway, August 25-28, 1998.

p. 115 *"Fish don't exist in a vacuum:* Commentary by Richard Haedrich in this and following paragraphs is from a series of personal communications with the author that took place during three interviews in St. John's, Newfoundland, the first on August 11, 1998, the second on December 2, 1998, and the third on December 10, 1998.

p. 117 *The net was in tatters*: for a technical description of the standard shrimp trawl and the basic design and operation of the

Nordmore Grid, see *Responsible Fisheries Summary*, June 1997, p. 7.

p. 120 *"Bernard Bromley, that's*: The interview with Bernard Bromley in this and following paragraphs took place in the offices of the *Northern Pen* on Thursday, December 3, 1998.

Chapter 9

p. 126 *One of the people that*: Personal communications with Dr. Donald G. Parsons in this and following paragraphs took place during two interviews, both in St. John's, Newfoundland, the first on August 9, 1998, and the second on December 11, 1998.

p. 127 *"Read our stock assessment report*: The report referenced in this paragraph is DFO Science Stock Status Report #C2-05, "Northern Shrimp off Newfoundland and Labrador," March 1997. The research document that this report is based upon is Canadian Stock Assessment Secretariat Research Document 97/05,D.G. Parsons and P.J. Veitch, "Regional Review of the Status of Northern Shrimp (*Pandalus borealis*) Resources in Areas off Newfoundland and Labrador (Divisions 0B to 3K)," 1997.

p. 130 *For the next few decades*: background information in this and following paragraphs about Olaf Olsen, Ches Crosbie, and the Olsen Whaling and Sealing Company are from Michael Harris, *Rare Ambition: The Crosbies of Newfoundland*, Penguin Books, Ontario, 1992, pp. 120-201.

p. 132 *In the summer of 1966*: background details about whaling activities at Williamsport after the Crosbies abandoned the site in 1959 are from three personal interviews, the first with former fish plant manager Claude Martin of La Scie, Newfoundland, on October 29, 1999, the second with Memorial University oceanographer Dr. Jon Lien of Portugal Cove, Newfoundland, on October 30, 1999, and the third with former whaling captain Bud O'Brien of Bay Bulls, Newfoundland, on November 2, 1999.

Chapter 11

p. 152 *Joe sat across the table*: Personal communications with Joe Wiseman reported in this chapter took place during two interviews with the author, both in Fortune Harbor, Newfoundland, the first on July 30, 1998, the second on December 7, 1998.

p. 153 *"People just assumed that this*: background information and production statistics for Atlantic Ocean Farms, Limited are from personal communications with the company's founder and president, David Walsh, during an interview with the author on January 18, 2000.

p. 155 *The answer to most of*: Statistics for current aquaculture activity in Newfoundland are from a series of personal communications with Paul James, Newfoundland Department of Fisheries and Aquaculture, during interviews with the author on February 28, 2000, and March 2, 2000, and from departmental statistics that he provided.

p. 156 *For growers like Joe Wiseman*: World organizations that have touted the technological "miracle" of aquaculture include the World Bank (whose spokespersons have called seafood farming "the next great leap in food production") and the United Nations Food and Agriculture Organization (FAO), whose managers have estimated that "under favorable conditions" global food production from seafood farming could increase by some 70 percent over 1998 levels by 2010.

p. 156 *A look at world production*: For statistics in this paragraph for world aquaculture production between 1977 and 1998 , see *The State of the World Fisheries and Aquaculture 1998*, Food and Agriculture Organization of the United Nations, Rome, 1999, pp. 3-12. For projection for the year 2010, ibid, p. 86.

p. 156 *Statistics are a funny business*: ibid, pp. 10-11, 82-83.

p. 158 *Perhaps the most benign form*: For a more detailed description of Chinese pond aquaculture, see Anne Platt McGinn, "Promoting Sustainable Aquaculture," in *Rocking the Boat, Conserving Fisheries and Protecting Jobs*, Worldwatch Paper 142, Worldwatch Institute, Washington D.C., June 1998, p. 45; also George L. Chan, "Aquaculture, Ecological Engineering: Lessons from China," in *Ambio*, November 1993.

p. 158 *In contrast, most western*: for water and waste statistics for cultivated fish, see McGinn, op. cit., pp. 49 and 51.

p. 158 *The most environmentally damaging*: For global production of tiger prawns, see McGinn, op. cit., p. 48. For destruction of coastal habitat, see Tracy Baxter, "The Hidden Life of Shrimp," *Sierra Magazine*, July/August 1998, pp. 56-57.

p. 159 *The environmental cost of this kind*: Ibid, p. 57.

Chapter 12

p. 167 *In the middle 1960s*: for a brief history of Joey Smallwood's relocation program, see Farley Mowat, *The New Founde Land*, McClelland & Stewart, Inc. Toronto, 1989, pp. 75-80.

p. 168 *For most outporters*: Mowat, op. cit., p. 80.

p. 171 *I knew a little about*: Personal communications with Dr .David Taylor in this and following paragraphs took place during two interviews with the author, both in St. John's, Newfoundland, the first on August 9, 1998, and the second on December 11, 1998.

p. 172 *According to Taylor:* for the history of the snow crab fishery in Newfoundland and statistics on quotas, landed tonnages, numbers of licenses, etc, see "Newfoundland Region: Stock Status Report Newfoundland and Labrador Snow Crab," DFO Science Stock Status Report #C2-01, April 1997, pp. 1-5.

p. 172 *As Taylor looked into*: ibid, p. 3.

p. 172 *Another observer of the snow*: for times and places of personal communications with Richard Haedrich as they appear in this and following paragraphs, see footnote, p. 115.

Chapter 14

p. 187 *Here, perhaps in the very*: for a more detailed history of Sir John Calker Crosbie's rise to financial and political prominence, see Michael Harris, *Rare Ambition*, Penguin Books, Toronto, 1992, especially chapter 5, "Sir John," pp. 58-102. For "powerful convoy of privilege," ibid, p. 60. For reference to the old Duder premises, ibid, p. 61.

p. 188 *After Sir John's untimely*: for the history of Ches Crosbie's years at the helm of the Crosbie empire, ibid, pp. 103-229. For statistics on the size of the Crosbie holdings at Ches' death, ibid, p. 243.

p. 188 *Thus it was that young*: for the history of Andrew Crosbie's economic misadventures, ibid, pp. 340-381.

p. 189 *John Crosbie appears to have*: for a discussion of Crosbie's bid for national leadership and "propensity to make insensitive remarks," ibid, pp. 322-340.

p. 189 *"administrative Clydesdale"*: ibid, pp. 301-02.

p. 189 *"the most pig-headed. . ."*: ibid, p. 272.

p. 190 *I moved past the woman*: personal communications with

John Crosbie in this and following paragraphs took place during an interview at his law offices on December 10, 1998. Later conversations with Crosbie and his wife Jane took place the same day at Bianca's restaurant, St. John's, Newfoundland.

p. 190 *"The story's all there:* Crosbie's reference in this paragraph is to Chapter 20, "Who Hears the Fishes When They Cry?" pp. 372-401, in John C. Crosbie, *No Holds Barred: My Life in Politics*, McClelland & Steward Inc., Toronto, 1997.

p. 191 *Not lied, exactly*: reference in this and following paragraphs is to Alan Christopher Finlayson, *Fishing for the Truth: A Sociological Analysis of Northern Cod Stock Assessments from 1977-1990*, Social and Economic Studies No. 52, Memorial University of Newfoundland, St. John's, 1994.

p. 193 *"This province hasn't been standing:* for Crosbie's published version of the importance of the Hibernia project and his part in saving it for Newfoundland, see Crosbie, op. cit., chapter 23, "Saving Hibernia," pp. 434-449.

p. 193 *But I didn't ask about*: for details about Crosbie Offshore Services Ltd., see Harris, *Rare Ambition*, pp. 344-346 and 359-364. For Freshwater Bay, ibid, p. 387. For Ches and Michael Crosbie, ibid, pp. 368-369 and 386-387.

p. 193 *He stepped around a carton of*: for times and places of personal communications with Richard Haedrich as they appear in this and following paragraphs, see footnote, p. 115.

p. 196 *Haedrich turned without speaking*: the editorial referenced in this paragraph, by J.A. Hutchings, Carl Walters, and R.L. Haedrich, is "entitled "Is scientific inquiry incompatible with government information control?" in *Canadian Journal of Fisheries and Aquatic Sciences*, May 1997, v. 54, pp.1198-1210.

Chapter 15

p. 204 *Ram Myers, who until recently*: for times and places of personal communications with Dr. Ransom A. Myers as cited in this paragraph, see footnote, p. 76.

p. 204 *Jeff Hutchings, now a colleague*: for times and places of personal communications with Dr. Jeffrey Hutchings as cited in this paragraph, see footnote, p. 77.

p. 204 *Perhaps the most outspoken opponent*: for Richard Haedrich's critique of the Fisheries Resource Conservation Council's recommended quotas for the 3Ps cod fishery, see Richard L. Haedrich and Johanna Fischer, "Thermodynamics for Marxists: New Ways at Looking at Old Problems," Retrospective Monitoring and TEK Projects, Eco-Research Program, Memorial University, St. John's, Newfoundland, p. 11.

p. 205 *In conversation, Haedrich*: for times and places of personal communications with Dr. Richard Haedrich, see footnote, p. 115.

Epilogue

p. 211 *Sadly, none of these events*: For the timetables and official rationale for the various openings and closings of the Newfoundland cod fisheries, see DFO Stock Status Reports for various breeding populations of the northern cod, 2003 and earlier. A summary and verification of such openings and closings was also provided to the author in a personal communication with DFO Resource Manager Leonard Knight during a telephone interview on January 25, 2004.

p. 211 *That same spring*: For the proceedings of the May 2003 meeting of COSEWIC as they relate to the Atlantic cod, see "COSEWIC Assessment—Atlantic Cod" as published on the organization's Web site at *www.sararegistry.gc.ca*.

p. 212 *For all three of the latter fisheries*: For estimates of the sizes of remnant populations of various breeding stocks of Atlantic cod, see Jeffrey Hutchings, "COSEWIC Status Report – Atlantic Cod," loc cit. On the subject of the reclassification of threatened species, readers may be interested to learn that according to a COSEWIC press release dated May 2, 2003, "the Western North Atlantic population of the Humpback Whale, previously listed in the "\'special concern' category, was removed from the [endangered] list [at the May 2 meeting], due in part to the success of recovery efforts. Fewer Humpback whales are becoming entangled in fishing nets, and people have become more proficient at untangling those that are caught. There are now about 10,000 Humpback whales in the Western North Atlantic."

p. 212 *The news from the snow crab fishery*: Stock assessments and predictions regarding future abundance in the Newfoundland snow crab fishery referenced in this paragraph can be found in DFO Stock Status Report C2-01 (2002) and DFO Science Stock Status Report 2003/021.

p. 213 *In the world of fisheries science*: see Ransom A. Myers and

Boris Worm, "Rapid worldwide depletion of predatory fish communities," in *Nature,* v. 423, May 15, 2003, pp. 280-283.

p. 213 *"In the past several years*: Personal communications with Dr. Ransom A. Myers contained in this and following paragraphs took place during a telephone interview with the author on February 3, 2004.

p. 214 *While Myers has been documenting*: Personal communications with Dr. Jeffrey Hutchings in this and following paragraphs took place during a telephone interview with the author on January 30, 2004.

p. 215 *In enumerating such strategies*: Andrew Rosenberg, former northeast administrator of the U.S. National Marine Fisheries Service and member of the U.S. Commission on Ocean Policy, is quoted as his words appear in this paragraph in "Murder of the Bounty: The Empty Seas," *Popular Science*, January 2004, p. 77.

Bibliography

Research for this book took place during a period of more than a decade and involved some thirty-thousand miles under sail, nearly a hundred personal interviews, and the perusal of countless published records, articles, and books. The bibliography that follows is not intended as an exhaustive listing of all published materials but rather as an aid to the general reader, listing only those sources most relevant to the book as it eventually evolved.

Aquaculture Production Statistics, 1986-1995, The Food and Agricultural Organization of the United Nations, Fisheries Circular no. 815, Revision 9, Rome, 1997.

Arnason, Ragnar, and Lawrence Felt, eds., *The North Atlantic Fisheries: Successes, Failures, and Challenges*, Institute of Island Studies, Charlestown, Prince Edward Island, 1995.

Bender, William and Margaret Smith, *Population, Food, and Nutrition*, Population Reference Bureau, Population Bulletin, v. 51, no. 4, February 1997.

Bengtsson, Jan, et. al., "The value of biodiversity," in *Tree*, v. 12, no. 9, September, 1997, pp. 334-336

Berrill, Michael, *The Plundered Seas: Can the World's Fish be Saved?*, Sierra Club Books, San Francisco, 1997

Blades, Kent, *Net Destruction: The Death of Atlantic Canada's Fishery*, Nimbus Publishing Limited, Halifax, 1995

Brawn, Vivian, "Reproductive Behavior of the cod (*Gadus callarias L.*)," *Behavior*, v. 18(3), 1961, pp. 177-198

Broad, William J., *The Universe Below: Discovering the Secrets of the Deep Sea*, Simon and Schuster, New York, 1997

_____, and Andrew C. Revkin, "Has the Sea Given Up Its Bounty?" in New York *Times*, Tuesday July 29, 2003, pp. C-1-2

Brown, Lester R., *Tough Choices: Facing the Challenge of Food Scarcity*, W.W. Norton & Co., New York, 1996

Brubaker, Elizabeth, "Cod Don't Vote," in *The Next City* Magazine, Winter 1998- 1999, v.4, no. 2, pp. 35-42

Canover, Robert J., et. al., "Climate, Copopods, and Cod: Some Thoughts on the Long-range Prospects for a Sustainable Northern Cod Fishery," in *Proceedings of Coastal Zone Canada*, v 4, Halifax, 1994, pp. 1732, ff.

Caron, David A., "An Introduction to Biological Oceanography," in *Oceanus*, v. 35, no. 3, Fall 1992, pp. 10-17

Chantraine, Pol, *The Last Cod-Fish: Life and Death of the Newfoundland Way of Life*, Jespersen Press Limited, St. John's, 1993

Cochrane, Candace, *Outport: Reflections from the Newfoundland Coast*, Addison-Wesley Publishers, Don Mills, Ontario, 1981

Cook, David G., "Editorial," *Canadian Journal of Fisheries and Aquatic Sciences*, v. 54, 1997, pp. iii-v

Cox, Betty, "Billions on TAGS, Problems Remain," in *The Ottawa Times*, no. 21, December 1997, pp. 1-2

Crosbie, John C., with Geoffrey Stevens, *No Holds Barred: My Life in Politics*, McClelland & Steward Inc., Toronto, 1997

Daley, Beth, Gareth Cook, et. al., "Sea Change: The New England Fishing Crisis," an in-depth report in four parts, Boston *Globe*, October 26-29, 2003

Day, Douglas, "Addressing the weakness of high seas fisheries management in the north-west Atlantic," in *Ocean and Coastal Management*, v. 35, no. 2-3, 1997, pp. 69-84

Dayton, Paul K., "Reversal of the Burden of Proof in Fisheries Management," in *Science*, v. 279, February 6, 1998, pp. 821-822

Development of the Cod Trap, Fishing Gear and Equipment Publication no. 2, Fisheries Development Branch, Department of Fisheries and Oceans, Newfoundland Region, 1983

Doubleday, William G., et. al., "Comment: Scientific inquiry and fish stock.. assessment in the Canadian Department of Fisheries and Oceans," in *Canadian Journal of Fisheries and Aquatic Sciences*, v 54, 1997, pp. 1422-1426

Drinkwater, K.F., "Atmospheric and Oceanic Variability in the NW Atlantic During the 1980s and early 1990s," in *Journal of Northwest Atlantic Fisheries Science*, v. 18, 1996, pp. 77-97

_____, "Interannual Variability in the Atmospheric and Oceanic Conditions in the Labrador Sea and their Association with the North Atlantic Oscillation," DFO Working Paper for the ICES/GLOBEC Workshop on Prediction and Decadal-Scale Ocean

Climate Fluctuations of the North Atlantic, September, 1997

"Eastern Scotian Shelf Cod," DFO Stock Status Report 2003/020, Halifax, Nova Scotia, February, 2003

Felt, Lawrence F. and Peter R. Sinclair, eds., *Living on the Edge: The Great Northern Peninsula of Newfoundland*, Institute of Social and Economic Research, Memorial University of Newfoundland, Paper 21, St. John's, 1995

Finlayson, Alan Christopher, *Fishing for the Truth: A Sociological Analysis of Northern Cod Stock Assessments from 1977-1990*, Social and Economic Studies No. 52, Institute of Social and Economic Research, Memorial University of Newfoundland, St. John's, 1994

"Forage Fishes in Marine Ecosystems," in *Proceedings of the International Symposium on the Role of Forage Fishes in Marine Ecosystems*, Alaska Sea Grant College Program Report N. 97-01, University of Alaska, Fairbanks, 1997

Grenfell, Wilfred T., *Labrador: The Country and the People*, The Macmillan Company, New York, 1909

Griffin, Nancy, "When Tradition Dies: Does a cod fishing shutdown in Newfoundland provide hard lessons to Maine?," in Bangor *Daily News*, February 10, 1998, pp. A-1, A-6-7

Hannesson, Rognvaldur, *Fisheries Management: The Case of the North Atlantic Cod*, Fishing News Books, Oxford, 1996

Harder, Ben, "Catch Zero: what can be done as marine ecosystems face a deepening crisis?," in *Science News*, v. 164, July 26, 2003, pp. 59-61

_____, "Sea burial for Canada's cod fisheries," in *Science News*, v. 163, May 17, 2003, p. 318

Harris Michael, *Lament for an Ocean: The Collapse of the Atlantic Cod Fishery: A True Crime Story*, McClelland and Stewart Inc., Toronto, 1998

_____, *Rare Ambition: The Crosbies of Newfoundland*, Viking Penguin Books of Canada, Toronto, 1992

Healey, M.C., "Comment: the interplay of policy, politics, and science," in *Canadian Journal of Fisheries and Aquatic Sciences*, v. 54, 1997, pp. 1427-1429

Hurrell, James W., "Decadal Trends in the North Atlantic Oscillation: Regional Temperatures and Precipitation," in *Science*, v. 269, August 4, 1995, pp. 676- 678

Hutchings, Jeffrey A., "Fisheries of Atlantic Canada: The Certainty of Technology and the Uncertainty of Science," address delivered to the Funding Committee of the Oceans Institute, Cambridge Library, Royal Artillery Park, Halifax, August 9, 1997

_____, R.A. Myers, and G.R. Lilly, "Geographic variation in the spawning of Atlantic Cod, *Gadus Morhua*, in the northwest Atlantic," in *Canadian Journal of Fisheries and Aquatic Sciences*, v. 50, no. 11, 1993, pp. 2457-2467

_____, Carl Walters, and R.L. Haedrich, "Is scientific inquiry incompatible with government information control?", in *Canadian Journal of Fisheries and Aquatic Sciences*, v. 54, 1997, pp. 1198-1210

_____, et. al., "Reply: Scientific inquiry and fish stock assessment in the Canadian Department of Fisheries and Oceans," in *Canadian Journal of Fisheries and Aquatic Sciences*, v. 54, 1997, pp. 1430-1431

_____, "Spatial and temporal variations in the density of northern cod and a review of hypotheses for the stock's collapse," in *Canadian Journal of Fisheries and Aquatic Sciences*, v. 53, no. 5, 1996, pp. 943-962

_____, and R.A. Myers, "The Biological Collapse of Atlantic Cod off Newfoundland and Labrador: An Exploration of Historical Changes in Exploitation, Harvesting, Technology, and Management," in *The North Atlantic Fisheries: Successes, Failures, and Challenges*, Ragnar Arnason and Lawrence Felt, eds., Institute of Island Studies, Charlestown, PEI, 1995, pp. 39-93

_____, and R.A. Myers, "What can be learned from the collapse of a renewable resource? Atlantic Cod, *Gadus morhua*, of Newfoundland and Labrador," in *Canadian Journal of Fisheries and Aquatic Sciences*, v. 51, no. 9, 1994, pp. 2126-2146

Johnston, Wayne, *The Colony of Unrequited Dreams*, Doubleday, New York, 1999

Katona, Steven, et. al., *A Field Guide to the Whales, Porpoises, and Seals of the Gulf of Maine and Eastern Canada, Cape Cod to Newfoundland*, Third Edition, Charles Scribners' Sons, New York, 1983

Kavanaugh, Patrick, *Gaff Topsail: A Novel*, Viking Press, New York, 1996

Kimber, Stephen, *Net Profits: The Story of National Sea*, Nimbus Publishing Limited, Halifax, 1989

Kurlansky, Mark, *Cod: A Biography of the Fish that Changed the World*, Walker and Company, New York, 1997

Lambert, J., et. al., "Etat des populations de crevettes nordiques (*Pandalus borealis*) de l'estuaire et du golfe du Saint-Laurent," Canadian Stock Assessment Research Document 98-102, DFO Science, Mt. Joli, Quebec, 1998

Martin, Cabot, *No Fish and Our Lives: Some Survival Notes for New-foundland*, Creative Publishers, St. John's, 1992

McCay, Bonnie and James Acheson, *The Question of the Commons: The Culture and Ecology of Communal Resources*, University of Arizona Press, Tucson, Arizona, 1987

McCloskey, William, *Their Fathers' Work: Casting Nets with the World's Fishermen*, International Marine/Ragged Mountain Press, Camden, Maine, 1998

McGoodwin, Russell, *Crisis in the World Fisheries*, University of Colorado Press, Boulder, CO., 1990

Meadows, Donella H, Dennis L. Meadows, and Jorgen Randers, *Beyond the Limits: Confronting Global Collapse, Envisioning a Sustainable Future*, Chelsea Green Publishing Co., White River Junction, Vermont, 1992

Momatiuk, Yva, and John Eastcott, *This Marvelous Terrible Place: Images of Newfoundland and Labrador*, Camden House Publishing, Camden East, Ontario, 1988

Morgan, Bernice, *Random Passage*, Breakwater, St. John's, 1992
_____, *Waiting for Time*, Breakwater, St. John's, 1994

Mowat, Farley, *Sea of Slaughter*, The Atlantic Monthly Press, Boston, 1984
_____, *The New Founde Land: A Personal Voyage of Discovery*, McClelland and Stewart Inc., Toronto, 1989
_____, *The Serpent's Coil*, McClelland and Stewart-Bantam Limited, Toronto, 1980

"Murder of the Bounty: The Empty Seas," in *Popular Science*, January 2004, pp. 76-77

Myers, RA., N .J. Barrowman, and J. A. Hutchings, "Inshore exploitation of Newfoundland Atlantic cod (*Gadus morhua*) since 1948 as estimated from mark-recapture data," in *Canadian Journal of Fisheries and Aquatic Sciences*, v. 54, 1997, pp. 224-235
_____, K. F. Drinkwater, et. al., "Salinity and recruitment of Atlantic cod (*Gadus morhua*) in the Newfoundland region," in *Canadian Journal of Fisheries and Aquatic Sciences*, v. 50, no. 8, 1993, pp. 1599-1609
_____, J. A. Hutchings, and N. J. Barrowman, "Why do fish

stocks collapse? The example of cod in Atlantic Canada," in *Ecological Applications,* 7(1), 1997, pp. 91-106

_____, and Boris Worm, "Rapid worldwide depletion of predatory fish communities," in *Nature,* v. 423, May 15, 2003, pp. 280-283

Naeem, S., et. al., "Declining biodiversity can alter the performance of ecosystems," in *Nature,* v. 368, 1994, pp. 734-737

Neary, Peter, ed., *White Tie and Decorations: Sir John and Lady Hope Simpson in Newfoundland, 1934-36,* University of Toronto Press, Toronto, 1996

Neis, Barbara, "Fishers' Ecological Knowledge and Stock Assessment in Newfoundland," in *Newfoundland Studies,* v. 8, no. 2, Fall 1992, pp. 155-178

"Newfoundland and Labrador Snow Crab," DFO Stock Status Report 2003/021, St. John's, Newfoundland, March 2003

"Northern (2K + 3KL) Cod," DFO Stock Status Report 2003/018, St. John's, Newfoundland, February, 2003

"Northern Shrimp (Pandalus borealis)—Div. OB to 3K," DFO Stock Status Report 2003/036, St. John's, Newfoundland, May 2003

Palmer, Craig T, and P. R. Sinclair, "Perceptions of a Fishery in Crisis: Dragger Skippers on the Gulf of St. Lawrence Cod Moratorium," in *Society and Natural Resources,* v. 9, 1996, pp. 267-279.

_____, and Peter Sinclair, *When the Fish Are Gone: Ecological Disaster and the Fishers in Northwest Newfoundland,* Fernwood Publishing, Halifax, 1997

Parfit, Michael, "Diminishing Returns: Exploiting the Ocean's Bounty," in *National Geographic,* November 1995, pp. 2-55

Pauly, Daniel, et. al., "Fishing Down Marine Food Webs," in *Science,* v. 279, February 6, 1998, pp. 860-863

_____, and Jay Maclean, *In a Perfect Ocean,* Island Press, Washington D.C.,2002

Platt McGuinn, Anne, "Charting a New Course for the Oceans," in *State of the World 1999,* W.W. Norton & Co., New York, 1999, pp. 78-95

_____, "Freefall in Global Fish Stocks," in *Worldwatch Magazine,* May/June 1998, pp. 10-11

_____, *Rocking the Boat: Conserving Fisheries and Protecting Jobs,* Worldwatch Paper No. 142, Worldwatch Institute, Washington D. C., June, 1998

Proulx, Annie, *The Shipping News*, Charles Scribners' Sons, New York, 1993

Prowse, D. W., *A History of Newfoundland from the English Colonial and Foreign Records,* Macmillan and Company, London, 1895

Roach, Thomas E., *Arn? Narn! Faces and Voices of Atlantic Inshore Fishers*, University College of Cape Breton Press, 1997

Rowe, Frederick W., *A History of Newfoundland and Labrador*, McGraw-Hill Ryerson Limited, Toronto, 1980

Russel, Dick, "Fishing down the food chain," in *Amicus Journal,* Fall 1995, pp. 16-23

_____, "Hitting Bottom: As trawling goes into high gear, undersea coastal habitat is being razed to the ground," in *Amicus Journal,* Winter 1997, pp. 21- 25

Safina, Carl, *Eye of the Albatross: Views of the Endangered Sea*, Henry Holt & Company, New York, 2002

_____, *Song for a Blue Ocean: Encounters Along the World's Coasts and Beneath the Seas,* Henry Holt & Company, New York, 1997

Sakar, Dibya, "The Ocean Blues: Navigating the Course of Population Growth," in *The ZPG Reporter,* v. 28, no. 1, January/February 1996, pp. 1-4

"Shrimp in the Estuary and the Gulf of St. Lawrence," DFO Stock Status Report C4-06, DFO Science, Mt. Joli, Quebec, 1998

Sinclair, Peter R.., *From Traps to Draggers: Domestic Commodity Production in Northwest Newfoundland, 1850-1982,* Social and Economic Studies No. 31, Institute of Social and Economic Research, Memorial University of Newfoundland, St. John's, 1985

State of the World Fisheries and Aquaculture, 1998, The Food and Agriculture Organization of the United Nations, Rome, 1999

Steele, D. H., R. Andersen, and J. M. Green, "The Managed Commercial Annihilation of Northern Cod," in *Newfoundland Studies,* v. 8, no. 1, 1992, pp. 34-68

Stevens, William K., "Long-line Fishing seen as Damaging to Some Fish and to the Albatross," New York *Times,* Tuesday, November 5, 1996, pp. C-1, C-8

Story, G. M.., W. J. Kirwin, and J. D. A. Widdowson, eds., *Dictionary of Newfoundland English*, Second Edition, University of Toronto Press, Toronto, 1990

Sutcliffe, W.H., et. al., "Nutrient flux onto the Labrador shelf from

Hudson Strait and its biological consequences," in *Canadian Journal of Fisheries and Aquatic Sciences*, v. 40, no. 10, 1983, pp. 1692-1701

Symes, David, "Conclusion: towards a regionalized management system for the North Atlantic," in *Ocean and Coastal Management*, v. 35, nos. 2-3, 1997, pp. 217-224

"The Northern Gulf of St. Lawrence (3Pn, 4RS) cod in 2002," DFO Stock Status Report 2003/021, St. John's, Newfoundland, March 2003

Thorne, Stephen, "Director Admits DFO Scuttled Seal Report," in Halifax *Chronicle Herald*, August 26, 1997

Warner, William W., *Distant Water: The Fate of the North Atlantic Fisherman*, Little Brown & Co., Boston, 1977

Wheal, Caroline, "No More Fish in the Sea: Lessons from New England," in *Calypso Log*, December 1994, pp. 14-19

Williams, Nigel, "Overfishing disrupts entire ecosystems," in *Science*, v. 279, February 6, 1998, p. 809

Woodard, Colin, *Ocean's End: Travels through Endangered Seas*, Basic Books, New York, 2000

Wright, Guy, *Sons and Seals: A Voyage to the Ice*, Newfoundland Social and Economic Studies No. 29, Institute of Social and Economic Research, Memorial University of Newfoundland, St. John's, 1952

Acknowledgments

During all the miles of travel required to make this book happen, large numbers of people conspired to help along the way.

Foremost in this group were the hundreds of Newfoundlanders who welcomed me and my shipmates into their villages, their homes, and their lives. Many of these became voices in the book. Countless others, unnamed or mentioned only briefly, were there to lend a hand, share a meal, offer a bit of advice, make a traveler feel at home. I owe an enduring debt of thanks to each one—as well as to Newfoundlanders collectively—the most hospitable and generous people I have ever known.

During the actual writing of the book, dozens of friends and colleagues contributed importantly to the development of the finished piece, suggesting ideas, sharpening images, correcting factual errors, polishing a bit of prose. Lynda Bogel provided me a virtual education in how to make a sentence sing. Sifford Pearre introduced me to many of his scientific colleagues, then, along with his wife Anja, contributed a careful editorial reading that helped shape the narrative in dozens of important ways. Carol Young, Joyce Yeats, Bill Alberts, Kell Achenbach, Mark Pendergrast, John Miller, Rennie Stackpole, and Amanda Lake all took part in shepherding the manuscript through various stages of its evolution. Skip Crane provided the wonderful maps.

Among the scientists who participated in the project, I owe special thanks to Ram Myers, Jeff Hutchings, and Dick Haedrich, all important voices in the book, all of whom also served as teachers and consultants for me as I tried to understand the current state of knowledge in the complex and sometimes mysterious world of fisheries science.

Don Parsons and David Taylor also shared their work with me and gave unflaggingly of their time during interviews, as did Jon Lien, Ken Drinkwater, and Craig Palmer. Craig and his wife, Fran, were also instrumental in introducing my wife, Kay, and me to the people of Flowers Cove, and in hosting us during a winter visit to that village.

For their help in various phases of the research for this book, I wish to thank John Gushue at the St John's *Evening Telegram*, Joan Ritchie and Colleen Field at the Memorial University Center for Newfoundland Studies, Carolyn Good at the CBC Tape Library, David Feltham at Gulf Seafoods Port aux Basques, David Walsh at Atlantic Ocean Farms.

I wish also to thank my wonderful agent Arnold Goodman for his unflagging efforts on behalf of this project, my editor and publisher Steve Carlson for his continual working of miracles, my cousin Ann Benoit for her inspiration, my friends Ted and Liz Brainard for their enthusiasm and good ideas, my fellow circum-navigators Jim and Jeanie Foley for their comradeship, my ship-mates, Amanda, Nat, Liz, and Richard, for their hard work and good company.

I wish to thank my parents, Chuck and Betsy Arms, to whom this book is dedicated—my father for teaching me to love the sea, my mother for teaching me to love the words. And finally and most of all, of course, I wish to thank Kay, who has always been there in person even when she isn't in the book, and who nurtures and sustains this peripatetic scrivener every day of his life.

About the Author

Educated with graduate degrees at both Yale and Harvard, Myron arms is a writer, lecturer, and professional small-boat sailor. He is author of several books, including *Boston Globe* best-seller *Riddle of the Ice,* and has published more than fifty feature articles in *Cruising World, Sail, Blue Water Sailing,* and many other sailing and adventure magazines.

A U.S. Coast Guard-licensed Ocean Master since 1977, he and his wife, Kay, have now voyaged over 130,000 sea miles, including two high-latitude crossings of the North Atlantic, a voyage to western Greenland, and eight summer sail-training voyages to the coasts of Newfoundland and Labrador.

As this book goes to press, he begins his ninth journey to northern Newfoundland with a group of new sail trainees. Readers may sample his other writing and may follow this and other sailing adventures on the Web at *www.myronarms.com.*

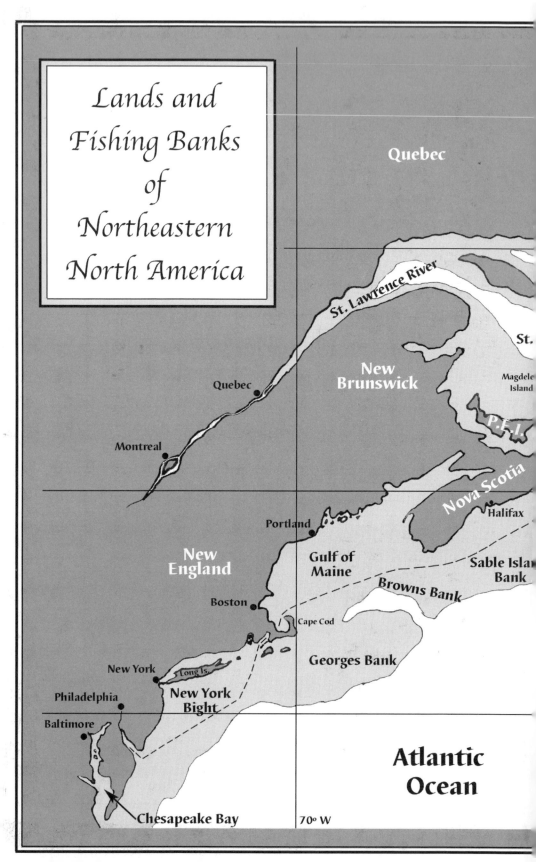